Michael G Kramer OMIEAust.

Full Story of the Anglo-Saxon Invasion

ISBN 978-1-7640-275-2-6

Copyright © 2025

Table of Contents

Introduction

Much is said about the longships and who invented what and when. The simple fact is that the longship was developed by both Danish and other Vikings and the Engel Tribesmen. It is known that the Engels used longships before 449 A.D., and that was hundreds of years before the first Viking raids upon Britain. In comparison to the Engels, the Saxons used two forms of shipping. These were the trireme of Greek origin and the twin masted Ceol. In both cases, the ships could be propelled using wind power of sails and or oars. The Saxons only used longships for ceremonial purposes. By the year 449 A.D., the Engels and Kimbern tribes had amalgamated with the Saxons, and this made their combined strength one powerful force. All three tribes operated autonomously, each under the orders of its own nobility but always under the banner of the Saxons.

The Engel tribe were living on both sides of a long fiord called Eckenforde, located in about the middle of the Jutland Peninsular. At the time, the entire peninsular was peopled by Germanic tribes. Eckenforde provides an excellent and safe harbour for shipping because it extends for a very long way into the peninsular. The original Engel homeland had Anglen as its capital, which is why English-speaking people tend to call the people who came from that region Angles. The north of the peninsular was peopled by the Kimbern tribe. This tribe was feared by the Romans, who called them Cimbri. In many older English texts, the Kimbern tribe are referred to as Jutes. While that may be technically correct, the fact is that the Engels came from the middle of the Jutland peninsular, and the Saxons originated from the south of it. Therefore, all these people can be called Jutes.

After 449 A.D., the original homeland of the Engel tribe was left totally deserted because the entire tribe had gone to Britain as a mass migration, which also left several of their longships at various stages of construction behind them. The Viking longship appeared off the coasts of Britain more than 150 years after the Engels had settled there. It is thought that the difference between the Engel longship and the Danish Viking version was that the Viking longships had a "T" shaped keel, which gave the Viking version of the longship much better handling characteristics in rough weather. On the other hand, the Engel longship had a keel plank.

What was the reason for the Germanic tribes settling in Britain? The actual reason is lost in time, but it may have been that the Saxons could not expand towards the west and the Rhine River because the Germanic tribe Called Franks were there. There was pressure coming from the Wends, who were also living on the Jutland peninsular, and the Danes who also needed to expand.

After the Engels left the Jutland Peninsular, so did many of the Kimbern and Saxons. All three tribes settled in Britain, with the Engels calling their new homeland Engel-land. That made the entire Jutland peninsular depopulated, a fact not missed by the Danes who moved in and made use of the deserted countryside. Centuries later, the Germans would take back most of the Jutland peninsular.

The Kimbern Tribe

Good day to you. I am the ghost of a Kimbern Prince and War Lord, my name is Horsa. The Kimbern tribe occupied the north of the Jutland peninsular. I died in the year of 455 A.D. because of battle wounds. I shall now tell the story of how the Germanic tribes came to Britain and one of the reasons for them doing so. Some of you readers may be familiar with the name of my twin brother, called Hengest. Some people also call him Hengist.

My father was named Wictgils, and he was the son of Witta. His father was known as Wecta. And his father is known to be the god Woden, which means that Thor is my Great-uncle. With such an impressive family line that is directly related to the gods, it is no wonder that the names of Hengest and Horsa have lived through the ages and are known in even the twenty-second century A.D...

I think that before we go much further, it may be a good idea to tell you the meaning of the names of Hengest and Horsa. The name of Hengest still means "stallion" in the German language. While Horsa is a variation of the Germanic name of Horst and that name had the meaning of "Trainer". Let's now digress for a while, and I will explain how I ended up with the name of Horsa. In my family and most other families in the Kimbern tribe, we had a tradition of being named twice. Once at birth and again at a later age when we were beginning to show our true characteristics.

Hengest and I were twins, and upon birth, we both received our initial names. In my brother's case, he was firstly named Ernest, while I was initially named Bern. When we were aged fourteen, Ernest was at the horse training yard of our main Kimbern horse training compound when a stallion broke from its tether and reared up, appearing to be threatening a girl who happened to be close by.

Ernest ran over to the stallion and proceeded to calm it down. Using low and soothing tones, he eventually gained the stallion's trust, and he proceeded to further pacify it by gently running his hands over it. When he had completely gained the animal's trust, he asked those present for a horse brush, and upon being given one, he began to gently brush the stallion, which was now very calm. After spending more time brushing the stallion and talking to it in a low voice, the animal trusted him to the point where it now followed him everywhere he went. That caused many of those who were present to begin talking about what they had just seen happen, and word of the event quickly reached the ears of our father. After we had both returned home, our father, called Wictgils, spoke to us both.

He said, *"After that display of courage and understanding of the stallion and how you, Ernest was able to gain the complete trust of the stallion and so save the little girl who was being threatened by it, I am so impressed by your actions that I am now going to give both you and your brother your warrior's names. Ernest, your name shall be Hengest which is the Germanic name for a stallion. Your brother's name will change from Bern to Horsa. That is because I have watched him training both himself and other young men as warriors. I am naming him Horsa because that means "Trainer" in our language. I have watched him as he trained himself and others, and I must admit that I like what I have seen.*

Even at his young age, he shows all the signs of being a great trainer of warriors and other occupations. I have had the joy of seeing him constantly putting himself and his companions through countless drills and possible tactical situations, which will result in instant action by the warriors without the necessity of giving them orders because every man in his units will know what he must do and when he must do it. Now go, my sons, I am most proud of you both!"

I urge you to think about it, and when you do, I am sure that you shall also conclude that a lord of the Kimbern[1] would also be a trainer of warriors he commanded. The training of my warriors is one of the things that I was famous for. I trained my men by putting them through so many practices and drills that everything was second nature to them, and they only required a minimum of orders to complete any given task.

I always bore in mind what was so ably demonstrated by the warriors of Armin when they wiped out Varus and his three Roman Legions plus supporting units in the Teutoburger Forest only four

---

[1] The Kimbern tribe were originally located in the north of the Jutland peninsular. They were fierce warriors they worshipped the gods of Wodin and his son Thor. Like the Danish Vikings, their language was old German. They shared that language with the Engels and Saxons with whom they amalgamated.

and a half centuries before now. Armin and his warriors beat the Romans because his warriors were lightly armed and armoured, allowing them to move at a higher speed than the Romans, who were burdened by the weight of their armour and weapons.

As well, all of Armin's warriors knew exactly what they had to do. An additional requirement of these warriors was that they knew the duties of the man both above him and below him in rank. By having men who could easily assume command if a commander was killed or injured, my warriors were never left leadless. That was something which was to prove very beneficial. All of this meant that the fight would go on, never losing its impetus and, the pressure upon the enemy would be unceasing. That is why I trained my men in such a way that they would all know what was always required of them and under all conditions. It is one of the reasons that both discipline and training are so important. These two factors will often make the difference between success and failure in battle.

The Britons Want Missionaries

In 167 A.D., the ruling Roman Emperor was Marcus Aurelius. A priest had risen from being the normal rank of Father, and he was in a position like that of the Cardinals of the twenty-second century. He became the Pope later during the year of 167 A.D. and held that position with great honour for fifteen years. He was Pope Eleutherius.

In June of 178 A.D., he received a letter written in Latin from the king of the Britons, whose name was Lucius. The letter said, *"Dear Holy Father Eleutherius, I am Lucius, the king of the Britons. I have been speaking to Roman merchants, soldiers, and sailors here in Britain, and they have told me of your god. He is said to be both kind and merciful and that he forgives the sins committed against him by the people who believe in him and accept his covenant of life and worship.*

For now, everyone here is a heathen and uses pagan practices. I beg you to immediately send missionaries to the islands of Britain to convert my people to the correct faith, that of belief in and the worship of Jesus Christ, the Lord. Please do not let my people continue to wallow in their misguided heathen practices! I would like to be the first person in Britain who is converted to your faith and baptised. I shall be most happy for your priests to baptise me in public so that my people can see their very own king being baptised in front of them. I am sure that such an act by me would be the best way of also converting large numbers of Britons and eventually converting everyone in this land to your Christian faith."

Accordingly, Pope Eleutherius spoke to some of the clergy staff around him. He said, *"Who do we have among us to send to the British Islands to do the work of God and convert the heathens in Britania to the true faith?"* He was immediately answered by the clergy around him, with one of them saying, *"Holy Father, I know of two priests who may be the answer that you are looking for. In both cases, these men are fearless, and I know that they would welcome an audience with you about this matter. I have heard them both speak, and I think that they both would jump at the chance to not just become your missionaries in Britania, but start things rolling with the baptism of Lucius, the king of the Britons. The names of the two priests that I have in mind are Father Faganus and Father Deruvianus. I know for sure that Father Deruvianus would love to build a church near Glastonbury.* Soon afterwards, both priests appeared before their Pope.

Pope Eleutherius said, *"Your task of converting the Britons will be made much easier by the fact that their king Lucius has asked for his people to become Christians and even for himself to be baptised in public! Such an act by a king of the gentiles will open the way for the conversion of all Britons who witness the baptism of their king. So, I suggest that you both go and see this king*

11

immediately and use his baptism as a means of making the other Britons follow suit. Remember that much of the success or otherwise of converting people from being heathens to becoming true Christians lies in selling religion. By having a public baptism of their king, it will be the way for the church to gain a foothold in Britain and become a strong religious force. Now, get out there and give Lucius, the king of Britons, what he wants, namely for him to be baptised in public and for your missionary work to really flower!"

So it was that in the year 179 A.D., Lucius, the king of Britons, was baptised in public in a shallow stream not far from the church at Glastonbury. King Lucius died twenty-two years later, and he was given a Christian burial, complete with much ceremony. The missionary work of the two priests continued with much success. With Britons successfully converted to Christianity, the stage was now set for misunderstandings and mutual religious intolerance that followed when the Germanic pagan tribes arrived.

Germanic Tribes

I found it difficult to trace the Teutonic branch of the present European population beyond the first conflicts between with the Romans. All that I was able to do is to confirm the opinions of historians that the Germanic tribes had a lot in common with the Cimmerian, Celtic and Slavic clans and that they migrated originally from the areas surrounding the Caspian Sea, extending from the foothills of the Caucasian and Median alps through Transoxiana to the steppes of the Ural and the Volga[2].

All these nations were known to Greek historians and geographers by the name of Scythians. That name was never used by those people themselves. In general, it may be said that the name

---

[2] Greenwood, 1836

Scythians was used to describe the many people who had the characteristics of being tall, robust, fair-haired, and blue-eyed. These people continued to occupy the plains of the Oxus and Iaxartes, and they were nomads or semi-nomads to almost the birth of Christ. They migrated and spread themselves over central Asia from the Caspian to the Great Wall of China and from the Himalayas to the Altai, settling eventually in areas of Finland and Sweden.

There is no doubt that the Germanic tribes are lineally descended from some of the more powerful and numerous of these tribes. They share the same personal appearances, customs, and languages. They also have other similarities with these people. The nomadic way of life is always the last to convert to civilisation, and in the case of the Germanic tribes, they stuck to their nomadic way of life until a long time after they were first noticed.

Their nomadic habits continued for a long time. I found that during their history, whole nations migrating with their herds of cattle and their families with about as much difficulty as experienced now in mounting military expeditions and/or campaigns. By the early Bronze age, Germanic tribes occupied the entire Jutland peninsula and all land through to what is now known as Switzerland and beyond. The alps and the region of Sarmatia to the east and their northern limit was the Baltic coast. Their western boundary was the Rhine River, but that was crossed many times by both the Germanic people and the Gauls[3].

Engels

These people are usually called Angles by many English-speaking people. Their capital was called Anglen, located about

---

[3] Greenwood, 1836

mid-way on the Jutland peninsula. Their language was old German, just like the language of their close neighbours, the Danish Vikings.

In the year of 407 A.D., the Romans abandoned what we now call England. That country was then constantly invaded and harassed by the Scots and Picts who were raiding it at will. Eventually, the king of the Britons obtained the help that he was seeking. The raids became a thing of the past for a long time. That came about because the Germanic tribes of Engels, Kimbern and Saxons had amalgamated. They were invited to Britain to protect the Britons against the invaders. The Engels were first mentioned by the Roman historian Tacitus[4] (5th Century A.D.) The seven tribes of the Suevic Nation, which included the Engels, worshipped the Goddess Nerthus, also known as Hertha or Mother Earth. The worship of this goddess always left a lasting impression upon all who saw her rites.

In the Baltic Ocean, an island had a sacred grove in which there was a consecrated chariot covered by a single robe that no-one except her priest was allowed to touch. In this robe, the goddess was supposed to reside. During times of religious festivities, the priest would bring out the chariot, which was drawn by cows. That signalled the arrival of the goddess, and that always resulted in great joy among her followers. Great festivities followed, and no war was entered into during that time.

The Engels lived along a very long fiord which almost cuts through the entire Jutland peninsular. It is known as Eckenforde and is in the Schleswig area of northern Germany. The Engels settled along both banks of Eckenforde and Anglen was located at the end of the fiord, on the narrow bit of land connecting the south of the Jutland peninsula, to the northern part of it. The Engels were known as warriors and sailors. There is a lot of argument as to who invented

---

[4] Greenwood, 1836

the longship, with some saying it was the invention of Danish Vikings, while others say that the Engels invented the longship.

What is known, is that the Engels left their original homeland on the Jutland peninsula and went to Britain using their longships. They did so as a mass migration, leaving several of their longships at various stages of construction behind them. The Engel version of the longship had a keel plank, and it was not as good during rough weather as was the Danish Viking longship, which had a "T" shaped keel giving it much better handling characteristics. The Viking longship made its first appearance off the coasts of Engel-land almost one-hundred and fifty years after the Engels has settled in Britain. They called where they settled, Engel-land because as they were approaching the coasts of the north of Engel-land they were surprised the find that it closely resembled the coasts of their original homeland. Therefore, they named it as Engel-land meaning Land of the Engels.

Given that Copenhagen is located barely thirty-eight miles to the east of the western side of Eckenforde and that both the Engels and the Danes spoke old German, it is highly likely that both Engels and Danes worked together to produce the first longship. Naturally, the Danes refined it and used the longship with devastating results during raids upon various parts of the world. The Engels continued their migration until the entire tribe was relocated to the northern and central parts of England.

Franks

Saint Jerome, when writing his book, "The life of St. Hilarion", in the fourth century, describes the Franks as people distinguished more by their strength and capacity than the number of their possessions. Before and after him, most historians called the homeland of the Franks Germania, while he called it Frankia. Both Greek and Roman historians agree the Franks were living within

Germania, between the Saxons to their north and the Alemanni to their south.

The Franks settled on the Rhine, and centuries after the Roman defeat at the hands of Arminius and Thusnelda, the Franks became the dominant Germanic tribe through the process of amalgamating with other tribes. Some of the well-known Germanic tribes to be part of this amalgamation were members of the Chauci, Cherusci, Chamavi and Chatti tribes, while some of the relatives of these same tribes chose to amalgamate with the Saxons. The members of the tribes who chose to join with the Franks became Franks and fought under the banner of the Franks. The name of Franks became identified with 'Wehrmannen' or warriors by other people. Meanwhile, the Saxons were also becoming a dominant force among the Germanic tribes through the process of amalgamation.

Aelbehrt had recruited a crew for his ship, which he was operating out of the mouth of the Weser River in northern Germania. He had assembled his crew, and he now stood before them as he spoke. He said, *"Welcome, gentlemen, to the crew of my pirate ship. We shall harry and plunder the coasts of Britania, the lowlands of the Dutch, the coasts of France and Spain and even well beyond those places as far away as Africa. You will all begin training as pirates, and you shall learn skills at arms, how to swim, and you shall know your places, and you shall learn to do exactly as you are told to, because I will not tolerate any lapses of discipline! As soon as you have completed your training, we are off to plunder the coasts of Britannia and France. Are there any questions?"*

Siegfried asked, *"For how long shall we be training before we can raid the people of Britania and Spain? I am asking because it seems to me that once we begin to actively plunder the coasts of northern Europe, the Romans will not take our presence lightly, and they shall come after us with the Roman Navy, which uses ships like the Greek Triremes."*

Aelbehrt answered, *"Siegfried, the training normally takes about fourteen days before you are considered ready to begin your duties of being the pirates of the Franks! Many other Frankish pirates are already operating from ports in Northern Germania, harrying the coasts of Britania and the western side of the channel all the way past Spain to Africa.*

All of that is Roman territory. I have it on good authority that the Roman General called Posthumius has been assigned the task of both stopping our pirates and clearing the bands of Frankish robbers from the roads of Gaul other places, including Spain. I have received word that Posthumius has said that he will clear away all pirates and robbers by the end of seven years. We shall make him wish that he had not even been born!"

Origins of the Saxons

Bear in mind that the ancient Germanic tribes did not have a written language of their own until after they defeated the Romans at the Battle of the Teutoburger Forest in September of 9 A.D., which resulted in the Romans leaving Germania and the beginning of the Germans using the Latin alphabet. Therefore, most knowledge about the Saxons before those times comes from ancient Greek historians who record the Saxons as having been part of the army of Alexander the Great. After the death of Alexander in Babylon, these Saxons dispersed and sailed to the coast of Northern Germania, settling on the coastal region of the southern part of the Jutland peninsula and near the mouth of the Elbe.

Much information about the Saxon origins comes from Witichind, Saxon, a monk of the Abbey of Corvey in Westphalia. In the tenth century, he collected and digested the early history of his people. He wrote the 'Saxons Annals' for his friend, Otto the Great. Witichind wrote, *"Opinion is divided on the matter of the origin of the Saxons, with some scholars believing the Saxons derived their origin from Danes and Normans. However, the teachings of ancient Greeks state the Saxons are the remnants of the Macedonian army of 'Alexander the Great', which after his death, was scattered to all parts of the earth. That may be, but it is certain that they were an ancient and noble people. They are mentioned in a speech by Agrippa to the Jews, which was reported by Josephus[5]. We know with certainty that the Saxons came in ships and that they came to Germania by sea, landing at the mouth of the Elbe and conquering the Thuringians who were there before them."*

Their ships of that time were the Greek triremes of the naval forces of Alexander the Great. These vessels were propelled using three decks of oarsmen and sails. Their first documented use was in 525 B.C... The trireme had a crew of one hundred and seventy rowers, twenty hoplites (heavily armoured and armed soldiers) and ten officers. It could be used as a warship capable of attacking and sinking other shipping by ramming the enemy ships and could also carry both passengers and cargo.

Due to the Saxons' invasion of the Thuringian territory, the resulting war between them was fought for many years with great bitterness on both sides. After a long time, a truce was put into effect by which the Saxons obtained permission to purchase provisions. Their money was soon spent, and when they ran out of it, they thought that peace was of no use to them.

So, the Saxons now invented a reason to continue fighting. One of their warriors called Wodenlieb dressed himself in his finest clothing and decorated himself with golden trinkets, golden chains, and bracelets. Dressed and decorated in this way, he walked toward

---

[5] Greenwood, 1836

the territory of the Thuringians, who mocked him as soon as they saw him. They then filled their laps with loose sand and dust from the ground and exchanged them for the golden trinkets he was wearing. The Saxon now returned to his ships and explained to his people that he had bought land and asked his tribe to follow him.

Carrying his newly purchased earth along with him, he scattered it over the land while in sight of the Thuringians, and he did so, as sparingly as possible to cover a greater area. After he had very sparingly spread the dust over a very large portion of land, he spoke to the Thuringians. He said, *"I have now taken possession of the land that I have purchased from you, and I have paid you for it with gold! That means that all the land over which I have sprinkled dust now belongs to the Saxons. Be assured that we shall defend this newly purchased land by force of arms, and if you want a contest, then we, the Saxons, shall provide you with the war that you want!"*

A warrior of the Thuringians spoke out. He said, *"My name is Eburwin, and I am aghast at what you Saxons have done! You have used trickery to obtain our land from us, and I do not recognise your ownership of Thuringian land. I am more than happy to fight you, Saxons, for the right to Thuringian land! I do not want to see you Saxons in this area again! I shall throw you, the foreign Saxon invaders, out of my territory!"*

That was followed by the Thuringians making a disorderly attack upon the Saxons. Present with the Saxons was the warrior commander Brecht and his son Dietz. Seeing the Thuringians coming as a disorganised rabble, Brecht said, *"It is high time to teach the Thuringians not to mess about with Saxons! Dietz, take thirty-eight archers to that little clearing to the right of the Thuringians and shoot your arrows into them. When you have used your arrows, withdraw from the Thuringians, and lead them toward the rest of us here! We shall be lying in wait for them to arrive. When they do so, we will annihilate them all!"* So, the Thuringian attack resulted in a slaughter of the Thuringian warriors present at that time.

Afterwards, the Thuringians proposed a conference that was to be attended by representatives of both sides. The representatives were to be unaccompanied and unarmed. Their purpose was to discuss common grievances and to try to find common ground upon which both sides could use to settle their differences and to find peaceful resolutions of their problems. At a meeting of the Saxon elders, the war with the Thuringians was discussed. A warrior chieftain called Egilhard spoke to the assembled gathering of Saxon elders. He said, *"Ladies and Gentlemen, so far, we have taken possession of some Thuringian land, but much more is required by us for our tribe to thrive in this area. The Thuringians are re-organising, and we should strike first before they can obtain help from their allies and try to kill us all!*

The peace conference that has been set-up by the Thuringians gives us the ideal opportunity to slay our enemies and take over this part of Germania completely. I propose that we attend the conference as stipulated without any escorts, but with our long knives called Sachs, hidden under our cloaks! When I sound my horn twice, that shall be the signal for our men attending the conference to draw their knives and kill all Thuringians present at the conference. We should then take-over as much territory as possible and safe-guard ourselves by forming alliances with other tribes and even amalgamating with them! I put it to you that we should use this opportunity and to become powerful from implementing it!

His words were having a great effect upon the Saxons listening to him. After some discussion among the elders, Prince Clovis spoke. He said, *"Fellow Saxons, I am in favour of the proposal put before us by Egilhard! It has come to my attention that the Thuringians shall attend the conference with all their princes present. That gives us the possibility of making them leaderless. All we must do is to hide our long knives under our cloaks as suggested by Egilhard, and the Thuringian enemy shall be driven from this part of Germania."*

A vote was taken, and it was agreed to wipe-out the Thuringians at the conference in that way. At the sound of the second blast from the horn of Egilhard, the Saxons attacked the astonished Thuringians and wiped them all out. From that time onwards, the Saxons became celebrated and inspired great terror in their neighbouring tribes.

The Saxon monk called Witichind wrote, *"Some people think that the name Saxons came from this ferocious deed because, in our language, the knives with which they performed the slaughter of such a great number of people are called Sahs.* That resulted in the Saxons obtaining territory and settlements along the Germanic coasts to the point where they were firmly established. At later times, the Saxons proved themselves to be good farmers. In keeping with the practices of most Germanic tribes, when the farming practices of sowing or reaping of crops was to be carried out, the entire tribe took part. For the remainder of the year, farming was left to individuals who would use the land correctly, and no houses or other buildings were erected on agricultural land. The other male members of the Germanic tribes would obtain their luxuries as plunder taken from enemies.

In their new settlements, the naval power of the Saxons thrived, and their wealth increased as they amalgamated other tribes. One of these was the Kimbern, the tribe of Hengest and Horsa. The Saxons also amalgamated with the Engels. Due to their habit of only growing enough gain to supply their needs of wheat or rye for their bread and barley for their beers, the Germanic tribes suffered famine at times. Through the continued process of amalgamation with other tribes, the Saxons moved great distances inland from the coasts. Inland, there is still a German state called Saxony as distinct from the coastal states of Upper Saxony and Lower Saxony.

While Valentinian was providing defence against Rome's external dangers, the internal state of Gaul was a source of constant fatigue and anxiety caused by numerous bands of Frankish robbers who infested all roads in Gaul. Meanwhile, the coasts of Holland, Britania and Gaul were ravaged by pirates who were both Franks and Saxons operating out of the northern German port areas. Both bands of pirates committed fearful slaughters among inhabitants of Britania and Gaul for a great distance from the coasts. They would usually attack at night after they had selected the richest looking house to attack. That was usually followed by looting the homes and killing the occupants of them[6].

That resulted in the Menapian commander of the Roman legions called Carausius being called in to attend a conference with the future Emperor Maximian. Carausius entered the villa where Maximian was and saluted him. Maximian said, *"Carausius, it is nice to see you. Your new most urgent duty to stop the terror of the Frankish robbers who are infesting the roads in Gaul, while both the Saxons and the Franks are causing many problems through the activities of their pirates who are constantly attacking the coasts of Britannia and Gaul on a constant basis! Get out there and stop these threats to Roman commerce and the well-being of Roman territory from happening. I do not care how you do it. Just stop the Franks and Saxons from robbing and killing Romans!"*

Carausius said, *"Give me the authority to go after those two Germanic tribes by laying waste to their homelands in Germania, and I will solve these problems for you!"* Maximian said, *"No, there*

---

[6] Greenwood, 1836

must be a better way than to invade Germania! Romans shall never go to that land where our legions were slaughtered. Roman law now forbids that! I shall give you the approval to send the legions to impede the Franks acting against Rome in Gaul, and I will give you the ships necessary for you to protect the coasts of Britania and Gaul, but you may not invade Germania! There is too much opposition to that from the Senate of Rome and from the Roman people!" So, Carausius did as he had been ordered ad eventually became successful in removing the Frankish robbers from Gaul and lowering the threat of the Frankish and Saxon pirates to the coasts of Britannia and Gaul.

He was later unjustly accused of being in league with the robbers and pirates. He was condemned to death by Emperor Maximian. Rather than submit to any charges and certain death, Carausius took control of Britania and declared himself to be the Emperor of Britania. He reigned as emperor of Britania until he was killed in battle in the year 293 A.D., and Roman rule was restored.

The Saxons in Germania worshipped Woden and Thor until they were converted to Christianity at about the same time that the Engels, Kimbern and Saxons in Britannia were converted, but the reasons that it happened were very different in the two counties. The Germanic tribes living in Britannia were converted by persuasion, whereas the Germanic tribes of Germania were converted at the point of a sword by the Franks at roughly the same time. The Saxons, like the Franks and Alemanni, stand out as a union of amalgamated tribes. The most distinguished tribe among them gave its name to the union of the tribes.

In the year of 449 A.D., the Kimbern chiefs of my brother Hengest and myself (Horsa) accepted the invitation of the weak British King Vortigern. So, we sent our powerful forces to aid the Britons and help them to expel the Picts and Scots who were constantly invading Britania and raiding the Britons. Having accomplished that task, we stopped being allies and just took over the country-side. After a few years, the amalgamated forces of the Kimbern, Engels and Saxons dominated the island of Britania. The different tribes tended to settle in different areas. The Kimbern settled in what is now called Kent.

East Angelia, Mercia and Northumberland were peopled by the Engels, and the Saxons populated Wessex, Sussex, and Essex as well as other parts of England. While at first, these formed separate kingdoms, they all eventually joined as a single country. The main driving force of that was King Alfred the Great of Wessex and his son named as Edward-the-Elder. The original Britons left those areas and moved to the Cornwall area, Wales, and the west coast of Northumbria.

Meanwhile, the Saxon name on the European continent replaced the more ancient tribal names of Chauci, Cherusci, Frisii, Amsivarii and others by simply amalgamating with them. The Saxons even persuaded some of the tribes that had joined the Franks to leave the Franks and become Saxons. However, while the Saxons were expanding and settling Britain and expanding their German territory, The Franks quickly became dominant in the western part of Germania near the Rhine River and expanded into parts of Gaul. Over time, they would become dominant and even invaded and conquer all of Gaul. Now that the background is complete, we can concentrate upon the actual story of the beginnings of England.

The King of Britons asks for Help

The king of the Britons was known as Wurtgern and as Vortigern or Wyrtgeon. He was indecisive and weak, watching helplessly while his people were being killed, raped, or plundered by both Picts and Scots. He was known to be pedantic, obstinate, and so lustful that he was open to every vice imaginable, even to the point of having constant sex with his own daughters. Having been informed of more raids being inflicted on the Britons by the Scots, he called for a conference of the nobles of the Britons to take place in year 443. The resulting conference took place at his castle in what we now call Sussex.

Being seated on his throne, he could see his people before him, and he started the conference. He said, *"Fellow Britons, ever since 418 A.D., we have been putting up with invasions and raids by Picts and Scots into our country! When the Roman overlords left Britannia in 418, they took their hordes of gold and silver with them but in many cases, they just buried it here in Britania. We have been fortunate in that we have been able to find some of the buried treasure which can be used by our kingdom to provide security. I have called you all here to discuss possible actions to improve the security of Britania and to keep our people safe! I need you all to come up with ideas of how to safe-guard our people from the unwanted attentions of Picks and Scots! I shall now invite all of you to float your ideas of how best to deal with our situation before we are wiped out as a sovereign state!"*

From the rear of the throne room came a reply. The leader of some tribes of the Britons located to the southwest of the Northumberland coast spoke. He said, *"My king, I am Arthur, the leader of three tribes of Britons living southwest of the Northumberland coast near the north of Wales! It seems to me that we may have two possible courses of action available to keep the invaders and despoilers of our women out of our territory. Firstly, you could try to get the Romans to return to install law and order in Britannia. If that fails, you could try bringing in warriors from elsewhere if you cannot get them from Britannia."*

Vortigern said, *"Thank you, Arthur, I shall draft a letter written in Latin to the Roman Emperor Valentinian. In the letter, I will outline our problems and ask for the return of the Roman Legions!"*

The next act of Vortigern was to order his scribes to come to him. When they arrived, he said, *"Gentlemen, I have important work for you that must be carried out with diligence and efficiency immediately! You are writing a letter to the Roman Emperor Valentinian in which you shall outline the plight of the Britons since the Romans left this land in 418 A.D... We must make sure that order is restored as quickly as possible! So that we can have order restored, we ask you to again send Roman legions to protect us!"*

He followed that by saying to the scribes, *"So, all of you, write letters in Latin to the emperor imploring him to send Roman legions back to Britania! I want each of the twenty of you to write letters, and the best ones shall be selected to be sent to Valentinian!"* The scribes got busy and drafted the letter to the Roman Emperor. It read, *"Mighty Valentinian the Third, the Master of the world, please do not let us, your loyal subjects in Britania, continue to suffer invasion, raiding and looting of our homes and towns by the lawless Scots and Picts, who pillage our people! We cannot stand against them! We implore you to allow Roman legions to once again bring law and order into Britannia!"*

Some two years passed before Vortigern received a reply from the Roman, and he did not like what the letter from Valentinian said to him! Valentinian wrote, *"My dear Vortigern, you must provide your own defences because I cannot help you. I have more than enough troubles of my own to deal with. The Germanic tribe called Goths sacked Rome earlier in the year 435 A.D... As you may or may not know, the Roman Empire has now been divided into the Western empire with its capital in Rome, and the Eastern Empire, with its capital in Constantinople. Because of the splitting of the Roman Empire into halves, there are many problems for both parts of it. The Germanic tribes have already sacked Rome once, and they are massing for further attacks against Rome. I get the impression that they are taking revenge for what Rome tried to do to the Germanic tribes in earlier times! There are now new incursions into Roman territory from the Visigoths, and I am very busy in trying to only defend Rome itself!*

Also, I have been informed that Romans will soon be facing new invaders called Huns. Apparently, they are new to Europe and have slits for eyes, and they are said to be very cruel but capable warriors and that they eat dogs! Although I cannot help you, I do sympathise with you, and therefore, I suggest that if all else fails, that you contact the Germanic tribes living on the Jutland peninsula, they are very capable and war-like warriors who could help you to turn the tide in your favour! Some of the tribes on the Jutland peninsula are called Engels, Kimbern and Saxons. These have amalgamated now, but each one of those tribes still has its own identity and ruler. All three of them fight under the banner of the Saxons! You may find that if you can gain the alliance of one of these, then you will also have the alliance of them all because of their amalgamation with the Saxons, but each tribe is still under the command of its own nobles. So, it is with regret that I must inform you that you must deal with your situation yourself because Rome cannot help you."

Becoming alarmed at the probability of continued invasions and raids by Picts and the Scots in Briton territory, Vortigern called a conference. At mid-morning, the conference got underway. Vortigern said, *"Fellow Britons, I have received the answer from the Roman Emperor! He says that Rome cannot send us any help because the Romans are now paying the price for their attacks upon the Germanic nations and that the Goths have sacked Rome itself! He has suggested that we ask the Germanic tribes of Engels, Kimbern or Saxons to help us because they have amalgamated into one powerful people! I am now turning this question over to you to*

27

gain your input and ideas about this. Please speak what may be on your minds!"

The first to speak was Arthur, who was leading his Britons in areas of Wales and the west coast of Northumbria. He said, *"My king, I realise that I am a young warrior leader, but we must be careful about whom we ally ourselves with. The German warriors are fierce, and I know that they will stop the incursions of Picts and Scots into our territory, but it will be at a cost! The Germans will not do anything for nothing! We shall have to pay them dearly if we go down that path! I feel that it will be better for us to simply erect fortifications where we must do so and to raise our own armies and to train them!"*

He was answered by another Celtic warrior leader called Caratacos. Caratacos said, *"Mighty Arthur, I agree that we should build-up our own defences and that we must have the fortifications that you speak of! However, time is short, and our people continue to suffer at the hands of the Scottish invaders from the north! We must make sure that our people do not suffer more of the attacks upon them. My sister has recently been married to a member of the household of the nobility of the Kimbern tribe located in the Jutland peninsula. I could send her a letter written in Latin asking her to get her people to send some warriors here to look at our situation and to help us out, even if we must pay them as being our mercenary soldiers! If things do not work out, we can simply tell them to leave!"*

That caused the warrior leader called Lugubelenus, to speak. He said, *"King Vortigern, Arthur, and Caratacos, I fully agree that we must do something very quickly before the Scots consume us all! I, therefore, believe that it is imperative that we contact Hengest or Horsa of the Kimbern and ask them to come here and see what needs to be done before they set a price upon their help for us to remove the Scottish threat! If we let them bring in their families, there should be no threat to Britons from doing this!"* A vote was taken among the assembled nobles, and messengers were sent to Hengest and Horsa, asking them to come to Britannia to meet with King Vortigern.

So, Britania now had the strange situation of its king being a self-serving, inactive man who was prone to all the vices of the flesh, and the Western Roman Emperor who was cowardly and vain, in fact, little more than a boy. Like the king of Britons, he indulged in most vices imaginable, and like his British counterpart, he was useless in all battle situations.

A Letter Arrives at the Kimbern

Hengest, who was leading the Kimbern Germanic forces, received the letter from King Vortigern of the Britons. I (Horsa) was leading the Kimbern warriors who were trained to mainly operate from longships at the time, and Hengest took the letter to me to read with him to save time and end any possible confusion. So, I read the letter out to him. It read, *"My dear Hengest and Horsa, I am Vortigern, the King of Britons, and I beg you for assistance in dealing with the marauding Picts and Scots who are constantly invading my country. They are always in the habit of raping the women of the Britons and killing my people as well as plundering them! I have vast reserves of both gold and silver, which has been left behind by the Romans when they abandoned Britania and returned to Rome a few years ago. Before they left, the Roman buried their hordes of gold and silver, but much of it has been found. If you come to my aid, I shall reward you with great riches!"*

Hengest said, *"My brother, I have heard of this King Vortigern! His reputation is that of a useless coward, and I do not like the idea of helping someone who is basically a coward. I have heard that he has no compassion for others and has the reputation of being a self-serving tyrant! All the same, I think it may be in the best interest of our people to go to Britania, during which time we can send back reports to the Engel tribe and the other two tribes about the land of Britania and its defences. What do you make of this, Horsa?"*

I now spoke to my brother. I said, *"Hengest, I believe that you are right. I think that what we have here is a plea from a coward who also happens to be a pity-less arsehole. It is my considered opinion that we must go to Britania and meet with this coward because we will get many riches by being his mercenary soldiers. We may even end up with land enough to resettle our tribes into Britania and provide the land necessary for living space that the members of the Kimbern, Engel and Saxon tribes are asking for! This is an opportunity for the gaining of riches and possibly the provision of new living space for all three of our tribes! I have spoken to the leaders of the Engel tribe, and they told me that the entire tribe wants to migrate to a new area".*

So, it was that my brother, a small band of two-hundred Kimbern warriors and myself, boarded five Engel longships and set sail for Britannia. Carrying our horses were the Saxon two-masted ships called Ceols. These were like a longship but broader and had a much deeper draft, allowing heavier loads. After sailing for two days, we arrived at Ipwinsfleet in the year of 449 A.D., and we landed on the islet of Thanet, where we set up our first camp and then set about meeting with the Briton King Vortigern. Hengest said, *"Horsa let's now go and meet with the weak king of Britons called Vortigern so that we can see what he is made of and get some idea of how rich or otherwise he may be.*

We must note all defences that we may see as well as the lay of the land and make maps accordingly. We should also commence writing reports about the land and its defences which we must send directly to the Engel headquarters at Anglen on the Jutland peninsula. After we have gathered enough intelligence about

Britannia and its defences, we should encourage our people in the three tribes to launch the necessary all-out invasions of Britania" I said to Hengest, *"My brother, as usual, you are correct, now, let's go and see this Briton despot ruler!"*

We eventually arrived where Vortigern was living in his castle, and we had a meeting which involved Vortigern, his translator called Ceretic, Hengest and me. It is just as well that the translator was there because his presence greatly helped our communicating with Vortigern. Vortigern began speaking through the translator, saying, *"Good day, gentlemen, you have the look of being both capable and able warriors. Both of you appear to move with grace, and you both give the impression of great latent strength and dexterity. Please tell me who you are and what your purpose for being here may be".*

After Ceretic had finished translating this to us, Hengest said, *"We are Kimbern warriors and Princes. Our people have entered an amalgamation with the Engels and the Saxons, which gives us great military strength! We come from the Jutland peninsula in northern Germania, and I am Hengest, while this is my brother, Horsa. We are both princes of the Kimbern people, and we are here in response to your letter asking for aid in stopping the incursions of Picts and Scots into your territory. Our father is Witta, and his father was Wecta, who is the son of Woden. So, my Great Uncle is Thor, the son of Woden!"*

Vortigern recognised that these men were, in fact, pagans and that caused him some discomfort. He also was overjoyed by the news that they were at his castle to answer the letter he had sent asking for help. He said, *"I can see that you Jutes are not of the true faith which is Christianity! Although I would like it if you became Christians, it is not necessary. I welcome you both because I need your services to stop the raids and invasions of my county by the*

31

Picts and Scots! Ever since the Romans left, we have had to put with these sorts of attacks upon our towns and cities. I have great wealth with which I can pay you for your services of protecting my people from the unwanted attention of Picks and Scots!"

Hengest now spoke again through the interpreter Ceretic. He said, *"Vortigern, my brother and I have a force of two hundred and seventy Kimbern warriors here with us who shall be placed into your service of stopping the invasions and other attacks by the Picts and Scots from occurring. To provide a good service to you, we must have a very secure base from which to launch our attacks upon the Picts and Scots! We must build a fortress on Thanet Island, and you shall provide both the labour force and the necessary stone to build it!"*

After he had considered this for about two minutes, Vortigern spoke to Hengest. He said, *"Kimbern Jute, I shall allow you to build a castle type of fortress within an area that can be enclosed by a tanned leather thong made from a single bull's hide. I am happy to provide the labour force and stone to do that because you will not be able to build much of a fortress within the area enclosed by a thong made from the hide of a single bull which I am providing. Those are my conditions for you to build a fortress on Thanet Island.*

If you decide to accept my conditions, you must firstly prove yourselves to me and permanently stop the invasions of the Picts and Scots into my territory! You now have my conditions, take them or leave them and depart from here if you decide to leave them!" I thought that Hengest was going crazy when I heard him answer. He said, *"Very well then Vortigern, I accept your terms, but firstly I need much information about the Picks and Scots. Whom you speak of, such as where are they normally located, what route do they usually take when attacking your country, do they have help from other areas or countries, what obstacles are in their path that could* be used and improved upon so that they will find increasing difficulty in attacking your country?"

Vortigern answered with, "Hengest, the resources of the Picts and Scots appear to be vast. They have help from their kin located in the Orkney islands off the coast of Scotland, and that makes dealing a body blow to these invaders difficult. They have roving bands of Pict and Scottish warriors who just cross Hadrian's Wall at will, now that the Romans are no longer here to guard the wall. In fact, they started to take down the wall in some places and then they have used the material to build homes at other sites.

The routes that they take are through the Roman openings in the wall at the former Roman gatehouses! These mostly have fortifications which can be used by your warriors, other than at the places where material has been removed from the wall to make homes for these people! Hengest said, "I see. I need some things, firstly maps where-ever possible, showing everything, we have discussed and the locations of Scottish settlements on the mainland as well as the Orkney Islands. I also need maps and charts showing trade routes as well as the locations of the Roman gatehouses in Hadrian's wall. Also, I must be allowed to send for more Kimbern warriors because the warriors you have supplied are close to useless!"

Vortigern said, "Once you have demonstrated your dominion over the Picks and Scots' and after they have sopped attacking and laying waste to my lands, then and only then may you build your fortification on Thanet Island. I will then also allow you to send for reinforcements of Kimbern warriors from Germania. So, the sooner you can bring the Picts and Scots to heel, the sooner you will have your fortress and your Kimbern reinforcements!

I note that both you, Hengest and your brother Horsa are Kimbern Princes. After you have made my country safe for my *people here in Kent, I shall be glad to make both of you generals in my army. I shall assign men to your commands as I see fit, but only after you and Horsa have made my country safe from the attacking enemies! Remember that the sooner you bring the enemies to heel, the sooner you shall have your fortress on Thanet Island, and the sooner you shall command my army!"*

That prompted Hengest to say, *"Firstly, Vortigern, you must make sure that the men you are assigning to my brother, and I have some knowledge of our German language. To help to achieve that, I shall run German language classes for the warriors you place under our command. When that happens, be sure to only give Horsa and me your very best warriors, for Horsa, and I shall constantly monitor their performances. Those who do not measure up to our expectations shall be returned to you immediately.*

I have had letters sent to my home base in Germania asking for more Kimbern warriors to be sent here. We must have these extra Kimbern warriors so that we can raid the Scots in their own homes, including on the Orkney Islands. The reinforcements that I have requested from home should be here within fourteen days or less. When they arrive, we shall silence the threat to your country that is coming from the invaders while simultaneously attacking other population centres of the Scots and Picks. After that has been done, there should be peace for a time. Now it is you who can take what I am offering you, or you can leave it, and the Kimbern force will depart immediately if you decide against allowing me my reinforcements!"

Hengest then said, *"If you answer is that my warriors and bother are to stay here assisting you, you shall get me all your map-makers, sailors and all good soldiers that you may have so that we can plan the assault upon the Picts and Scots. To be successful against them, we will not just have to beat them in the field when they cross into your territory. We must also attack them in their own homes and in all areas where they think that they are safe from attack by your forces! In short, we must make them feel very insecure, even when they are in their own homes on the Scottish main-land or on the Orkney Islands!* After considering what had been said by Hengest, Vortigern said, *"Very well, Hengest, you have what you want. I give approval for you and Horsa to bring in more Kimbern warriors!"*

Hengest & Horsa Fight Invaders

It was always in the areas of planning and negotiations that Hengest was totally supreme. His nature was that of a cold, calculating and highly disciplined man who would always observe what was happening before making a considered decision. He could make quick decisions that were always to his advantage, even when other people thought that they had the better of him. As planned, he now obtained the maps provided by the staff of Vortigern. He then studied those maps until he was familiar with everything on them. He then spoke to other officers of Vortigern's army, and from them, he learned about the routes usually taken by the Picts and Scots when they were raiding the Britons. It was during this time that Hengest and me (Horsa) were to write letters in the Latin language to their German comrades at home and completely unknown to Vortigern, Ceretic and others in the forces of the Britons, Hengest also wrote letters to both his people in Germania and to his daughter Rowena.

To his people, Hengest had written, *"The land here in Britania is rich, and it can sustain far more people than it currently supports! The king of the Britons is a lazy, cowardly, and inferior man who is known to be open to every vice imaginable, and he does not want to fight. He only wants others to do the fighting for him! Because of his cowardly nature, we now can have new lands for our people by simply taking over his locality in the Britania area known as Kent. To be successful in this, I need many more warriors!*

The letter from Hengest to the elders of the Engel, Kimbern and Saxon tribes continued. It said, *"After we have successfully ridded Vortigern of his Pict and Scottish enemies, I shall ask for increasing amounts of warriors from Germania and for our women to join us here in what our Engel cousins now call Engel-land when the time is right. In due course, I shall make representations to Prince Eomaer, the current leader of the Engel tribe, for him to also bring the Engels to the island's north, where the Engels said they wanted to settle and they will from now on called this land Engel-land, and they will find new and suitable productive land for them to use."*

To his daughter Rowena he had a letter written which said, *"My dearest daughter, I am going to prepare things for you to become the Queen of Britons, and I shall give you the details of this when you join me here in Kent, located in southern Engel-land. I will let you know the details when you arrive here later. For now, ready yourself for your coming role of being the Queen of the Britons. Before that happens, there is much to be done by many people. I shall be in touch with you about these matters again later when things are closer to needing to be completed. Greatest and love from your father, – Hengest."*

At a meeting between Hengest, Vortigern, Ceretic and me (Horsa) in the morning a week after the following day, Hengest spoke. He said, *"Gentlemen, Horsa and I have closely studied the maps you have provided, and we have gone to extraordinary lengths to completely reconnoitre the entire length of Hadrian's Wall from the east coast to the west coast of Britania! We have discovered three more probable routes which are bound to be used by the Picts and Scots when invading your country. Also, we have reports written in Latin by officers of the Briton army. Combined, these things give us an edge over the Picts and Scots. We can use this intelligence to organise ambushes and give the invaders a nasty surprise!"*

Speaking now directly to Vortigern through the interpreter Ceretic, Hengest spoke. He said, *"Vortigern, Horsa and I shall each lead forces made up of one hundred and thirty-seven Kimbern warriors who have been reinforced by the addition of another one hundred and thirty-seven Briton warriors from the army of Vortigern. The two forces shall bring to heel the invaders who are causing you so much grief! All these men are volunteers for this mission. The Britons who have volunteered for this expedition have been trained in the Saxon arts of war and our German language so that they shall understand their orders! We are taking this fight directly to the Picts and Scots, who will not understand what has hit them when we actively ambush the Pict and Scottish routes of attack through the wall and into your territory!*

I shall lead the first units of warriors. We are ambushing the invaders at locations of breaks in the wall. About fourteen miles to the north-west of Carlisle, where there is a sharp bend in the wall. And where there are beaks in I, it is weak! Many of the breaks in Hadrian's wall were put there by the Romans to let commerce flourish between the Britons and Scots! Horsa will take another group of warrior units numbering one-hundred and thirty-seven Germanic warriors. As well as the same number of Briton warriors to the area of an old Roman fortification and a break in the wall, located approximately halfway along its east to west length. Located some forty-two miles to the east from Carlisle in the west. That is another major route taken by the attacking enemies of the Britons!

By ambushing the Picts and Scots as they come into the land of Britons, we should be able to stop further attacks from occurring for a time. After that, we must go after the Picts and Scots, no matter where they may be living. To successfully mount offensives against the enemies of the Britons, I need vastly increased numbers of Germanic warriors than I currently have here. Vortigern, I am asking for your permission to bring in as many Germanic warriors as are needed to reinforce my warriors! They are needed to make Britania safe for your people!" Vortigern now spoke with the aid of the interpreter called Ceretic.

He said, *"Hengest, you are welcome to bring in more Germanic warriors to help in ridding my country of the Pick and Scottish pests! I will consult with you further on this subject later when we discuss your fee for providing protection for my people and what we must provide you and your forces with. That discussion shall take place after you have dealt with the enemy using the ambushes you have described and other punitive actions against the enemies of my kingdom! We shall also discuss what further action must be taken against my enemies when you have completed that, as well as any additional reinforcements that you may need to bring to my country!"*

So, it was that Hengest and his small, combined force of Kimbern and Briton warriors went to the old Roman barracks and fortifications near Carlisle. At the same time, I and my combined force of Germanic and Briton warriors, which also totalled two hundred and seventy-four men went to a point about halfway along Hadrian's wall. Here there was a break in the wall to allow commerce to pass through it as well as a barracks to house the previous Roman soldiers. All the buildings were abandoned but still usable.

Both small forces now made themselves as invisible as possible. That was done by not allowing any outward signs of occupation of the former Roman barracks and other buildings. No fires were allowed, and the members of both forces were ordered to remain silent unless new orders were given or a tactical situation needed to be discussed between the warriors. I was pleased to see that the Briton members of our forces were becoming accustomed to the discipline of the Kimbern and they were performing much better than both my brother and I expected.

Normal conversation between warriors was forbidden, and that resulted in the men speaking to each other in whispers in case the marauding Picts and Scots became tipped off about our presence. Sentries were assigned and rotated every hour. That allowed everyone in our ambush units to be fresh and rested. After the middle of the night, a large force of three hundred or more Picts was observed by my warriors stationed in their ambush positions about half-way along Hadrian's Wall. I was notified about the situation, and I quietly moved to join the sentries to see for myself what was happening.

I saw that the Picks were all heavily armed and that their main protection was their large and heavy shields which they had strapped onto their backs. I quietly sent the word down the ambush line that my warriors were to let the enemy reach the limits of our position before we sprang the ambush. As the enemy was continuing to advance, I quietly moved to the end of the ambush site. When I got there, I began counting the passing Pict warriors. After I had counted twenty of them, I gave orders. I yelled, *"Archers and spearmen, kill the enemy! Other warriors, attack and slay the Picts with your battle-axes and swords! All warriors are to line just one side of the track leading past us so that we do not accidentally wound our own men with arrows or spears! By all of us being on the same side of the track, there will only be enemies before us!"*

It was now that I became thankful that I had the foresight to personally train all my warriors, including the Britons who had been assigned to my brother and me by King Vortigern. I had the satisfaction of seeing that all my warriors had high degrees of battle readiness and skills at arms. All the men in my units and sub-units knew their tasks and the tasks of the men immediately above them and below them in rank and station. That resulted in every warrior knowing exactly what he was to do in all situations. An added benefit of this was that in the event of a chief or a sub-chief becoming a casualty, someone else would automatically take his place, thereby allowing the battle to continue my terms.

I had placed one archer with every four other warriors, with these men being located about twelve feet away from the track and spaced at eight feet apart. It was night-time, but we could see reasonably well because of the bright moonlight from a full moon. As soon as the arrows were shot and the spears had been thrown, we all engaged the enemy using our battle-axes and swords. The result of our ambush was that many Picks fled, leaving two hundred and eighty-four of their comrades lying dead on the track near Hadrian's Wall and the opening through it

Our attack was over in a heart-beat, and I ordered the men to go out to where the Picts were lying and to kill those who were not already dead. That was quickly done, and in some cases, my warriors cut the throats of the Picks, using the Saxon long knives. In some other cases, the enemy was dispatched to the next world by my warriors using battle-axes while some other Kimbern warriors drew their long broad swords out of their sheaths and then used them to kill the enemy! To have some idea of what had been accomplished, we counted the bodies of our dead enemies. Meanwhile, at the ambush site near Carlisle, which Hengest commanded, a force of three hundred Scottish warriors was approaching the position where he and his warriors were lying in wait for them. Hengest used similar tactics to those that I had used in that he also had a mixture of archers and spear-throwers launch the attack on the Scots.

As the morning twilight turned into full sunshine, my men and I left our ambush site and proceeded to travel to the location of my brother and his warriors. We arrived at his Carlisle location the following afternoon. Finally arriving, I spoke to Hengest. He said, *"Horsa, we will be in conference with Vortigern, his translator and advisors, in due course. I shall take the opportunity to tell him that our mission of harrying the Pick and Scottish invaders of his country has been successful and demand that we bring in more Germanic warriors. I shall also demand that he pays us gold and provide provisions for our warriors. I shall also demand that all materials and the work-force to build the fortress on Thanet Island are provided by him immediately!*

Also, I have secretly had one thousand and eight hundred more Kimbern warriors selected for service with us here in Britania. When they arrive here, my daughter Rowena shall be with them. She will become the ruling Queen of the Britons, and I have sent word to Prince Eomaer, the leader of the Engels, to take up land in Britania to the north of us here in Kent. He answered my letters to him, and he has indicated that he shall soon be arriving together with all his people! Now rest my brother, tomorrow we shall see Vortigern, and we shall get what we want!"

A new meeting with Vortigern and his staff was arranged, and during this meeting, Hengest firstly reported our victories against the Pick and Scots. He said, *"Vortigern, my brother and I have wiped out two units of Pick and Scots which had a combined strength of five hundred and eighty-four warriors! That shall bring peace to your country for a time but remember that the problem of the Pict and Scottish invaders is still out there, patiently waiting for more opportunities to attack your country and its people!*

It is only my warriors that stand between the invaders and your people. I am now going to tell you about our demands for giving you and your country protection from invaders, no matter where the invaders may come from! You and your people must provide my warriors with food and other provisions that may become necessary for us to continue our work of ridding your country of the invading Picts and Scots! We need to have a strong fortification upon Thanet Island, which will also house my command centre. Do you give permission for work to start on this?"

Vortigern replied, *"I grant you permission to build a tower or other fortification on the rocky part of Thanet Island, but that must be no greater than the area that a single leather thong can enclose."* Hengest immediately replied with, *"Thank you, Vortigern, after we have taken more action against the invaders of your country, we shall get to work in laying out my fortification. Which I call the Thong Castle because of the restrictions which you have placed upon it."*

What Vortigern did not know was the Hengest had already obtained five very large bulls which would be used to both provide a feast and the hide from which to make the leather thong which was to be used to mark out the area of his fortifications. Hengest was planning to use the meat from bulls at a feast he was planning. He wanted to have the court of Vortigern attend the feast, which was to be held after his reinforcements and his daughter Rowena arrived at Thanet Island. They, at last, arrived in eight longships which were propelled by a combination of oars and sails, crewed by Engel warriors. The longships were accompanied by six redesigned triremes and two twin masted Ceols, which were Saxon ships.

Hengest watched as the ships arrived at Thanet Island and were anchored. He waited until the one thousand eight hundred Kimbern warriors had disembarked, and then he set out to find Rowena. Finally, he saw his beautiful daughter, Rowena. He then waited until she was rowed ashore, and then he embraced her. He said, *"Rowena, my lovely girl, I am so happy to see you here! Come now, I have your living quarters ready for you, and I have assigned you some Britons as servants. Make sure that you keep a close watch on the Britons and do not trust them!*

They give the appearance of being most untrustworthy, and many of them appear to have no morals at all. Yet, they constantly criticise us for being what they call pagans and not worshipping their god, who is so weak that the people who believe in him hanged up their god on a Roman cross! The King of the Britons is both weak-willed and open to many vices, including having sex with his own daughters! That is both disgusting, and against the moral principles of our people as well as that, even the religion of the Britons calls such acts incest! Because Vortigern is so weak, I am sure that when you marry him, that you will dominate the Britons as their queen. Always remember that you can always count upon the services of myself and your uncle Horsa to make things happen for you. I will go into all of that with you in detail later. For now, rest and I will see you at tonight's evening meal which shall take place in the mess-hall just over there to the right!"

Having said that, he left. Hengest now came over to me and said, *"Horsa, I am going to stage a feast to which all the ruling Britons will be invited. I will get Rowena to make sure that Vortigern, the king of Britons, has as much ale and wine as he can drink. The object is to get him drunk so that his guard will be down. Rowena will be constantly supplying him with whatever he needs, and she will be very attractive to arouse his interest in her.*

The five large bulls I have obtained will be killed and their meat cured, ready for the feast. The hide of the five animals shall be cured and made into one continuous thin leather thong. The feast will take place right after you have taken the war to the Scots, right where they feel most secure, namely, your forces will attack the Scots in their homes on their Orkney Islands

While you are leading the raiding of the Orkneys, I shall be leading our new invasion of the Scottish mainland. After both new operations have been completed, we shall use the leather thong to mark out our castle on Thanet Island. Keep on training your warriors, brother, because we shall soon be back in action. I want you to get rid of the Britons who are warriors in your forces and replace the one hundred and thirty-seven of them with some of the Kimbern warrior reinforcements who have just arrived. The remaining new Kimbern warriors will bolster my force, raiding the Scottish mainland while you are busy in the Orkneys. I already have the locations of some Pick villages, and they will not be spared! After you have also returned from raiding the Orkneys, the feast shall take place. That shall be followed by us making further demands upon Vortigern and the Britons!"

That resulted in having my warriors practising embarking and disembarking the ceols, triremes and longships. The longship being the favoured method of shipping used by the Engels. These things were practised all over Thanet Island and on some of the islands located in the English Channel. I had my warriors practise quietly disembarking from the ships and storming ashore during the night in both calm and rough weather so that all warriors would know exactly what was required of them when the real invasion and raiding of the Orkneys took place.

I was practising this with my warriors because, as their leader, it was of great importance for me always to be always seen at the head of my warriors. It is because of this, "Leading from in front and thereby setting the example", my warriors would always do whatever I asked of them. After all, the sight of the leader going forward without hesitation and doing what he is asking his men to do is always the best way to ensure that the men will have a total commitment to the task at hand and that they will follow the example of their leader.

I kept my warriors in training by practising at least two sea-borne assaults per night. I was always with the men, and they loved me for doing that. I always shared their hardships, and when we were victorious against an enemy, I shared the booty taken from the enemy with my men. After another four nights of this training and rehearsing, I felt that we were ready to take the war directly to the Scots located on the Orkney Islands. I had a meeting with my twin brother Hengest. I said, *"Hengest, everyone in my force of Kimbern sea-raiders knows what is expected of him, and we are ready to take the war directly to the Scots located on the Orkney Islands!"*

Hengest said to me, *"Horsa, let us now pray to Woden so that he will grant us fair weather and a moonlit night for our attack upon the Orkneys in seven days from now! You may think that you and your men have all the training that is necessary, but I want you and your men to keep on practising the night-time sea-borne invasion of the Orkney islands, although you could cut these practices down to just one every second night between now and when you sail!*

A traitor to the Scots has come forward with information from which a model and some maps of the Orkneys and their settlements are now being prepared. He said, *"As soon as the model and the maps are ready, I need you to assemble all your warriors and then I will personally take each man through both the maps and the model, making sure that they understand exactly what they must do and when they must do it once we launch the raid upon the settlements on the Orkneys.*

You must make sure that each man memorises the lay-out and the locations of buildings on the Orkney Islands. You shall also be responsible for the assignment of duties to each warrior. So, take each of your warriors through what must be done, how to do it and when it must be done!" That was completed, and the warriors now found themselves assembled outside a mess-hall. I asked the warriors to come forward in groups of four men. They would go into the mess-hall and study the model of the Orkneys and their settlements. I now ensured that I was standing close to the model and answered the questions that each warrior may have had.

After each man had memorised the lay-out of the Orkney Islands and their settlements, roads, tracks, and obstacles such as streams and drains, I would quiz each man to make sure that he knew everything that needed to be done, when to do it and how to do so. A warrior said, *"Horsa, I suggest in the time that is left before we sail on this punitive raid against the Scots on the Orkneys, that we build a replica of the two villages on the Orkneys and make many practise raids upon both, by both day and night! That would make us an unstoppable force!"* I was in agreeance with that. I said, *"Well suggested Kurt! That is what we shall do!"* so, we practised raiding the two villages by both day and night for every one of the next few days.

After a long time, I was sure that everyone in my command knew what was happening and his part in achieving the successful outcome. With great joy, I spoke to Hengest. I said, *"Brother, my men are totally ready for action right now! In fact, they are eager to complete the invasion and raiding of the Orkneys! They all know what is to be done and how it must be done!"* Hengest replied, *"Good! Let your warriors know that we shall be providing a large feast in five days from now and that they shall be able to eat and drink as much of whatever they want! Tell them that both beer and wine as well as roast pork and beef shall be provided!*

I have already ordered some men to begin preparing things by slaughtering and butchering the five bulls and the pigs. Five days shall be long enough for the meat of the bulls to cure and set. As soon as they have been slaughtered, the hide of the bulls shall undergo the tanning process. When the leather has been cured and is ready for use, narrow strips of the bulls' hide will be turned into the leather thong with which we shall mark out our fortifications on Thanet Island. Once we have the very long leather thong, we shall invite Vortigern to see us marking out our castle using it. That will remove his possible objections to the size of it. As for the Picts and Scots, you and your warriors are to sail to the Orkneys immediately while my warriors and I depart to deal death and destruction to the Picts and Scots on the Scottish mainland!"

Hengest now went to his daughter, Rowena. He spoke to her. He said, *"Rowena please pay attention to what I am about to tell you. Tonight, we launch two simultaneous attacks upon the Pict and Scottish foes of the Britons. Your uncle Horsa is even now on his way to the Orkney Islands, where his forces will attack the Scots in their own homes at night! I am leaving in a few moments to attack the Picts in their own base areas at night also! We shall attack the Pick areas and settlements north of the wall. We know exactly where they are, and we have their locations marked on accurate maps. After marching directly to these base areas and Pict settlements, we shall attack their homes during the morning twilight, when they are still half-asleep!"*

Your uncle and I may be gone for as long as three to four days. While we are gone, I need you to prepare for a feast to which the court of King Vortigern have been invited. That has been scheduled for five days from now, and it will begin in the late afternoon. During the feast, you are to constantly supply Vortigern with as much ale and wine as he wants! You must be very alluring and looking your absolute best! If he wants to fondle you, let him so in such a way that he will always want more of you! I suggest that you even let him expose one of your magnificent breasts and let him both fondle your beasts and even let him insert his fingers into your vagina.

You must make him desire to marry you more than he likes life itself! Once he is married to you, I will take up my power over him due to him being my son-in-law. He shall then have to obey my commands according to Kimbern law! So, Rowena, this is a very big and very important task for you! Do you think that you can handle it?" Rowena replied, *"Pappa, you know that I can do so! I will make sure that Vortigern is totally beguiled and smitten by my presence. Rest assured that I shall be his wife, no matter what other members of his family may think! As you have mentioned to me, this will make me the ruling Queen of the Britons, and they will from then on swear allegiance directly to me as well as to Vortigern or even instead of Vortigern!"*

Now that all was completed on the domestic front, Hengest and his forces got underway to the closest Pick settlements on the northern side of the wall while my forces and I set sail for the Orkney Islands. We had sailed for a long time, and I was peering through the night-time fog, trying to see where we were. Suddenly, the fog lifted, and there was now brilliant moonlight! I could see some light shining out of openings in dwellings on the Orkneys, and we now steered our ships towards the settlements. With my fleet of forty ships now split into equal halves, we proceeded to attack both settlements we could see. All my units or their sub-units went to the homes of the Scots and attacked them by bursting through the doors if the houses had them. The startled inhabitants tried to resist us, but they were quickly overcome.

My warriors were raping the Scottish women, and we carried away a lot of plunder and booty as our reward for the night's work after we had killed many Scots with our two-handed battle-axes and swords. I now addressed my warriors and said, *"Men, tonight you have excelled yourselves! We have successfully carried the war to the Scots on the Orkney Islands, and I wager that this lesson shall not be forgotten! There shall be equal shares of all booty that we have taken tonight as soon as we get back to Thanet Island!* My warriors rejoiced upon hearing me say that. They began to chant, *Hail Horsa! Long live, Horsa!* The happy sound of my warriors pleased me.

After sailing back to Thanet Island, we found that Rowena was already well towards implementing her father's plan of action. There were already very large amounts of beer and wine in the storerooms where it was securely kept. We were waiting for Hengest and his warriors to return from harrying the Scots on the mainland. Soon, there was the sound of trumpets heralding the approach of Hengest and his warriors. We saw Hengest approach us, and he was quickly embraced by Rowena.

He said to Rowena, *"How are things progressing for the feast which will be held in about two days from now?"* she said, *"Pappa, I am happy to inform you that we have as much ale and wine as any man or group of men can drink and much more! All of that is safely stored away from unauthorised persons. The five bulls have both been slaughtered and butchered. Their skins are undergoing the tanning process in compliance with your orders. The meat is in secure storage away from flies, and it is undergoing the processes of setting and curing. It shall be ready for consumption in two days from now. Is that what not you wanted?"* Hengest answered, *"Yes, my daughter, it most certainly is!"*

The Feast is a Huge Success

Hengest noted with satisfaction that the members of the court of Vortigern were arriving and were being seated in the main mess hall, which was also being used by his warriors. The five bulls were on spits that were being slowly turned over the fires under them, and the pleasant smell of cooking beef filled the air. There were also twenty pigs being roasted on spits, and that would give the guests a choice between the main courses of beef or pork or even both.

49

Hengest had seen for himself how the hide of the bulls was being cured and was in the process of being turned into leather by tanning the hides. That was to be followed by cutting the hides into thin strips and making one continuous leather thong out of them all.

It was late afternoon, and Hengest spoke to Rowena. He said, *"Rowena, my girl, I think that you could start the feast because Vortigern and his court have arrived here. That is him over there, accompanied by his four current wives. I think that you should put on your white velvet dress with the gold thread stitching and gold leaf stitched into the collar areas. Wear your golden chains, rings and other trinkets, so that Vortigern and his entire court will be dazzled by you and what you are wearing!"*

Rowena replied, *"Yes, Pappa, I will change into the clothes and apparel that you speak of and wash and anoint myself, give me a few moments!"* having said that to her father, Rowena went to her quarters, washed herself, and changed into the clothing and followed that by putting on the jewellery like she had been told and then anointing herself. After some time, she re-emerged from her room, and Hengest was most impressed with the way his daughter now looked. As well, she had a pleasant and seductive smell about her from the fragrance she had applied to herself. Her white velvet dress and its trimming complimented her fine slim body, which was made even more visually appealing by the jewellery that she was wearing. She had the look of someone who could take away the breath of a crowd.

Hengest said, *"By Woden, my girl, you look so very beautiful and desirable! If the way you look does not interest Vortigern and cause immense jealousy of you among his current wives, then nothing will! I now want you to attend to Vortigern and make sure that he ends up becoming drunk. Make sure that you are always within his sight and let him know that you are a serving princess of the Kimbern nation from the Jutland area of Germania and that you would like to be the very effective ruler of Britania! Make sure that he knows that to have you, he must get rid of his four current wives!"* Rowena simply said, *"Yes, Pappa"*, and then she went over to where Vortigern and his companions were seated, and she began speaking to Vortigern's translator called Ceretic.

To Ceretic, she said, *"Good day, sir, I am the serving Kimbern princess from the Jutland area of Germania, and my name is Rowena! My father is Hengest, and that is him, over there. Pappa has instructed me to personally look after you and the court of Vortigern and to make sure that you all have whatever you may need. May I now fill your goblet with either ale or wine?"*

That was answered by Ceretic, who was impressed by the alluring looks of Rowena, as was everyone else who was present at the feast. He knew that his king was always interested in beautiful young women, and he was very aware that a possible marriage of Vortigern to Rowena could provide the badly needed union between the Britons and the Germanic tribe that was protecting the Britons from Picts and Scots. He spoke to Vortigern. He said, *"Sire, please allow me to introduce Princess Rowena of the Kimbern nation on the Jutland Peninsula. She is the daughter of Hengest, whom you already know as your military advisor and commander of the forces who are protecting us from the Picts and Scots. Hengest has ordered that Rowena shall be waiting upon you and your immediate party!"*

Vortigern was already becoming affected by the alcohol he was consuming, and he threw caution to the wind and began to flirt with Rowena as best he could, bearing in mind that he did not speak her language, whereas she was always a step ahead of him in that she had by now learned some of the basic language spoken by the Britons. That allowed her to understand much of the conversation between the Britons. She immediately understood what Ceretic and Vortigern were saying when she heard Vortigern say to Ceretic,

"What a beautiful girl! I want her, and I need to fuck her as quickly as possible, even if I must marry her and make her a true ruling queen of the Britons!" Ceretic was mindful of the weak military situation the Britons were in, and so, he cautioned Vortigern.

He said, *"Vortigern, my king, I urge you to exercise patience! I remind you that in you getting married to a Kimbern Princess, you may find that you shall be subject to the laws of the Kimbern and that they may then give you orders! You could find yourself subject to the laws and traditions of the Kimbern nation rather than the laws and traditions of Britania!"* Having overheard what the two men were saying and understanding it made Rowena smile in the sure knowledge that the plan was beginning to take shape.

She kept on serving wine and ale to the immediate family and party of Vortigern, all the time making sure that Vortigern could plainly see her. Whenever she served wine or ale to Vortigern, she would do so by coming up very close behind him and then she would lean forward, pouring the wine or ale into his goblet. That allowed him to look down her cleavage, and by so doing, he could see her magnificent left breast and nipple, which excited him to the point that he completely forgot that he was in s public feast. Much to the dismay of his four current wives, and his translator, he put his hand up the dress of Rowena, who opened her legs a bit wider, and she allowed him to insert his index finger into her vagina and begin an up and down motion with it, effectively 'finger fucking', her.

She allowed him to continue doing that and even allowed him to feel around under her dress and fondle her beats with his left hand while the index finger of his right hand was still inserted into her vagina. She now said to Vortigern, *"Well Vortigern, enjoy your finger fucking of me because that is as close to the real thing as you will ever get, unless of course, you get rid of your current four wives and then, marry me!*

You shall have to make me the sole Queen of the Britons, and you shall have to see to it that I have real power by proclamation, or else you shall never have me! As I was hearing Rowena say that I was thinking, *"Well done, Rowena, you really are your father's daughter! He should be well pleased by this display of how much like him you are!"* Having enraptured Vortigern successfully, she now served other guests of the feast until Vortigern sort an audience with Hengest. He agreed to the audience with Vortigern, who as always was accompanied by the translator, Ceretic. Vortigern was the first to speak. He said, *"Hengest, I am very attracted to your daughter, Rowena, and I want her to be my queen. Will you give your permission for me to marry your daughter?"*

I always knew that Hengest would turn everything to his own advantage because of his cold and calculating manner. I heard Hengest say, *"Vortigern, my answer is no! you shall not marry my girl because you are already married to four other women! Get it through your rather thick head that Germanic women have the same rights as their male counterparts! That also means that Germanic warriors have one wife!*

The only way for you to ever have Rowena as your wife is to firstly get rid of all four of your current wives. That must be done three months before you marry Rowena, who shall stay with me until such time as you firstly marry her and hold her coronation service on the same day! So, think it over! If you want Rowena as your Queen, she must have her coronation as the ruling Queen of Britons on the same day as you marry her, and you will proclaim in public that Queen Rowena now commands the army of the Britons! Now go and think this over! Be sure you mean it if you still want to go ahead and marry Rowena after you have thought it through because when you do marry her, she shall have real power. She will always have the entire resources of the Saxon confederation both here and in Germania available to her to impose her will upon anyone, anywhere! I shall give you two days to think it over! After two days have elapsed, I will assume that you have decided to accept my terms for you to marry my daughter. When that happens, you shall find that you will from that time onwards be governed by Kimbern law because I shall be your father-in-law!"

After two days, Vortigern could no longer control his overwhelming desire for Rowena, and he, therefore, sent word to Hengest that he agreed the terms of the marriage set by Hengest and added, *"Please let me marry your daughter immediately and I shall make her the ruling Queen of the Britons as you have asked. I shall firstly get rid of my current four wives if the priests let me do so! If not, then their official positions shall be downgraded so that they officially stop being my wives and become 'Comfort Women'. The coronation of Rowena as true Queen of the Britons will be scheduled for the same day as my marriage to her.*

When we get married, Rowena will have her coronation as the Queen of Britons immediately after the wedding. During the wedding ceremony, I shall announce that Rowena is now the commander in chief of the army of the Britons! When Rowena is married to me, she will have real power and be in joint control of my armed forces with me."

Vortigern agreed to the acceptance of the demands of Hengest, resulting in both the wedding and the coronation of Rowena being held on the same day. A conference between the two men at a later time of the same day concluded with Vortigern saying, *"When you come to my castle to see me, I would prefer the time of day to be when the sun is high in the sky tomorrow, please also have your demands for the continued protection of my people ready, and we shall also set in motion, the construction of your thong castle on Thanet Island!"*

That pleased Hengest very much, and he then came to me and said, *"Horsa, take some men and mark out the entire thong castle on Thanet Island using the one continuous leather thong we have had made. Closely inspect all joins to make sure that they are all sound and invisible. We will take Vortigern to the location, and he will tell his workers to begin construction, even if he is surprised at the sheer size of it. He will do my bidding because that is the only way he will ever be able to have my daughter, Rowena, with whom he is enchanted. He wants to make her his Queen, and when he does so, she will have total power over Britons!"*

I said to him, *"By Woden and Thor, Hengest, you sure do know how to get your way, and that is very good for our people! Do you think that we have anywhere near enough warriors here? I am thinking that sooner or later, Vortigern's own people will tire of us foreigners being here and he will be forced to act against us at some point in the future, so we must be ready if we are to stay in this country!"*

I need not have worried about things because Hengest, as usual was right on top of the situation, because in the meantime, Hengest had been in contact directly with Prince Eomaer, the leader of the Engels. In Latin, he had written to Eomaer. His letter read, *"Prince Eomaer, gather up your entire people and come hither to Britania. The land is rich, and the Britons are a lazy and unworthy people. There is much to be gained by your people in this, and it will be best if you bring them all as quickly as possible. I shall be very happy if you and your Engel warriors and sailors were to settle in the northern part of this from a city called York right up to the Scottish border."*

Within the long harbour of the fiord known as Eckenforde there were now one hundred and ten Engel longships. They were being made ready and maintained for the mass migration to Britain of the entire Engel tribe! The leader of the Engels, Prince Eomaer was in command, and he kept his fingers on the pulse of the coming mass migration of his people.

Now that the time was here, he spoke to his people. He said, *"The entire Engel tribe shall go to new lands which I have named as Engle-land and take up new territory there! We will firstly send our best warriors in the first fleet of one hundred and ten longships, and we shall repeat that as many times as necessary to move our entire people to the new territories! That shall leave our current home along the banks of Eckenforde on the Jutland peninsula abandoned.*

There are some longships which are under various stages of construction that shall have to be left here because we are operating to a tight schedule! I am hoping that we can successfully move the entire tribe to Engel-land using just three movements of our one hundred and ten longships! However, we shall complete the move using as many trips of the entire fleet as may become necessary! Even our animals will be taken with us to our new territory in Engel-land!"

So, it was that the first fleet of one hundred and ten Engel longships sailed for Britannia carrying men, women, children, fowls, cats, dogs, horses, and other things necessary for the Engels when they arrived at their new homeland. As the ships were nearing the coast of what we now call Northumbria, Prince Eomaer spoke to those around him. He said, *"Æthol and Konrad, and look over there toward our front and towards the west, does it not remind you of the coasts near Eckenforde?"* Both warriors answered, *"Yes it does, why are you saying this?"* Prince Eomaer said, *"Gentlemen and fellow Engels please look upon our new homeland! I hereby name this new countryside as "Engel-land".* (Land of the Engels).

News of the arrival of the new-comers quickly reached the ears of Vortigern who became alarmed, and he went to see Hengest to speak to him about the new-comers whom he thought could be a threat to the security of the Britons. When he met with Hengest, he said, *"Hengest, I am alarmed that new people have taken up territory to the north, and the east and west of us. I need you to see these people and if you think that they are a security threat, then you and the warriors you have must push them back into the sea where they have come from!"*

By now, Hengest and I had both learned to speak the complicated language of the Britons, but Hengest pretended to not be able to understand or to speak the language. Instead, he insisted upon the presence of the translator called Ceretic in all dealings with Vortigern. Speaking via Ceretic, Hengest said, *"Vortigern, my brother, our warriors and I have now been in your service for almost a year! During that time, we have nullified the threats to the existence of Britons from both Picks and Scots! So, believe me when I say to you that there is no threat to the security of Britons coming from the newly arrived Engels!*

They have come here at my request to do so in order that the threats to Britons from the Picts and Scots will be permanently silenced! To provide total security to all parts of Britania peopled by Britons, I have also asked the Kimbern brethren called Saxons to come to Britannia and settled towards the north of us and west of us here in Kent. When that happens, your security will be complete!"

Vortigern asked through the aid of Ceretic *"Hengest, will you give me permission to marry Rowena?"* Hengest replied, *"Certainly, have the priests of your religion set everything in motion and we shall have the Royal Wedding right here on Thanet Island. Now, we must go on to other matters! Firstly, we, the Kimbern are providing the feast and the drink necessary to celebrate your wedding to my daughter! There should be more than enough meat, wine, and ale for every man and woman to eat and drink his or her fill!"* Vortigern replied, *"Thank you, Hengest, I now want to inspect your marked-out site for the construction of the fortress that you want my workers to build for you!"*

Hengest agreed and both men went to the marked-out construction site. Vortigern could not understand how such a large area could be marked out using a single leather thong. So, he asked Hengest about it, all the time expecting some sort of trickery. Hengest simply said to him, *"Vortigern, I have done as you asked. Please inspect the leather thong and you will find that there are no joins in it that you can see, because this is one continuous leather thong, just as you wanted in the first place! Now then, if you truly, wish to marry Rowena, I shall give both of you my blessing and I shall continue my role of being the protector of your people."*

That satisfied Vortigern. He said, *"All right Hengest, we will get on with building your castle that you have laid out. The labour force and materials for that shall begin arriving as of the morrow morning!"* It was just as well that the two leaders had worked out their differences because the Engels were now arriving in Britannia in force. Vortigern was as good as his word and the promised materials as well as the labour force arrived at the construction site on Thanet Island slowly over the next one hundred and twelve days.

Vortigern said to Hengest, *"I have spoken to my priest, a father Germanus, and he says that he can organise the Royal Wedding to take place in two days from now. I both love and desire Rowena. I have dissolved my marriage to my four former wives just as you have demanded of me and I shall continue to do whatever it takes to have her, including having to take orders from you as my Father-in-law!*

It is now necessary for you to submit to some Briton customs! The major condition is that Rowena must convert from being a pagan who worships Woden and Thor to becoming a full Christian and taking up the ways of the Holy Catholic Church. That means that she must be baptised in public so that my people can see that their new Queen of Britons is a Christian just like the people themselves! That is very necessary because my people have been Christians for a long time now, that occurred while the Romans were still here! Now then Hengest, do you still give me your blessing to marry Rowena now that you know she will be converted to the Christian faith?"

Hengest replied, *"Yes Vortigern, I shall compromise, and Rowena will convert to your Christian faith! For that to happen, have your father Germanus come to see me so that we can organise this public event! I fully realise that Rowena must be baptised in public and that that must take place before the Royal Wedding can proceed but proceed it shall!"* Soon afterwards, Father Germanus was ushered into the presence of Hengest. He said, *"Hengest, I am told by king Vortigern that you have given your blessing to Rowena being baptised and taking up Christian ways before she is officially married to Vortigern. Today is Monday and I am happy to baptise her in public, at midday at the shallow river near here in one day from now.*

If you agree with that, I shall begin announcements during services of my church that this is the case! That should result in many people coming to see the baptism of the future Queen of the Britons!" Hengest replied, *"Please go-ahead Father Germanus, I agree with what you are proposing!"* Hengest, was still insisting on the use Ceretic to interpret what was being said by the Britons and him, and that was just pretending, for he was able to understand what was being said. At the next meeting he had with Vortigern, he again used Ceretic to interpret. He said, *"Vortigern, by you marrying my daughter, you will be my son and therefore, I shall become your confidant as well as your general, your advisor and your father-in-law! Make sure that you always listen to what I say and do what I tell you to do, for it is all for the best for you to do so!"*

The larger than expected thong castle became a landmark on the Thanet Island and that was used as a navigation mark by the Engels who kept on arriving in large numbers and then moving on to populate the east, north and central parts of Northumbria, Mercia, and East Anglia after first fighting with the Britons who were there before them and expelling them. Rowena was baptised a day afterwards. Due to the Britons knowing that their future queen was going to be baptised in the shallow river, many people were present to witness the event which had been given a lot of publicity by Father Germanus.

There was another meeting of Vortigern and Hengest. Hengest said, *"Vortigern, if you want Rowena and she in turn wants you, then you shall give me all of Kent which shall become peopled by members of the Kimbern people of northern Germania. That of course means that the Britons must move out of Kent! So, Vortigern, do you really want my daughter and are you willing to give me all of Kent for her?"* Vortigern said, *"Yes to both questions Hengest, I want Rowena, and I shall make her the ruling Queen of the Britons. As I have already told you, I no longer have other wives, and Rowena shall be the only wife that I shall have from now on! Rowena will have the power of a true ruling queen and as a wedding present to you, you shall get all of Kent!"*

Next, the Royal Wedding of Vortigern and Rowena took place at the church building used for these events by the Britons in Kent. So, it was that Rowena and Vortigern were married with great ceremony with Father Germanus of Auxerre doing the officiating and conducting of religious rites of the ancient Catholic Church of

Rome. As Vortigern had been true to his word, the thong castle was becoming ever larger. Suddenly, there was the sound of trumpets which made me look into the area where shipping was anchored. I could see that another forty ships had arrived. Some of them were the Saxon Ceols while others were Engel longships. On board these was another of my brothers. He was Ochta and he was accompanied by the son of Hengest called Esc.

During that time, Vortigern slept with Rowena, and he deeply loved her. After another three weeks has passed, she began having cravings for strange combinations of food as and after another month, she was certain that she was pregnant due to her missed periods. After a normal pregnancy, Rowena gave birth to her daughter, whom she named as Desiree.

Britons and Germanic Warriors Fight

All these things were happening over seven years. Vortimer, the eldest son of Vortigern and his two brothers so strongly objected to the continued subservience of the Britons to the Germanic warriors that they voiced their objections directly to their father, Vortigern and they then broke the terms of the truce between the Britons and the Germanic warriors after it had been in force for seven years.

Vortimer, went to his father and spoke to him. He said, *"My father, the Engels and Kimbern are draining the wealth out of our country. Our people are tired of having to supply Hengest and his people with gold, furs meat and grain and I think that we should make war upon these foreigners and get rid of them, because they are no longer required. The Picts and Scots who were attacking us once, no longer do so, and our people want their former lands back. We all want to be rid of the foreigners now living among us, so let's get rid of the foreigners and do so right now before they bring in even more warriors and keep our people down!"*

So, it was that the truce between the Germanic warriors and the Britons was broken by Vortigern and his Britons seven years after the arrival the Germanic warriors. In the year 455 A.D., the first of four major battles occurred. It was at Aylesford that a son of Vortigern called Katigis and I came into direct conflict. Katigis was carrying a large crucifix, and it was because of it that I was easily able to identify him. Having seen him, I yelled out in a mixture of Briton Celtic and old German, *"Hey you weak as piss Briton, come here and get some fighting tuition or are you as afraid and gutless as your gutless father? Come here and face me, for I am Horsa, a Lord of the Engels, Kimbern and Saxons!"*

Katigis yelled back at me. He yelled, *"Horsa, I look forward to closing with you and killing you, you bloody German prick! Prepare to die, you foreign arsehole!"* As a result of those few words, we ran towards each other, both of us determined to kill the other! We met in the middle of the stream on the ford, and Katigis tried to kill me by making a wide swing with his sword. I was able to see that coming and immediately jumped to the side of him. At same time, I bought down my two-handed battle-axe in a downwards motion from his head towards his feet. That cut him in two!

I was feeling elated by this victory over one of the leaders of the Britons and so, I began chasing down the other Britons who had become badly affected by the loss of one of their leaders so early in the battle. As I was closing in on another of the Britons, I heard Hengest yell out a warning of, *"Horsa, look out! There are another three Britons behind you!"* Hearing that resulted in my sharply turning around and facing my attackers who were trying to get me from behind. That prompted me to say to Britons in their own language, *"Oh come now. Do not be shy! Come forward and try your luck against me in a fair fight, or can you Briton low-life people not handle a direct attack when the one being attacked can fight back? Come forward and get some high-grade Kimbern steel into your guts!"*

Having yelled out those insults, I ran towards the three Britons, who were armed with swords and shields. I was armed and dressed in the typical Saxon mode. That is that I was wearing my Saxon steel helmet. Chainmail armour, red cloak, my sah, (Saxon long knife) and attached to my back, was my large round shield. Also attached to my waist was my long broadsword. In my hands, I was holding my favoured weapon, the Kimbern two-handed battle-axe.

As I got closer to the Britons, I could not help trying to incite them into something stupid. I yelled out, *"You useless Britons, you and your kind are totally unworthy people, and you should all be exterminated! I am the sort of warrior who will rid the world of the presence of the likes of you! Now you die!"*

I was hoping that the Britons would become enraged, which they did, and by doing so, they were lowering their own caution and fighting abilities. I was now close enough to begin my attack against them. I swung my battle-axe directly down from the head of the nearest Briton towards his feet. That had the pleasing result of my enemy being cut into two pieces. I was so busy that I did not notice another two Britons joining with the original three of them. That meant that I was now facing four enemies.

After the heated encounter with the Britons, three of them were lying on the ground, but while I was despatching the third one, the fourth member of the group managed to plunge a spear into my back. He was joined by another Briton who swung his sword and that struck me on the side of my neck, cutting my carotid artery and so, I bled to death. Since both sides had now lost one of their leaders, they both withdrew from the battle-field. A truce was arranged, and both sides removed the bodies of their slain leaders from the field.

So, it was that the Britons carried the body of Katigis, the son of Vortigern away from the battle-field so that he could have a Christian burial with the rites practised by the Britons. Funeral arrangements were carried out on behalf of Katigis who had died the death of an honourable warrior. The Britons were Christians, and therefore, the officiating of the funeral of Katigis was carried out by Father Germanus, who was now the Bishop of Auxerre. Bear in mind that this was the same man who had celebrated the wedding of Rowena and Vortigern just seven years before.

Rowena wanted to know the location of the grave of Katigis, so she asked Vortigern where it was. Vortigern said, *"The grave of my son Katigis is known only to a few, why do you want to know its location?"* Rowena said, *"I need to know the location of the grave of Katigis so that I can fulfil my duties of mourning him as is expected by the Britons, because not only am I your wife, I am also the Queen of the Britons!"*

Vortigern said, *"Katigis is buried at Caer-Reputi, under the Roman arch. He has been placed there by our druids and other religious leaders as a talisman to keep the Germanic tribes away from that area!"* Rowena immediately passed on the information to her father, Hengest, who had his warriors dig up the body and then rebury it in Caer-Ludein (London). Likewise, my body was being carried from the battlefield by the warriors of Hengest and me. Seven years had passed since Hengest, and I first set foot upon the land of Engle-land. My funeral began and this was a typical Germanic funeral in which my body was cremated along with all my weapons, armour and even my war-horse. That was so that I could use these things in the after-life.

My funeral was one of the last ones to be conducted along Germanic lines, because my people quickly took up the ways of the Britons, whose country we had now become a part of. That happened because like other Germanic migrations, after we had been in Britania for some years, my people slowly began to intermarry with the local Briton tribes and over time our language would slowly become different, with some of the Celtic words and some words of Latin left over from the previous Roman masters of Britannia. As well, my people were slowly taking up the customs of the Britons, one of which was to bury their dead, rather than cremating the dead, as was the Germanic custom. (Engels, Kimbern and Saxons are from now on collectively termed as Saxons, Anglo-Saxons, or English.) From this time, we all become the English people prior to the coming of the Normans.

Another two years passed, and the year was now 457 A.D., when at Crayford, Hengest was able to engage the Britons in battle. Hengest and his son called Esc were mounted on their horses when Esc said, *"Pappa, I have noticed that the Britons appear to be massing near the stream and swampy areas downhill from here. What do you want our forces to do?"* Hengest answered, *Esc, my son, have I not always told you to take and hold the high ground at all costs? Have you done so? I shall explain why that is so important later.*

Esc said, *"Yes Pappa, I have done as you wanted, and we hold the high ground. Please tell me now why that is so important!"* Hengest said, *"Esc, it is always of major importance to hold the high ground because it makes it more difficult for spear throwers and archers to reach our men with their weapons. As well, when the enemy mounts an attack and does so going uphill, they will find increasing difficulty in closing the gap between them and us. It is far easier to press against an enemy when going downhill because the pressure that we can apply to enemies will be greater and the effort required by our warriors will be less by attacking downhill!"*

Hengest went on with, *"Esc, inspect you men and make sure that each one of them knows the job and can perform the duties of the man above him and below him in both rank and station. Make sure that each man knows exactly what to do and when he must do it. Form up a large grouping of you warriors and have them occupy the top of the hill over there! See to it that these men are in plain sight of the enemy.*

I also want you to hide most of your warriors in the wooded areas of the hill out of sight of the Britons. Next, those of your warriors who are within the sight of the Britons should bare their behinds and then bend over with their bums facing the Britons while they attract the attention of the enemy by calling out to them and patting their bums. That is a wanton insult, and I am hoping that the Britons will become enraged by that insult and then try to attack your men whom they can see at the summit of the hill.

Now listen carefully, when you hear one long blast from my horn, your warriors are to begin shooting your arrows at the Britons as well as throwing your spears at them! As soon as your men have used their arrows and spears, make sure that you give a long single blast from your horn. Now repeat to me what your must do and when you must do it!" Esc did as his father had instructed and then he asked, *"Alright Pappa, now that we have sorted out what I shall be doing, may I ask what you will be doing during that time?"*

Hengest answered his son with, *"Esc, I will be with the best cavalrymen we have, and we shall be already located at the top of a close-by neighbouring hill. Our task shall be the elimination of the Britons in the woods in the on the slopes and bottom of the hill we are talking about. As soon as you sound your single long horn blast, I shall answer it with two short blasts of my horn! That will also be the signal for the cavalry and me to sweep down the hill and kill the enemy!"*

When the battle was over, the Britons had lost four thousand warriors killed inaction, while the English had lost very few men due to their tactics and their knowledge of warfare, abilities, and their preparation of the battleground where they held the high ground. The Britons then retreated out of Kent and fled to London in an exasperated and weary condition. Meanwhile, the war between the Germanic tribesmen who were now called themselves English, and the Britons continued.

Vortigern Commits Incest

Fourteen years after the birth of the daughter of Rowena and Vortigern, Rowena became ill, and she could no longer satisfy the sexual wants of her husband Vortigern. She was confined to her bed to recover. Vortigern, forever a sexual predator, found himself being aroused by his daughter and he plotted to have sex with her. On her fourteenth birthday, Vortigern spoke to his daughter. He said, *"Desiree, you have the looks and charms of your mother with whom I cannot lay because she is ill. I badly need a root, and I desire to fuck you right now. So, get your clothes off and we can have an enjoyable sexual time right now!"*

His daughter named Desiree said, *"Pappa, what you are proposing is wrong and against all the teachings of Woden, Thor and even against the teachings of the Christian faith of the Britons. I shall not let you fuck me unless you agree to replace my mother as the Queen of Britons with me!"* Vortigern considered her demands for a moment and then he said, *"Very well, Desiree you shall have what you want, now undress and we will fuck!"* They made love and as a result Desiree gave birth to their son nine months after that.

Vortigern had lost his son called Katigis during his fight with me (Horsa). That troubled him and now, another one of his sons called Vortimer had been the main instigator of the war between the Britons and the Germanic tribesmen. Vortimer wanted his father to die so that he could become the King of Britons. That was known to Desiree. She invited her half-brother to a feast which had both wine and entertainment provided. He accepted the invitation and bought his taster with him. Vortimer was certain that no poison was present in the wine because his taster did not show any ill effects from tasing it. However, Desiree had obtained a very slow acting poison that would take up to four days to kill who-ever swallowed it without the victim showing any obvious signs of poisoning. During the night, four days later, both Vortimer and his taster died. When Vortimer died, the strength of the Britons died with him, resulting in the war declining into occasional skirmishes.

Rowena is Replaced by Desiree

Rowena had by now completely recovered from the illness that ailed her, and she set about resuming her duties as Queen of Britons. In attempting to resume her royal duties, she clashed with her daughter Desiree. Rowena was harshly spoken to by Desiree. She told Rowena, *"Mother, I am now the Queen of Britons! I have had constant sex with my father Vortigern, and he has replaced you with me because he thinks that I am much better in bed than you are! Has he not yet told you that I have given him a son, whereas you were only able to provide a daughter to him?"*

That news was most distressing to Rowena, who although a pagan, was deeply honourable and the thought of the incest as practised by her husband and her daughter sickened her. Rowena knew that she had to get away from the castle occupied by her husband and daughter lest she was murdered. So, Rowena went to live with her father, Hengest. Before she left, she wrote a letter in Latin to Germanus, who was now the Bishop of Auxerre.

In the letter she wrote, *"My dear Bishop Germanus of Auxerre, I am Rowena the rightful Queen of Britons and I have disturbing news to tell you. My husband, King Vortigern, has been constantly committing incest with our daughter called Desiree. She is currently nursing the son that she had after being impregnated by*

Vortigern. I do not know the name of the son of them both. I only know that he was the product of incest which is not permissible by anyone in the eyes of God! Even the Germanic tribes have similar laws to the Christians and those laws are expressed by Wodin and Thor stipulating that people must not commit incest!

As you may recall, I took the catechism of the Church and was baptised and accepted into the Church of Rome. I am now living at my father's castle on Thanet Island, and I shall never return to the immoral castle and home of my husband, King Vortigern and our daughter. I strongly urge you to do something about the disgusting situation that lets the adulterers and practitioners of incest be the king and queen of the Britons!"

After more time had passed, Bishop Germanus finally received the letter from Rowena. Soon after that, the news reached him that King Vortigern had taken his daughter Desiree as his wife and that she was now performing the duties expected of "Queen of the Britons" these things combined to make Bishop Germanus very angry, and so, he began to actively work against both Vortigern and Desiree!

Arthur Leads Britons

In the north of Engel-land lived a capable and war-like leader known as Arthur. He was the very same Arthur as authors wrote about in novels such as "The Knights of the Round Table". However, those are just imagined stories. What is fact about Arthur is that he upheld the sinking spirit of the Britons and roused their broken outlook, reviving their spirits and urged them on to fight the English. After several reversals in the fortunes of both the English and the Britons, Arthur went to see an artist whom he asked to paint an image of the Holy Virgin Mary to the inside of his shield.

The artist did as Arthur wanted him to do, and then Arthur went to see Bishop Germanus. At the meeting of the two men, Arthur spoke first. He said, *"Holy Father, Bishop Germanus, I am about to take on the forces of the pagan Hengest and his forces of Germanic pagans whom we now call the English!"* Before the bishop could answer him, he began to show the bishop, the image of the Virgin Mary which had been painted on the inside of his shield. He now said, *"Holy Bishop and leader of the church here, I beg you to bless this image of the Virgin Mary on the inside of my shield. I also beg you to bless my warriors and me in this glorious quest to rid our country of the English pagans and their Germanic reinforcements!"*

The Bishop of Auxerre was most impressed both by the confident, daring outlook of the young and war-like leader of the Britons as well as the image of the Virgin Mary he had on the inside of his shield. Accordingly, he went over to where Arthur was and said, *"Arthur, my son, please kneel so that I can place my hands upon your head and then begin the process of blessing you and your quest!"* Arthur did as the bishop had asked, and he knelt before him, resulting in the bishop placing his left hand upon Arthur's head while his right arm was raised towards the sky and he spoke to God.

He said, *"Lord God, I, your faithful servant upon earth both beg and beseech you to bless this warrior leader called Arthur, for he is a true warrior who is steadfast in his service to you oh Lord! He and his men shall drive the English pagans and their Germanic allies from the lands of your Christian people called the Britons! I also am begging you, Lord; to bless the image he has of your earthly mother Mary. That image is on the inside of his shield, so please bless both this warrior and the image of your mother located on the inside of his shield!"* That was followed by Bishop Germanus going into a trance and he then began to speak in a loud authoritarian voice that sounded as if someone else was speaking. The voice said, *"I am the Lord, your God and if you need me to have a name, you may call me either Yahweh or Jehovah! Arthur, I hereby bless the image of the Virgin Mary on the inside of your shield. When you find yourself in deep trouble, just kiss her image and my help will be forthcoming! I hereby also give you the quest to cleanse the English and their Germanic allies from all Celtic parts of engel-land! Remember to call upon my aid when that is needed!"*

Shortly after that, Arthur who was helped by Ambrosius, surrounded a large force of English (they were mainly Engels) and so, Arthur and his forces laid siege to them. That happened at a place called Mount Baden, near the city of Bath. The English had great defences in that they were holding the high ground, and they were armed with the long Saxon battle-axes and spears as well as long swords. They also had many archers whom they assigned based on one archer to every four other warriors. These being armed with long broadswords, and battle-axes. In addition, each man also had five spears per man and English cavalry units were in reserve. After three attempts had been made against the English forward positions, the was no progress in the battle because of the refusal to give ground by the English.

Ambrosius sought an audience with Arthur, which was granted. He said, *"Arthur, we are at a stalemate situation and our progress against the enemy has been halted! Our warriors are now fearful, and I feel that it's time for you to use the much-talked picture of the Virgin inside your shield, because that will greatly help cause. It will help our cause greatly for you to be seen many times by our warriors to be kissing the image of Mary on the inside of your shield and to you to loudly ask for the help of God to remove the English from all parts of the territory of the Britons!"*

That caused Arthur to say, *"Thank you for the idea, Ambrosius, that is what shall happen!"* Having said that, Arthur strode forward and while he was in sight of many warriors, He kissed the image of the Virgin on the inside of his shield! That having been done, he called out to God. Arthur yelled out, *"Heavenly Father, The English forces are beating our attacks on their positions! Why have you forsaken us, you loyal Christian followers? We beseech you, Jehovah to aid us in our attack upon the English!* He then again kissed the image of Mary and that was seen by many of his warriors.

Arthur spoke to Ambrosius. He said, *"Ambrosius, I am leading our attack upon the English positions during the morning twilight! That means we must all get into position for the attack while it is still dark! I need you to find some-one among your men who has a very deep and convincing voice. Find that man and bring him to me! I want him to act the part of God answering me while it is very dark! I shall say, 'God help us to now cleanse the English heathens and their German allies from the land of the Britons, for we are your people, while they are heathens!'"*

Ambrosius said, *"Yes Arthur, I do have such a man, his name is Tarquin. I shall send him to you as soon as I can find him. Before he comes to you, he will already know what you want him to do and say. All the same, you should go over it all with him because you now have a god-like status among our warriors and we must build upon that!"*

Having said that to Arthur, Ambrosius left. An hour later, Tarquin reported to Arthur. The two men conferred and decided upon the final wording of what had to be said while Tarquin was impersonating God. Tarquin said, *"Arthur, I think that our acting the part of God will carry more weight with the warriors if we have a visual effect as well as me pretending to be God talking to you in such a way that all of our warriors and even the English will hear it!"*

72

Arthur said, *"A visual effect at the same time? Please explain what you mean!"* Tarquin said, *"Once we are in position outside of the English defences, I propose that we have a small bright fire well behind you that shall make you appear to have a sort of a halo effect surrounding your body. I shall be well hidden in the dark! Let us hope that we have some light rain of drizzle just after you are seen by the warriors and they hear God talking to you! Such a combination of things must surely both build up your status with our warriors and make you appear to be God-like among the heathens opposing us!"* Arthur agreed and then all the forces of the Britons moved to positions of advantage against the English in the darkness.

Arthur moved to his position and was delighted when he noticed that a small fire was brightly burning behind him. The English warriors could see Arthur from their trench positions and they became fearful when they noticed that they could see Arthur because he appeared to have a glow surrounding him. The glowing effect was further enhanced by the very light drizzle that began falling. By now, Arthur looked as if he was surrounded with a halo.

Then Arthur loudly yelled, *"Our Father in heaven, who have you forsaken us? We are your children and the true followers of Jesus Christ! Aid us now that we are so badly in need of your help!"* Unobserved by the English and Briton warriors, Tarquin had placed himself into position on higher ground to the east of Arthur. Tarquin now said, *"Arthur, my son and warrior of God, firstly face your men and then kiss the image of the Virgin Mary on the inside of your shield! When that has been done, you must turn toward the English and then again kiss the picture of Mary inside your shield. When that has been done, trumpets shall sound from your side and then you shall lead the attack upon the English. You shall win the battle!"*

All of that was seen and heard by both the Britons and the English warriors. The Britons took heart, while the English became dispirited and many of them were confused and fearful. Ambrosius spoke to Arthur. He said, *"Arthur, I am most eager to bring our English foes to battle! It is high time for them to get the taste of Briton steel into their guts!"*

Arthur was in front of his army and he held open his shield and kissed the painting of the Virgin Mary on the inside of his shield. That was seen by many of his warriors. Arthur yelled, *"We are the warriors of God! I have been blessed by the Bishop of Auxerre and before all of you, I have kissed the image of the blessed Virgin Mary, she is on the inside of my shield!"* That was followed by Arthur again kissing the image of Mary painted on the inside of his shield. He then yelled in a loud voice. He said, *"Men, follow me and stay close to me, for I am arrow proof because I have again kissed the image of Mary. We now attack the English and their German allies, and we shall remove them from the land of the Britons! Now attack the English and wipe them out!"*

What followed was that with Arthur leading his army from in front of it, the Britons closed with the English force made up mainly of Engels. Arthur was on his own as he attacked and killed nine of the English enemies. He and his army were successful in dispersing the English who had suffered a slaughter of their warriors. Arthur was aided by the attack upon the Anglo-Saxons by Ambrosius.

Meanwhile, due to having suffered several reversals, the English prayed to the Engel goddess Hertha or to the Gods of Wodin or Thor after which they re-entered the fight with renewed vigour which reversed the situation! That resulted in the forces of Arthur becoming scattered and retreating Britons were left scattered all over the northwest of Engel-land. Vortigern was still alive and in power, but he did not even consider fighting against his former allies. Meanwhile, Hengest had returned to Germania and raised an army of three hundred thousand warriors and then he and the new army sailed for England. They finally landed on Thanet Island.

Hengest approved a plan by his sub-ordinates to inform Vortigern of the arrival of this new Germanic force.

The Night of the Long Knives

Hengest called for an assembly of his warriors. Having assembled them he spoke. He said, *"My fellow warriors, we have achieved much since we first arrived here in Engel-land! However, the unworthy Britons have decided to make war upon us, after they welcomed us in and enjoyed our protection of them and their families! They have attacked us and even killed many of the Engel, Kimbern, and Saxon tribesmen who have been fighting on their behalf! That is treachery and the sort of thing that I have grown to expect from these unworthy people!*

These unworthy people are so strange that they even worship a god whom they hanged up on a Roman cross and made him die like a common criminal! Do you hear that? Their god is so weak as piss that he could not even get himself off the Roman cross and attack his enemies! He just died on the cross and these strange unworthy people worship him! We shall be doing to the Britons what they are trying to do to us! In two days from now, at the time of the afternoon when the shadows are long and evening approaches, we are staging a large feast to which the nobles of unworthy Britons have all been invited!

All of you will be serving the gathered nobles of the Britons with food, wine, and ale! Be prepared for the sight of even our own Germanic women being fondled by these Briton arseholes, but make sure that you do not interfere and simply let the Britons have their way! While you are serving the nobles of the Britons, make sure that you give them as much wine and ale as they want! The more drunk that the Britons become, the better! Make sure that each one of you have your sahs[7] in the special sheath that you have on the inside of your leggings/boots or else attached to your waits and see to it that you cover you sahs with your red cloaks! Either way, make sure that you conceal your Sahs! The reason that you will have your sahs concealed is because when the Britons are well and truly drunk, I will give one long and continuous blast on my horn. That will be the signal for all of you to draw your Sahs out of their scabbards and for you to kill all the Britons' nobles!

Now then, are there any questions you may want answered and is there anything that is not clear to you?" The warrior called Otto immediately answered. He asked, *"Is there anyone whom we are not to kill during this killing spree?* Hengest answered his warrior with, *"Just make sure that no-one harms or interferes with Vortigern, the king of the Britons or the members of his family! We are going to make him our prisoner and for the Britons to have him given back to them, they must pay the price of land territory from which, the Britons must immediately depart! We shall demand vast land masses."*

Hengest continued, *"We shall also take over all towns and cities within those locations and elsewhere!"* That resulted in the Germanic warriors chanting. They chanted, *"Hail Hengest, our great leader! Hail Hengest the mighty! Long live Hengest!"* So, a temporary mess-hall was set-up on the Salisbury plain and it was made ready for the feast. The nobles of the Britons were travelling towards the Salisbury plain and the location of the feast. Some of them arrived twelve hours ahead of the rest of them. At the site of the feast, the five bulls and twenty-two pigs were being readied for roasting on spits and that was scheduled to start after six hours had passed. These things required the attention of thirty of the Kimbern

---

[7] The Saxon long knife. It was usually carried in a sheaf attached to the belt of the warrior or within his boots.

warriors. The rest were to act as waiters and servants answering the beck and call of the Britons' nobles when they all arrived.

Hengest now ordered that the women he had organised to play up to the Britons be brought in and that they should start to immediately seduce the nobility of the Britons. Some of the Britons were pious men and they found the acts of the women in in throwing themselves at them to be disturbing as they were both married and Christians. These men immediately left the feast and its festivities because they felt that what was happening was immoral. As the five nobles left, more of the women began entertaining the Britons' nobles and the feast began with the serving of the first of the wine and ale. The serving was being done by the warriors of Hengest who all had their long shas with them, concealed in their boots or attached to their waists, but hidden under their cloaks. Many of the nobles present were as base and self-serving as King Vortigern. Six of them had exposed the breasts of the young women attending the feast. Vortigern, true to his weak and self-indulgent character, had his index finger in the vagina of a young woman. He was rapidly becoming ever more drunk, and his guard was down!

Next, Hengest's warriors were moving among the Britons with offerings of more wine and ale as well as roasted meat. Another hour passed during which the nobles of the Britons were becoming ever more drunk. Hengest put his horn to his lips and blew one long and very loud blast into it. He then yelled out in old German, *"Take up your sahs and kill all the nobles of the Britons who are here! Make sure that their leader, King Vortigern remains unharmed but is taken prisoner and bound with strong rope. Once he has been securely bound in that fashion, he shall be placed under guard just inside the entrance to the main dining area."*

The actions of the English warriors in attacking the Britons surprised the unsuspecting and very drunk Britons who were taken aback by the attack upon them by the Anglo-Saxon warriors. Some of these warriors were still appearing among the Britons serving out meat and drink. As ordered, the English warriors had simply opened their cloaks before reaching down and drawing out their shas or else they had reached down to their boots for them. They then used their shas to stab or cut the throats of the astonished Briton nobles. Four-hundred and sixty barons and other nobles of the Britons died during what became known as "The Night of the Long Knives"

Hengest was very satisfied with the night's work, and he was happy in the thought that all the nobles of the Britons had been killed. Eldol who was the Duke of Gloucester, had managed to escape by using a stake which was holding a tent to the ground. He pulled the stake out of the ground and then drove the stake into an eye of an Anglo-Saxon warrior using all his strength. That action allowed him to escape! That was to have profound repercussions for the English at later dates.

At about midday of the following day, Hengest had the prisoner, King Vortigern bought before him. When Vortigern was brought into the presence of Hengest, Vortigern was still bound with rope. Hengest shouted at his warriors. He said, *"Warriors, release King Vortigern from his bounds immediately!"* As soon as Vortigern had been set free of his bounds, Hengest spoke to him. He said, *"Vortigern, you are now my prisoner. I am going to demand that your Britons pay me and the other Germanic tribal leaders a ransom for your safe return!"* Vortigern asked, *what are your demands for my safe return to my people, the Britons?"*

Hengest said, *"The ransom that your people must pay to ensure your safe release is that the Britons shall immediately give all the areas known as Essex, Wessex, Sussex, and Middlesex plus all the towns, cities, castle and other fortifications within those areas to the Anglo-Saxon people, of which my warriors and I are part of! As well, you and all Britons shall leave those areas immediately and none of you shall be permitted to return. If the ransom is not paid immediately, My Kimbern warriors and those of the Engels and Saxons shall lay waste to your entire country and we will kill all people living in it other than our own people! So, the choice of whether that happens is entirely up to you and the Briton people!"*

Having heard what was said by Hengest and not liking it, Vortigern quickly thought the matter through and decided to accept the terms and conditions set by Hengest. He said, *"Very well, Hengest, you win! You and your Saxons shall have Wessex, Essex, Sussex, and Middlesex including all fortifications within those areas and all towns and cities within those areas! For me to follow this, I must have my Royal Seals which must be used to make royal proclamations and laws of this land. Hengest you and your warriors are making the people of the Britons and me move into places such as the Cornwall, west coast of Northumbria and Wales areas!"* Hengest replied, *"Certainly, Vortigern, I agree that you must have your royal seals and other things that you may need to pass laws and make proclamations! My warriors and I shall escort you back to your former castle so that you can obtain your Royal Seals!"*

Next, Hengest spoke to his daughter. He said, *"Rowena, I would like you to accompany me and my warriors to Vortigern's castle where the Royal Seals are kept so that he can then use the seals to make laws and to officially grant all land, fortifications, towns and cities in the areas known as Wessex, Essex, Middlesex, and Sussex to the Germanic tribes known collectively as Saxons or Anglo-Saxons or English!* However, Rowena was furious and incredulous at the suggestion that she return to Vortigern's former castle. She was in fact afraid that her daughter Desiree could be present and Rowena wanted to avoid her daughter at all costs! So, she said to her father, *"Pappa, you must be joking! I shall never again in my life go anywhere near my former husband called King*

Vortigern or our daughter called Desiree! Did you not know that Vortigern has been fucking his own daughter and that she has given him a son?

Not only that, but the two of them conspired against me and stripped me of my rightful title and power as the ruling Queen of the Britons! Vortigern has now married his own daughter whom he continues to fuck! He removed me from my post as Queen of Britons and installed Desiree into the position of Queen of the Britons! So, if you must go to Vortigern's castle, go on your own, for I shall never go there again! Nothing is as disgusting as a man who fucks his own daughter!"

So, it was that Hengest went to the castle of Vortigern without Rowena and upon getting there, Hengest immediately said to Vortigern, *"Vortigern, we are here at your castle. I have waited long enough, now stop stalling and get the Royal Seals and issue the proclamation that Britons are to immediately leave all areas of Wessex, Essex, Middlesex, and Sussex and that the Britons must go to areas in Cornwall, the west coast of Northumbria and Wales. You are to have this proclamation read out during all your church services and your people must be out of those areas that I mentioned by the end of next month or they will all die, as will you!"*

Vortigern answered with, *"Hengest, it will be difficult to inform my people of all of this, even when you have the help of your proclamation being announced during church services, but still, announcing the proclamation during church services is the best way to get your message across!"* Hengest replied, *"Fine, that is what we shall do!"* And so, the royal proclamation was read out during church services in all the churches controlled by the king of the Britons. That resulted in Britons immediately beginning to leave the areas stipulated by Hengest and it made the Kimbern Prince happy. Hengest now set Vortigern free. Vortigern immediately fled to Cambria.

Enemies Fight the Anglo-Saxons

As a result of being informed of the incest between King Vortigern and his daughter Desiree, the Bishop of Auxerre, Bishop Germanus began his campaign against Vortigern by publicly condemning him during church services held at Auxerre, during which he said, *"My friends, it is with great sadness that that I must inform you that your King Vortigern is actively committing treason against you, his own people!*

He has also directly offended God in that he has committed the great sin of incest by having sex with his own daughter! He has been given a son from that unholy act! That is not just a sin, it is a direct affront to God! I urge all of you to rise-up and depose Vortigern! He will keep on committing incest with his daughter, Desiree but that must stop immediately! When you rise and depose King Vortigern, you must also punish his lustful slut of a daughter and strip her of her position as Queen of Britons!

I am now going to contact Aurelius Ambrosius and others, including Uther Pendragon, to be fighting for us. I am going to invite Aurelius Ambrosius to take up the position of King of the Britons so that we shall not be leaderless when Vortigern is deposed! Regarding both Aurelius Ambrosius and Uther Pendragon, they both hate Vortigern because he had their father and brother killed. In the case of Aurelius, he is already an outstanding soldier, and he has battle experience that he gained while fighting for the Romans! His help for us against Vortigern and his English Allies will prove to be invaluable! Already, they have taken the fight up to the invaders of Britania, the Anglo-Saxons!

Bishop Germanus now said, *"My people, I have assumed direct control of our military forces until such time as Aurelius Ambrosius is crowned King of Britannia! Now please join me in prayer to bring down the self-serving, weak, and cowardly*

81

Vortigern and to get rid of the current Queen of Britannia, Vortigern's slut daughter who is aiding and abetting him in committing of incest! Join me in praying for an end to the current evil Briton monarchy and for the installation of our new royal leaders who will bring us back to Mother Church. We shall also pray that God aids us in expelling the English who are just Germanic pagans under a different name! If we can get rid of the English pagans, then all of Britania will again be God fearing!"

He went on to say, *"Let us all join in prayer. Holy Father, we the people of Britania who have been down-trodden and maligned as well as having to suffer the ravaging of our country by foreign based pagans who are now called the English, hereby beseech you to deliver us from the evil which is being done by our puppet King Vortigern! He is merely a puppet of the Germanic invaders now called the English! Lord God, we beg you to send a great ball of fire to wipe out Vortigern and his queen. The queen is his daughter Desiree and they both commit incest together! We therefore beg you to cleanse this country by sending a fireball and killing both as well as destroying the castle where they live as husband and wife!"*

According to legends, that is what happened, but I know that to not be correct! How do I know that? I know it because I am the ghost of Horsa and as a ghost, I can move backwards or forward in time and space. I saw what really happened. It was mainly due to the efforts of the Briton warriors led by the Bishop of Auxerre, Aurelius Ambrosius and Uther Pendragon that Vortigern's castle in Cambria was finally burned to the ground and all inhabitants died in it. No-one escaped!

That resulted in the death of Vortigern and his daughter with whom he had committed the great sin of incest as well as their toddler sized son. Rowena was not there, she had long left that castle when her very own daughter informed her that she had a son to Vortigern, who was her father and that she was now her father's wife as well as replacing Rowena as queen of Britons. Because of her disgust at what was happening between Vortigern, Desiree and herself, just after the downfall of Vortigern and Desiree and their son, Rowena left to return to Germania.

Arthur, Aurelius and Eldol

Aurelius Ambrosius was a high-born soldier of the Romans who had stayed in Britannia when the Romans left. He served the Roman army outside of Britannia and returned to that place after he retired from the Roman army. Due to his service in the Roman army, he had a lot of battle experience. Both he and his brother known as Uther Pendragon (Welsh nickname) had a deep hated for Vortigern who had done much against the family of these two men. As a result, they very much enjoyed watching the burning of the castle housing Vortigern, his wife Desiree and their toddler son. They were pleased that those three people were within the castle as it burned!

Soon after that event, (about 480 A.D.), Aurelius with the help of Arthur had surrounded a force of English (Engels) and they were laying siege to them. The English force had great defences in that they were holding the high ground and were armed with the long Saxon battle-axe and spears. They had many archers who were assigned based on one archer to every four warriors who were armed with the battle-axes, spears, and long broadswords. As well, the English had cavalry forces in reserve.

After three assaults had been launched against the English positions and repelled by them, Aurelius and Arthur conferred. Aurelius said, *"Arthur, we are at a stalemate situation and our progress against the English has been halted! Due to the much-discussed blessing of you and the picture of the Virgin on the inside of your shield, I think that it would greatly help our cause for you to again lead our attacks upon the English in person!*

I want to see you lead our forces against the English positions with the attack to begin as soon as daylight arrives and if you can launch the attack during the twilight hours of the morning, so much the better! That means that you and your 'Warriors of God" must move into position while it is still dark, so that all of you will be in position and ready to attack the enemy before the twilight of the morning begins to set in."

Arthur answered, *"Aurelius, I am most eager to bring the English foes to battle! It is high time for them to get the taste of Briton steel into their guts!"* after that meeting, both leaders of the Briton forces retired for the night. At about an hour before twilight, Briton warriors moved about their position, waking other warriors in preparation for the coming attack upon the English. The warriors successfully moved to their positions and were in them while it was still dark. The morning twilight was beginning, and Arthur was in front of his army. He addressed his men. He yelled, *"We are the warriors of God! I have been blessed by the Bishop of Auxerre, and I have kissed the blessed image of the blessed Virgin Mary! That gives me special powers! Do not be afraid of the English or their Germanic allies, because they are pagans and therefore, they do not have the protection of God, like we have! Please watch me as I again kiss the image of Mary on the inside of my shield!"*

With that, Arthur kissed the image of Mary on the inside of his shield in such a way that it was seen by many of his warriors. He then called out in a very loud voice, *"Men, follow me and stay close to me, for I am arrow proof because I have again kissed the image of the Virgin Mary. Now attack the English and wipe them out!"* What followed was that Arthur was leading his army from in front of it and setting the example to his men. The army of the Britons closed with the English force and a great slaughter resulted. The Briton warriors were attacking the English with vigour. Meanwhile, Arthur single-handedly took on and killed nine hundred of the

English enemy and he was successful in dispersing them. With the English position taken by the Britons, Arthur and Aurelius conferred. Aurelius said, *"Arthur, we have taken the position of the English, but we must not rest! I have received word that Hengest, and his army are in a field called Maisbeli, near Sheffield. We should march toward there immediately!"*

The Briton force did so, and soon after arriving at Maisbeli, they rested after having posted sentries. It was during the late afternoon that a warrior who was a sentry went to Arthur. He said, *"Sir, we have just been joined by a noble who wants to speak to you urgently. He says that he is Eldol, the Duke of Gloucester. He told me that he wants to join our cause because he is the sole survivor of "The Night of the Long Knives".*

Arthur replied, *"Sentry, bring Eldol to me, I look forward to speaking with him!"* the warrior departed and soon returned having Eldol in his company. Upon seeing Arthur, the warrior spoke. He said, *"Sir, this is Duke Eldol of Gloucester!"* He then departed. Eldol said, *"Arthur? I am Eldol the Duke of Gloucester! I am the only survivor of the treachery practised by Hengest and his cronies at "The Night of the long Knives! I greatly wish to meet Hengest the Kimbern in battle and to kill him!*

At that feast, which turned out to be an ambush, four hundred and sixty nobles of the Britons were killed! I am the only survivor of that awful event, and I want revenge! The only reason that I survived is that God showed me a stake which I was able to get hold of and then use it to drive it into the eyes of a Kimbern warrior.

That killed him and so, I took his weapons and then killed four more Kimbern warriors before I managed to get away from that awful place where our nobles died! Please let me join your forces against Hengest and his warriors for I need to kill Hengest!" That was agreed to by Arthur and later Aurelius as well.

The Death of Hengest

It was now the year 488 A.D., thirty-nine years after the arrival of the Germanic tribes in Engel-land during which time, they had become the English. Hengest was alarmed by the defeat and death of Vortigern moved his army from Cambria to new positions past the Humber River. Hengest began moving his men towards Aurelius hoping to surprise the Britons at Maisbeli, but that was anticipated by Aurelius.

Meanwhile, Hengest was placing his warriors into position and walking through his formations of warriors in a bid to give comfort and reassurance to the members of his army. He said, *"Men, you are originally either Engel, Kimbern or Saxon warriors, all of which have been amalgamated into the Saxon confederation! As Saxon warriors have the reputation being capable and fierce warriors, the warriors of the Britons are of a lesser calibre than you. Therefore, you must be able to close with and kill the Briton enemies easily! The warriors facing you are weak men who have a weak leader, and who is prone to every vice imaginable! Their king Vortigern even constantly fucked his own daughters, even though he had four wives! So, stain the ground with their blood and kill them all, for they are most unworthy and do not deserve to live!"* With both armies now formed up and battle ready, the fight between the Anglo-Saxons and the Britons began, resulting in the killing of many warriors from both sides!

On the side of the Britons, Arthur could be seen plainly seen at the head of his warriors rallying them to greater efforts. He yelled, *"Men, the enemy is close at hand! These English are the former allies of King Vortigern, but now, they are taking over our country! These foreign pagans are despoilers of our country and our women! We must cleanse Britania of them! So, close with and kill the enemy before he does that to you!"* Having yelled that to his warriors,

Arthur charged his horse straight into the nearest group of English warriors.

Meanwhile, Eldol was looking for Hengest everywhere and he could not find him. Some Anglo-Saxon warriors were giving the Britons a hard time and the Briton attack upon the English positions stopped. Large numbers of Britons were lying dead or dying upon the battlefield in front of the English who held the high ground. Eldol saw what was happening and he then prayed to God for help. He prayed, *"Lord and Heavenly father, please help us, the Christian Britons to defeat the English pagans who oppose us and are holding the summit of the hill before us. I beg you to send a lightning bolt to wipe out the English Saxons!"*

Suddenly, the sky clouded over, and it began to rain. The force of Eldol tried again to take the summit of the hill and again, they were driven back with alarming casualties. Eldol was despairing when he again prayed. He said, *"Our Father in Heaven, why have you forsaken us?"* Eldol now saw a vision of Saint Peter. Saint Peter said, *"Eldol, God has heard your pleas, and he shall grant you victory. You and all your warriors must vacate this area immediately, for God is sending a series of lightning bolts all over this locality! That will wipe out the English pagans!"*

Eldol ordered, *"Sound the retreat all Britons are leaving this locality and the work of slaying the English shall be done for us by God!"* Trumpets and horns sounded the retreat which was at once put into effect. No sooner had the Britons put a safe distance between them and the English position, than the sky darkened immensely and a long series of thunder bolts began to strike into the Anglo-Saxon positions at summit of the hill.

Arthur was also watching what was happening. Seeing the English positions at the hill's summit being subjected to a series of thunderbolts, he yelled out to his soldiers. He yelled, *"Look at that!*

God is on our side, and he is wiping away the English so that you can go and kill the enemy and rid our country of their presence forever! Now go and kill as many Englishmen as you can!"

Knowing that Kaerconan could not possibly hold against Aurelius, Hengest stopped outside the village and spoke to his warriors. He said, *"Fellow warriors of Woden and Thor, the Britons have managed to bring up unexpected reinforcements and we are now being threatened with extermination! We have all faced similar situations to this before and we will fight our way out of this one, as we have always done before now! Now join me in praying to Woden, Thor and Frea, the wife of Woden for total victory against these unworthy Britons. They are strange people who worship a god whom they, themselves, hanged up on a Roman cross! To arms my brothers, it is time for us to again close with and kill the Britons!*

His speech was met with rousing cheers as the Anglo-Saxons resumed their fight against the Britons. A furious fight between the Britons and the English came next, with the result of the English holding their ground, despite heavy losses of men and equipment. Eldol, who was still trying to find Hengest, knew that the day had been won when he saw the arrival of Gorlois, the Duke of Cornwall and his army. Eldol finally found Hengest. A great fight between them began during which Hengest had knocked Eldol to the ground and was smashing Eldol's face with his shield. For a moment, Eldol was stunned and almost helpless.

He then prayed to God for aid. He said, *"Our Father who is in heaven, be with me now and give me the strength to win!"* Eldol was suddenly filled with energy, and he managed to poke his fingers into the eyes of Hengest. Hengest was temporarily blinded and stepped back. That allowed Eldol to get up and he successfully applied a neck hold on Hengest. Now feeling much stronger, Eldol dragged Hengest into the ranks of the Britons. The English, seeing their leader thus defeated and dragged into the Briton positions, broke off their attack. Ochta, a son of Hengest now retreated to York, while his kinsman Eosa, retreated to Alclud (Dumbarton). Three days after the battle, Aurelius called an orders group[8].

The discussion got underway. The brother of Eldol was known as Eldad. He was the Bishop of Gloucester. He said, *"Although some people here think that Hengest should be set free, I want to see him cut to pieces! The prophet Samuel is my warrant. When Samuel had Agag, the King of Amalek in his power, he chopped him into small pieces saying, "As your sword has made women childless, so shall your mother be childless among other women. For that reason, do to Hengest what he has done to others and kill him, for he is a second Agag!"*

That was at once followed by Eldol dragging Hengest out of the village and then cutting off his head. Having the head of Hengest now lying on the ground at his feet, Eldol took off the Kimbern Warrior's helmet and grabbing the head of Hengest by its hair, he held it up in the air so that all could see it. The assembled crowd of warriors and people much appreciated what Eldol had done and so they all began to clap and chant. They chanted, *"Eldol, Hail Eldol, Thank you, Eldol the mighty!"*

Aurelius who always showed moderation in his conduct said to his advisors and commanders, *"I want Hengest to be given a funeral in the Germanic style. That means that we shall cremate him along with his helmet, weapons, and his warhorse. After we have burned his body, his remains shall be covered by a mound of earth. By giving our former enemy, the pagan funeral of his ancestors, we are also respecting these people with whom we shall come together over time and forge a new nation and people!"*

---

[8] An orders group is a discussion about the tactical situation during which ideas are exchanged, and orders are given.

After that, Aurelius accepted the surrender of the sons of Hengest, Ochta and Eosa who was his confederate. It was now that Aurelius entered an honourable treaty with both, which granted them all of the country bordering Scotland and so began a covenant with them. Hengest was succeeded by his son called Octa. Some people called him Oscar. Oscar was more intent on defending rather than enlarging his territory. He ruled Kent for twenty years. In year 508 A.D., Oscar died, and he was succeeded as King of Kent by Ermenic.

Æthelbert I Becomes King of Kent in 558 A.D...

Upon the death of Ermenic, he was succeeded by his son called Æthelbert 1, who became the king in 558 A.D... He was thought of as a weak ruler by his neighbouring rulers and was at war with some of them. Soon after he had become the king, he overheard some members of his court speaking. They said, *"King Æthelbert 1, has now lost two battles! He is currently seen as being so weak and indecisive that the neighbouring kings hold him in contempt! He can barely defend our own frontiers, and he must be taught to govern correctly and how to win wars, so that we, the people of Kent can live in prosperity like we deserve to do!"*

After hearing the way his people were openly talking about him, he decided to obtain the advice and guidance of his senior army officers in how to wage wars. His general said to him, *"Sire, to be victorious against an enemy, you must make sure that you hold most of the advantages! That always means taking and holding the high ground at all costs! Also, it is of vast important for you to always have strong and secure lines of communication between all your military units and for that, you shall also need a capable and force which is effective in using boats and ships to keep open your lines of communication and resupply!"*

You need to have highly mobile armed units of warriors who and be either infantry or cavalry or a mixture of both. The important thing is that these units must always keep your roads and other lines of supply and communication open and safe! The security applies also to your wharves and ports, including river ports. You must learn to act decisively and quickly, for if you do not, then your enemies most certainly will!"

That resulted in Æthelbert speaking. He said, *"Thank you for your advice general, I shall perform as you have advised me to, and I shall begin by taking the war to all our enemies immediately. During this time, I will be conferring with you repeatedly, so that I shall better learn the 'Arts of War' and I shall apply your advice at once! As of now, let no-one ever doubt my resolve or the abilities of the armed forces of Kent!"*

Afterwards, he applied what he had said and made every kingdom of the Angels, other than the area of Northumbria his own. A letter which was written in Latin arrived and it was taken to Æthelbert to whom it was addressed. The letter was from Charibert, who was the King of the Franks. The letter invited Æthelbert to the court of Charibert in Paris. The result was that Æthelbert called for his scribes to draft a letter for him.

He said, *"I want you to immediately write a letter to Charibert of the Franks in Paris. The text of the letter is to be: 'My dear Charibert, I, Æthelbert of Kent hereby accept your kind invitation to attend your court in Paris and I shall be travelling to meet you next month, if that is also your will. Can you please let me know as quickly as possible if this shall fit into your plans and if what I am proposing is convenient for you?'"* An answering letter arrived four days later in which Charibert answered, *"Yes, Æthelbert of Kent, please come next month and have some scribes with you because there is much that I would like to discuss with you that shall be of great benefit to both of our nations!"*

So, to obtain foreign connections and alliances, he became a friend of Charibert, King of the Franks. Time passed and one evening, Charibert spoke to Æthelbert. He said, *"Æthelbert, this is my daughter, Bertha! She is a Christian, and I think that you should also become a Christian before you marry her. Please talk to her and get to know her and the Christian religion".*

Bertha said, *"I am pleased to meet you, King Æthelbert of Kent! My father told me much about you before we met, and I must say that I like the man whom I see before me! I do not believe in waiting to be asked for anything; therefore, I am straight out asking you to marry me! My father needs you to ask him for my hand in marriage which will strengthen the position of Kent in all things!"*

That was followed by Æthelbert speaking. He said, *"Charibert, I am strongly attracted to Bertha, and I hereby ask you to give me her hand in marriage! As you have pointed out, she is a Christian, while I still worship the Gods of Woden and Thor! I do not know of your religion and therefore, I think it would greatly help me to learn about it. So, Charibert, how can I quickly learn about your religion and therefore become a better husband to Bertha?"*

Charibert answered, *"To aid you in understanding the rites and beliefs of the Holy Catholic Church, I have assigned the Bishop of Luidhard to teach you and help you to become Christian. The bishop has been placed on permanent assignment to you as the spiritual advisor to you and Bertha! Now then, I believe that when you return to Kent, you should announce your coming marriage to my daughter to your people. That will have the result of you being held in a higher esteem among the other kings ruling different parts of Engel-land!"*

After his return to Kent, his coming marriage to Bertha was announced and scheduled for six weeks afterward. That caused much joy among the people of Kent. Bertha arrived as scheduled and the marriage between her and Æthelbert was celebrated with much joy in Kent. Æthelbert was converted to Christianity and he issued the first code extent of the Anglo-Saxon laws, a code that set up the legal position of the clergy and many secular regulations. By the end of his reign, his kingdom included all of England south of the Humber River.

The Pope Wants Conversion of the English

In 596 A.D., Augustine was the prior of the Benedictine Monastery in Rome, and he was intrigued when a messenger ran to where he was reading the Holy Bible. The messenger spoke to Prior Augustine. He said, *"Prior Augustine, I have an urgent message for you from Pope Gregory the First! You are to at once leave here and travel to the Holy See, where you shall have an audience with Pope Gregory the First, who is also known as Pope Gregory the Great! Go immediately, for the Great Pope does not like to be kept waiting by those people whom he outranks, so go quickly!"*

So, Prior Augustine did as he had been instructed, and he walked to the Holy See which was within the city of Rome as is the Vatican. After much walking, he found himself being ushered into the presence of the great Pope. As soon as Augustine saw the Pope seated upon his throne, Augustine spoke. He said, *"Your Holiness, I am Augustine, and I have come to do your bidding as instructed by you! I could have been here sooner, but I was right in the middle of completing a tricky translation of the Holy bible from Greek to Latin when the messenger arrived! I felt that I had to complete the translation because there were only three more Greek words that needed translating! I therefore decided to complete the translation before coming here!"*

Pope Gregory the Great smiled and then he spoke. He said, *"Augustine, your reputation precedes you! I have been told of your many deeds on behalf of our Heavenly Father, and I have a major task which I am sure that only of your devotion to duty and your great ability can handle! Are you familiar with the situation in Britania?*

Augustine answered his Pope. He said, *"No, your Holiness, I am not familiar with what has happened in Britania, but I am sure that I can quickly learn whatever is required and then do whatever it is that needs doing!"* Pope Gregory the Great explained. He said, *"The religious situation in Britannia is strange and it worries me! The original people of Britania are called Britons, and they have been Christians since 178 A.D., when their King Lucius sent letters written in Latin to Pope Eleutherius begging him to send missionaries to Britania and to baptise him in Public. That made the converting of the Britons much easier for us! The sight of King Lucius being baptised in the shallow river near the church building made the watching Britons clamour to also be baptised! After that, we were able to convert most Britons to the Christian Faith!*

Soon afterwards, the Holy church flourished in Britania. Things were fine until 418 A.D., when the Roman empire decided to remove all Roman soldiers from Britania because they were urgently needed here to defend Rome! After our Roman soldiers left, the Picts and Scots began raiding across Hadrian's Wall and they spread terror among the Britons. King Vortigern of the Britons turned to the Kimbern warriors from the Jutland peninsula for help!

The Kimbern tribe is the same Germanic tribe who we Romans call the Cimbri! They live at the northern tip of the Jutland Peninsula. They are fierce warriors as are their neighbours, the Danish Vikings, The Engels, and the Saxons! These tribesmen are pagans who worship Woden and Thor! Due to the history of these pagans, they now full control all of Kent!

The Pope went on with, *"Since those times, a Kimbern King of Kent has married the daughter of the King of the Franks. Her name is Bertha, and she has managed to get her pagan husband to accept the teachings of Mother Church! As well, King Æthelbert of Kent has sent me a letter asking for him to be baptised in public and for the Church to send missionaries to the part of Britannia called Engel-land by the Germanic tribes! Once you arrive in Engel-land, you shall need to travel to the southern parts it, known as Kent and also for more missionaries to be sent to the Engel controlled Northumbria regions. I want you to select a team of monks to help you and I want to see you and your team leave for Britannia by June of 596 A.D...*

Augustine said, *"Your Holiness, I have been studying the beliefs of the English and their former countrymen in Germania. They mainly worship the pagan gods called Wodin and his son, Thor! The date of birth of Thor is said to be the 25th of December in an unknown year! The Germanic tribes and their cousins the Nordic Viking tribes are fierce warriors, but by us telling them that they have been mistaken about the identity of their gods, we should be able to instil God and his son, Jesus Christ into the places currently held by Wodin and Thor!*

Currently, we are celebrating the birth of Jesus on the 18th of December, which is when Venus was very close to the earth and shining very brightly! The men who wrote the New Testament recorded Venus as "The Star of Bethlehem". Therefore, Your Holiness, I propose that we change our current teaching from the birth of Jesus being the 18th of December to the 25th of December. If we do that, it will fit in with what the pagans already believe, and we will be able to convert all the people of Britania and the entire European continent within a very short time.

Your Holiness, you honour me by giving me such a wonderful opportunity to spread the word and teaching of God! However, you have only looked at Britania so far! By combining the conversion of the King of Britons with our missionaries going into Germania and converting the Germans in Europe, the work of the Church shall really flower!

Getting back to the situation of converting the Pagans of Kent, it should be easy after the people there see their own king being baptised! So, Your Holiness, If you approve me having a team of forty monks, I and my team of monks shall travel to Britania and later, Germania where we shall perform the work of God! As most Germanic tribes worship Wodin and Thor, their conversion is almost guaranteed if you change the date of birth of Jesus from the 18th of December to the 25th of the same month!"

Pope Gregory the Great was intrigued by what he had heard. He said, *"Very well Augustine, I am about to issue an epistle which changes the birth of Jesus from the 18th of December to the 25th of December. As well I am authorising you to have whatever you may need from the resources of the Church for your preaching the word of God to the masses in Britannia and Germania.*

I have already authorised you to have a team of forty monks to go with you to Britania to do God's work. Another team of forty monks and friars shall go to Germania and convert the people there before going on to the areas held by the Danish and other Nordic people! Thank you, Augustine, for your foresight and vision! After you have converted the English, I may send you to Germania to help with the conversion of some of the Germanic tribes who currently worship Hertha instead of Wodin and Thor!" And so, Augustine and his forty monks left Rome and travelled to southern Gaul. When they arrived there, they were warned of many dangers awaiting them if they went ahead to Britania, and so, they temporarily returned to Rome.

Back in Rome, Pope Gregory the Great encouraged Augustine by writing a letter of commendation about Augustine and his team to Æthelbert, the King of Kent. The letter was dated 23rd of July 596 A.D... The letter said, *"Dear Æthelbert, please note that I am approving your request for monks to evangelise you and your people in Kent! Please know that I have sent you the services of Augustine and his staff of forty monks to hep accomplish this great work of God! Your conversion to the Christian faith and your baptism will take place as soon as possible after Augustine and his party arrive in your country. Please make sure that you grant them a place where they can live and provide them with food and other things, including a place where they can preach the gospel. If you need to have anything about the Christian faith explained to you, be sure to ask your Queen Bertha, her bishop or Augustine when he has arrived."*

Public Baptism of Æthelbert of Kent

And so, Augustine and his team of forty monks arrived at Thanet Island and were met by King Æthelbert at the shores of the island. Augustine and Æthelbert began to converse with each other in Latin, because it was the only language that both men understood! During their discussions, it quickly became clear to Æthelbert that during church services, interpreters were required to translate the Latin church service into what the English could understand, Namely Old German.

Speaking in Latin, Augustine spoke. He said, *"Good day to you, King Æthelbert of Kent, I am Augustine, and I am here to begin God's work of converting you and your people as well as people from other parts of Engel-land to Christianity! I am being helped in preaching the gospel and baptising people by my team of forty monks and friars. All church services are celebrated in Latin because that is the universal language which can be understood without change anywhere in the world."*

Æthelbert answered him in Latin. He said, *"I speak, read and write Latin, so you can use Latin in your conversations with me, thereby ending the need to have a translator. How may I help you achieve your great quest for which Pope Gregory the Great has sent you here?"* Augustine answered, *"In order for people to follow the lord Jesus Christ, the Holy Father in Heaven and the Holy Ghost, we will have to sell the Christian religion the people.*

Only a few of my monks and friars speak both German[9] and Latin, so it will be a great help if you can release everyone in your country of Kent into my service so that these people can translate what is being said by the priest conducting the church services in Latin. I fear that we shall not be able to convert anyone to the correct faith if the people cannot understand what is being said!" That was followed Æthelbert speaking. He said, *"Thank you for pointing that out! I was going to raise that point with you myself, but now that you have raised it, I do not have to. I totally agree that my people must understand what is being said to them.*

Now then, let's get back to planning the conversion of my people from being pagans to becoming Christians! I have already sent messengers to many locations in my kingdom of Kent asking all people who can speak both German and Latin to report for service with you and your team of missionaries! These men and women will directly report to you and your team at church building that you have been granted at Canterbury. You are to use this building that you have been granted, to hold your first church services. You will find a shallow river close by where you can hold baptisms!

The translators whom I have placed into service with you should start arriving between now and the next six days. I want you to use these men and women to help spread the word of God! Also, Pope Gregory asked me to provide you and your entourage with

---

[9] At this time, the English language was almost pure old German.

food and lodgings. That has been done, and you shall find your lodgings are also in Canterbury, not far from where the church that I have allocated to your group is situated!

As for the necessary publicity to get large numbers of people to attend my baptism, I have ordered that town criers from every town, village or city in Kent shall announce the baptism of me and my being accepted into the Holy Church of Rome by making at least three loud public announcements per day Today is the twenty-eight of November. We have scheduled my public baptism to take place at the river near Canterbury, at midday, when the sun is high in the sky on the 25th of December 597 A.D..."

King Æthelbert went to Canterbury with Augustine and his entourage. When they arrived there, he formerly gave the group of missionaries their housing so that they could live comfortably and he also gave them the building used for church services by the Britons many years before. That church was called Saint Martin's Church, and in that way, he fulfilled his promise to Pope Gregory the Great. Due mainly to Augustine and his team being highly thought of and supported by King Æthelbert, Augustine and his team were kept busy in making conversions to the Christian faith and baptising these people.

Because King Æthelbert had town criers shouting out that he was going to be baptised in public in the river outside of Canterbury, many people knew that this event was taking place at midday, on the 25th of December in the Year of Our Lord, 597, and they attended his baptism in huge numbers. So, on Christmas Day of 597 A.D., Æthelbert was the first of his people to be converted to Christianity and he was baptised in public. He waded into the middle of the shallow stream where Augustine was waiting for him. As Æthelbert approached, Augustine spoke. He said, *"Æthelbert, do you hereby pledge your loyalty, obedience and love to God, do you hereby take the covenant of God and do you believe in the Heavenly Father and the saviour, Jesus Christ, who is the son of God, who was crucified, died and was buried, and rose up to live again, and free all of us from our sins? Do you also believe in the Holy Ghost? Will you give yourself, your soul and your very own being to God and his service?"* Æthelbert answered, *"Yes to all of your questions Augustine, I most certainly will!"*

That was followed by Augustine saying, *"Come over here, and I shall now baptise you in the name of the Father, the Son and the Holy Ghost!"* Æthelbert went to where Augustine was, and then Augustine held Æthelbert and quickly thrust him under water and immediately pulled him upright again. He said, *"In the name of the Father, Son and the Holy Ghost, you are baptised, and you must learn the ways of the Son, who is the Lord Jesus Christ! The best way to do that is for you to speak about God to both your wife, the Christian Queen Bertha, and her bishop. Also, please attend as many church services as you can at the church at Canterbury!"*

The sight of the King of Kent being baptised had a great effect upon the watching crowds of people, resulting in thousands of them cueing up to take up the new Christian religion and to denounce their former pagan religion involving the worship of Woden, Thor, Frea and Hertha. Many more conversions from the pagan religions followed and as a reward for his outstanding services to the Church, Prior Augustine was consecrated as a bishop by Saint Virginius at Aries.

Augustine discussed converting all people living on the island of Britania with both Pope Gregory the Great and Saint Virginius during a meeting between the three of them at Aries, immediately after the consecration of Bishop Augustine. The Pope said, *"Augustine, you have done well! All people living in Kent are now calling themselves Christians and they are attending church services in Canterbury and other localities in Kent! We now need you to continue your good work and concentrate on converting those parts of Engel-land which have not so far been converted to Christianity! After you have successfully converted the Germanic tribes of the Engels, Kimbern and Saxons in Engel-land, it will be time to start converting the Scots and other people living in the north of Britania!"*

Augustine replied, *"Your Holiness, I have been giving a lot of thought as how best to convert everyone who has not already been converted! I strongly believe that we must translate what is being said by our priests when they are conducting the Holy Mass, because the entire service is in Latin and most people will not understand what is being said! The main problem with that is that if people do not understand what is being said or laid before them, they will just walk away! For that reason, when I go into the countryside to preach, I shall have with me, translators who will immediately translate whatever the priests say, so that my congregations can understand the word of God!"* Both men agreed and so, Augustine began preaching as he had said, with the aid of translators who explained was happening during the church services to all people present.

The first example of preaching with the aid of translators explaining what the service was about took place at Canterbury. Augustine decided to firstly teach the members of his congregation at Canterbury the 'Lord's Prayer' and what it means. As the Mass was beginning, he said, *"My fellow Christians, I shall now teach you the 'Lord's Prayer'. I shall also explain what it all means. The 'Lord's Prayer's the prayer that was taught to us all by the Saviour, the Lord Jesus Christ, while he walked upon this earth! I am going to recite short sections of the prayer and explain what is meant by it as we go along!*

We start by saying 'Our father who is in heaven, hallowed be your name'. That means that we are talking to God, who is in his home called Heaven, but he can both see and hear everything we do! Is everyone clear about what is meant by the opening words of the prayer?" There were no questions, so he continued with, *"Hallowed by your name".* He said, *"That means that we love, respect and fear God and that we shall obey him at all times!"*

He followed that saying, *"Your kingdom come".* He went on to explain that it means, *"We, your followers and servants on earth are looking forward to the time when we can join with you God, in your kingdom of Heaven!"* He now said, *"May your will and not our will be done!"* He explained, *"Here we are saying to God, 'We want you to have your will carried out because God is always right, but man is not. Therefore, the will of God must prevail!"*

Augustine now said, *"Give us today, our daily bread, and forgive us for our sins, just as we forgive those people who sin against us."* He explained to the people, *"Here we are asking God to provide our food daily and to forgive us when we sin against him. By saying 'Just as we forgive those who sin against us' we are recognising that our forgiveness of our sins is conditional upon us forgiving the sins of others against us!"*

He continued, *"Do not lead us into temptation, but lead us away from all evil!"* He now said, *"That simply means that we want God to enable us to see what is good and what is just a temptation inflicted upon us by the evil Satan! By saying, 'Lead us away from all evil", we are rejecting Satan and his evil followers. My people, you must all learn the 'Lord's Prayer' by rote, and you must all say it every time you attend the Holy Mass! Are you all clear on what you must do?* He was greeted by silence, so Augustine assumed that his congregation understood his preaching.

Because no questions were asked, Augustine said, *"My people, my team of monks and friars including myself shall now go forth with you all and you shall all be baptised in the stream in the name of the Father, the Son and the Holy Ghost!* And so, the entire congregation went to the shallow river and the mass baptism was successfully carried out at the place where King Æthelbert had received his baptism. Augustine was happy with that progress, and he gave thanks to God.

These events caused Augustine to send two of his monks to Rome to directly report the good news of Augustine's successes to Pope Gregory the Great. They both returned to Kent in 601 A.D., with the pallium which was the symbol of jurisdiction for Augustine from Pope Gregory. The two monks had also bought with them, even more missionaries and these included Mellitus, Justus and Paulinus. Gregory was in direct correspondence with Augustine and asked him to purify the pagan temples for Christian worship and to consecrate another twelve bishops over whom he was to have full authority. So it was that the evangelization of the kingdom of Kent gathered pace.

Augustine was speaking some members of his team of friars and monks. He said, *"Brother Lazarus, I am considering building a new church at Canterbury as well as two monasteries. The new church shall in fact be a cathedral and it shall be named as Christ's Church or Christ Church! The two monasteries shall be known as the Saint Peter and the Saint Paul Monasteries! I want you to come up with attractive and workable designs for these new buildings.*

Lazarus replied, *"Thank you for your confidence in my abilities Augustine, I shall get to work, and I should be able to give you some of the sketches and plans for this wonderous undertaking the evening meal of today. So, if you would like to see them and make changes, then see me at our mess hall this evening!"*

Augustine met Lazarus at the mess hall that evening and the pair of them went into discussion about the planned building project. Lazarus said, *"Augustine, here are the sketches and some of the stretch plans for the cathedral you are going to call Christ Church. Please look closely at these and let me know what you think. It is critical that we get the design right before we start construction. As you shall see there are two entry/exit points into and out of the building on this plan. We need to decide if those shall be enough and if the windows that I have put into the design are sufficient or if we need more windows to have more light coming into the proposed church.* So, it was that the cathedral that became known as St. Augustine's after the death of Augustine was planned and built. Saint Augustine's Cathedral is also where the early archbishops are buried.

Augustine held a conference of the clergy in Kent. Addressing the assembled clergy, Augustine spoke. He said, *"My brethren, we have been asked by Pope Gregory the Great to make the Church of Rome the only religious force operating in Engel-land! Even though we have been successful in converting the people of Kent to Christianity, it must be remembered that the original Britons have been practising Christians ever since 178 A.D., and they have many existing buildings which they use to hold church services. I propose that we unify our church with that of the Britons so that we shall have church buildings in many places on Britannia and the good work done by the original missionaries becomes strengthened by us joining with the Britons for all religious matters! I now invite you all to vote upon this subject."* The vote was taken, and its result did not please Augustine.

The result was that the other church people working with Augustine voted against the idea of unifying the church in Kent with the other churches which had been set up by the Britons. As more Germanic tribes such as Saxons were still arriving in Britannia, the stage was set for more bias, religious intolerance, and apathy to flourish, and so render much of the work of Augustine and his team to be ineffective for some time. It was for these combined reasons that Augustine thought that he had failed. King Æthelbert of Kent had become a Christian and followed the true faith, enacting laws in his native language of old German and he gave rewards to those who were true Christians and believers. After a successful reign of fifty-six years, with the latter twenty-one years as a Christian, he died in 616 A.D., and the throne was then left to his son called Edbald.

Æthelbert had a second queen who was not as well-known as is beloved Bertha. The second queen was therefore the step-mother of Edbald. It was just as well that very few people knew that for years before the death of Æthelbert, his son was having sex with his step-mother called Adalgiso, thereby committing incest.

Edbald Succeeds Æthelbert as King

After Edbald took the throne of Kent in 616 A.D., he found himself evermore sexually attracted to his step-mother. She was a beautiful woman, and he desired her. He went to her and spoke to her. He said, *"Step-mother, how I yearn for you, you are so very attractive!"* Having said that to her he began to undress her.

After a time, she spoke. She said, *"Edbald, your attempt to expose my tits is rather clumsy. So, I will help so that my blouse and other garments are not ruined by you!"* having said that, she began to undress herself and then stood naked in front of him. That had the effect of immediately arousing him, and he immediately began to gently suck on both of her nipples. That in turn also aroused her sexually and she once again forgot about the fact that she was his step-mother and that sex between them was forbidden by Church doctrine. So, they then made love, but the church considered their love making to be an act of incest, and therefore they kept it as secret as possible. That was not the first time he had sex with his step-mother, and that activity was to continue for many years. It was because the couple had become careless in hiding their sexual activities, that they were seen having sex on two occasions by members of their court.

The hand maiden called Annabelle was taking some completed embroidery work for approval to the second queen when she saw both Edbald and his step-mother having sex. She was shocked by what she had witnessed, and she spoke about it to some of the other Ladies-in-waiting. Before much longer it was common knowledge that King Edbald of Kent was constantly having sex with his step-mother. That resulted in some of his people openly criticising him. They said, *"Our King Edbald is reputed to be a "Mother-fucker!"* The damage to the reputation of King Edbald quicky gathered pace and soon it was common knowledge both within Kent and outside of that place, that Edbald was having sex with his step-mother. That was to have serious consequences for him.

In time, that news reached the ears of some of the princes who had been beaten in battle by his father. They revolted and so, he lost some of the territory what had been gained by his father. Many of the rebels were saying, *"We will not pledge allegiance to a mother-fucker who is also a practising Christian. The Christians are a weird sect that worships a god who was hanged up on a Roman cross by his own people, yet they worship him! We therefore urge all people forget about the Christian religion and return to the embrace of Woden and Thor! We have sent our demands that King Edbald go back to the worship of Woden and Thor, directly to him! He knows that unless he does so, he shall lose his authority over everyone and possibly must fight against other kings for the right to govern Kent!"*

Meanwhile, Laurentius had succeeded Augustine as Archbishop of Canterbury when he heard the news of what King Edbald was doing, he became very offended by the conduct of the king who was still practising incest with his step-mother, as well as the fact that he had reverted to the pagan worship of Woden and Thor instead of being the baptised Christian King that he was. So, Laurentius despaired as to what he should do about things. After he had sent away all his companions, he considered abandoning Engelland and the Church altogether before he meditated upon the problem.

It was during his meditation that he received a vision from God. In the vision, saint Peter appeared and spoke directly to him. Peter said, *"Laurentius, stop being a coward and complete what you are supposed to be doing! I know very well that the tasks of getting Edbald to stop committing incest with his step-mother and go back to the Church both appear to be impossible! However, you must try giving that you best shot and God shall aid you in that! You will be surprised at what you can now achieve, so, get out there and speak to this wayward king! Only by so doing can he be brought back into the fold of the Church and Jesus Christ! When that happens, see to it that you once again, baptise him in public, using the shallow stream near Canterbury! Now stop feeling sorry for yourself and get out there, doing the work of God!"*

Laurentius went to see King Edbald, with amazing results! The king was easily convinced to convert back to Christianity, and he agreed to another public baptism of himself. He also broke off his incestuous relationship with his step-mother. Although the Church had forgiven him, it was only with great difficulty that he was able keep his territories. Many of his enemies still thought of him as a *"Mother-fucker"*.

All the same, he had amended his ways and for the rest of his life, he was of the true faith and his reputation became vastly better. The monastery founded by his father was ennobled by him with gifts of large estates and other valuable presents. After some more time, he was married to Emma, the daughter of the king of France. In time, Emma bore him a son whom they called Erconbert. He succeeded his father after he had reigned for twenty-four years. Both his father and grandfather had failed to destroy the idols and places of worship of the pagans, but that was quickly rectified by Erconbert who either levelled every temple of the pagans or else he had the temple building consecrated as a church for the worship of God.

Augustine was still in good health, and he went to Canterbury where he ordained Laurentius as the archbishop so that the new religious community of what was now known as England would not be without an archbishop when he died. After him, Mellitus who had been the Archbishop of London became the Archbishop of Canterbury. Erconbert appeared to be protected by the favour of God, resulting in everything being done according to his wishes to the point where he grew old in uninterrupted tranquillity. His daughter named Ercongotha, who was emulating her father in virtuous qualities became a leader in the monastery of Kalas in Gaul. His son named Egbert, did nothing memorable during his nine years of reign as the King of Kent. He was followed by a succession of weak and puppet kings until he was taken prisoner and put into chains by the Mercians. After some time, the Mercians set him free, but he was not received by his subjects, and it is unknown how or when he died.

Cuthred, who was the next heir to the throne of Kent, ruled in name only for eight years and he was followed by Baldred, who went into exile following his defeat by Egbert the King of the West Saxons. So, it was that the kingdom of Kent which had started to become English in 449 A.D., ceased to exist because it had been annexed by the West Saxons.

Cerdic and Cynric Arrive in Engle-land

Arriving at the southern of Engel-land during the year of 495 A.D., Cerdic was a German born Saxon of noble blood lines. He was the tenth descendent of Wodin and he had formed the opinion that he should leave Germania and obtain fame using daring and skills at arms. He spoke to his son, called Cynric. He said, *"Cynric, my son, I have the ambition to obtain riches, glory and new lands for our Saxon people and ourselves. There is much competition for everything here in Germania and I think that we must move to new land territories which we shall call home!*

I have been told that there are many opportunities for men like us on the islands of Britania! I was told that by Hengest when he was here last time for the purpose of raising an army of two-hundred thousand warriors to bring the Britons to heel. By using daring and our knowledge of the arts of war, we should always prevail over all our enemies, no matter who they may be! So, tell me Cynric, do you also have the opinion that we should take up new lands and enrich ourselves?"

Cynric answered with, *"Yes Pappa, I fully agree that we must take up new lands and that we should look at the possibility settling in the islands of Britania, so let us start training for night-time sea-borne assaults. In fact, I think that it would be a good idea to reconnoitre the coastal areas of Britania to find the most suitable area of where to launch our invasion of the island!"*

That so pleased Cerdic that he said, *"Cynric my son, I am so very glad that you have my outlook on life and that you are as fierce as me. In the morning, I will personally begin training all warriors, including yourself. All warriors shall practice attacking enemy using the Saxon long handled battle-axes. I want all warriors to practise using both hands to this heavy battle-axe down through the head of an enemy, towards his feet! As well, there shall be constant rehearsals of embarking and disembarking from ships onto shores while it is dark. All archers and spear throwers must practise their marksmanship to ensure that our arrows and spears hit our targets!*

Discipline shall be constantly applied and monitored, for it is critical to our success! After we have reached my desired level of proficiency in the use of all Saxon weapons and tactics, we shall go forth at night and practice landing upon the soil of Britania as silently as possible! Now my son, go to your training and after that, obtain replacement items for anything that is not completely serviceable. All other warriors shall be doing the same. We leave for the practise landings on the shores of Britania during the night in one month from now. During the meantime, we shall use our own shores to practise landing upon the shores of the Britons! We will practise both daytime and night-time landings! I pray that Wodin and Thor shall be with us!"

And so, after training for the next three weeks, it was time to reconnoitre the coasts of Britannia. The Saxons boarded the five Ceols[10] and set sail for Britannia. As the ships got closer, Cerdic issued orders. He said, *"We shall use the cover of darkness! No lights from us are allowed! We must not be seen by the enemy!"*

Arriving at the English shoreline where Cerdic wanted to practise the real landing, he quietly ordered his warriors. He said, *"Warriors, you are all to run for a distance two hundred and fifty paces, and then immediately return to our ships! We shall do this several times, and each time that we carry out these exercises, I want the time taken to be shorter than the time taken to complete it before. It is critical that we do this as quickly and as quietly as possible! Any man found to not be applying himself totally to this task will be dealt with severely! Now go and complete the first*

---

[10] Ceols were the two masted Saxon ships. They also use a redesigned Greek trireme.

practice landing!" That was completed and Cedric was happy with the result.

After another three of these landing practices, Cedric again spoke to his warriors. He said, *"Men, it makes me happy that you are all following your orders and you are functioning well! Tomorrow night will be a night of bright moonlight because it shall be a full moon! Our ships will be in position here, so that we can arrive when the night is darkest. We shall seek out all Britons and kill them! Our objective is to obtain new lands for Saxons to live in! For that to happen, the Britons must die so we can live! Now everyone is to return to our ships and rest."*

In 495 A.D., five ceols arrived at the coastal place that is now called Cerdic's-ore. As Cerdic had said, there was bright moonlight and the visibility was good. The Saxon warriors left the ships and as predicted, as the morning twilight was beginning, it got darker for some time before the twilight set in. The warriors left the ships and moved inland. It was not long before they came to walled town about five thousand paces from the shoreline. The warriors could see a bored sentry who was asleep on duty.

The warrior called Helmut said, *"Look at that! A sentry who is asleep on duty! Let's get him!"* That said, he went to the sleeping sentry and killed him using his Sah. This was repeated with most of the other sentries and the Cerdric took over the town. Cerdric had obtained a map of the countryside around the town. It showed the location of strong forces of Briton warriors. As 495 A.D., was just eight years after the death of Hengest, Cerdric and his Saxons wanted to avenge him. Cerdic split his force into equal halves. Of resulting two forces, one was commanded by Cedric while the other one was under the command of his son, Cynic.

A warrior came to Cerdic and spoke. He said, *"Sir, I have found the Briton force. It is large and totally disorganised! I think of its warriors as a disorganised and undisciplined rabble that we should be able to put down immediately without much trouble, even though they outnumber us by about eight to one!*

Cedric took out his map. Then he said, *"Show me upon this map where you have located the force that you speak of!"* The warrior did so enthusiastically, and he spoke. He said, *"Here where there are hills marked, they are bordered by a plain and a river which has been marked here".* As he was pointing to an area on the map. He said, *"The hills on this map mark the background and the river is here, as marked and the river has about three hundred paces width of trees along the banks ".*

That prompted Cerdic to say, *"Cynic, take your men and head towards the enemy, here ",* while he pointed to a location on the map. Cerdic continued speaking. He said, *"But do not engage the enemy yet, I need you and your men to remain as active reserves until I and my warriors have gone to this point behind the enemy, where the river forks. It does not matter how deep or fast flowing the river forks may be, we shall cross them and attack the enemy from their rear. Prior to my attack upon the enemy, I will sound one long blast from my horn! That is also the signal for your warriors to begin their attack on the enemy forces.*

It will still be daytime when we get to that point, so be alert for, and when you hear my horn blast, use it as a signal that my force is in position. When you hear the horn blast, attack on the enemy with all your arrows and spears, followed by the typical Saxon attack using the two-handed battle-axes and wipe the enemy out! I and my warriors will be doing the same to the enemy forces from behind them!"

As the day passed into afternoon, Cedric and his warriors did indeed cross both forks of the river completely unobserved mainly due to the lack of attention which was being displayed by the

Britons. So, Cerdic was able to reflect some strong sunlight off an old Roman mirror. That was seen by his son, Cynric, who immediately got his warriors ready for action by issuing the command, *"Stand to"*.

On the other side of the enemy position, Cedric took his horn and let out one long and loud blast from it, knowing that it would be heard by his son and his warriors. As soon as the horn blast had finished, Cynric ordered, *"Throw all your spears and release all your arrows into the enemy! After that has been done, attack the Britons using your Saxon battle-axes!"* The same order was repeated at the position of his father, Cedric, resulting in annihilation of the Britons present at the battle-field. The few survivors of the Briton force fled from the battle-field.

The result of that and some other actions like it was that the Britons never again dared to attack Saxon forces and accepted the dominion of the Saxons over them. Cedric did not waste his time and after he had been in Britania for twenty-four years, he was the absolute master of the southwestern part of England which he called West Saxony. Many people afterwards called it West Saxons, and it became Wessex.

Cedric spoke to his son, Cynric. He said, *"Son, you shall be my heir, and you will have the kingdom of West Saxony! To your cousin, Withgar, I am leaving the Isle of Wright because he is the son of my beloved sister, and he has helped our forces greatly during our conquest of these lands! I want both of you to work together towards building a new strong and just country!"*

Cynric was as illustrious as his father, Cerdic. Cynric had married and he was in the company of his son called Ceawlin in 556 A.D., when both he and his army of Saxon warriors encountered a large force of Britons at Beranbyrg (Barbury). The Saxons destroyed the Briton force. After ruling Wessex for twenty-six years and enlarging it, the kingdom was left to Ceawlin.

Two years later, in 558 A.D., Ceawlin the King of West Saxons and his brother Cutha were involved in a dispute with King Æthelbert the First of Kent. The dispute developed into war which was won by Ceawlin. Ceawlin spoke to Cutha. He said, *"Cutha, we are going into action against the Kimbern located to our west and south, and north. We are going to take Gloucester, Cirencester, and Bath! I have heard that the public baths at Bath have a choice of hot or cold water and that the water is health giving and rejuvenating! I assume that these reports are true, and I want to try out these things and we shall see if they are truly fit for a king!"*

That was followed by Cutha and his son who also had that name being killed by the Kimbern warriors whom they were fighting against. The loss of his brother and his nephew resulted in Ceawlin often lamenting the loss of both. Over time, he made enemies of both the Kimbern and the Engels who joined forces against him, and he lost his kingdom after ruling it for thirty-nine years. He was succeeded by Celric who was king for the next six years. Celric was succeeded by Ceolwulf who ruled for the next fourteen years. Although only aged seventeen years, he maintained the protection of his kingdom and expanded it.

Penda of Mercier

After him, his sons of Cleric, Cynegils and Cuichelm effectively and jointly ruled the kingdom. They were in many battles against the Britons and the king of Mercier called Penda. Penda was a great warrior who had the love and respect of his warriors. He was speaking to the warriors. He said, *"Men, it is time to expand the kingdom of Mercia! We shall do so by firstly taking Cirencester from the three kings of Wessex!"* The resulting battle for Cirencester was a complete disaster for Penda! It resulted in only a few of his followers and himself barely managing to escape the vengeance of the three kings of Wessex.

Cuichelm spoke to a man who was a professional assassin and willing to kill Edwin, the king of Northumbria. Cuichelm said to the assassin, *"I am willing to pay you very well to kill Edwin, the king of Northumbria! That man has been a constant pain in the neck for my brothers and me! He has taken a lot of territory from us and therefore, he must die!"*

Meanwhile, the assassin who had decided to tell King Edwin about the plot by Cuichelm to murder him was speaking to Edwin. He said, *"King Edwin, you may find it interesting that Cuichelm, one of the three kings of Wessex, has asked me to kill you on his behalf!"* King Edwin of Northumbria said, *"So, the leadership of West Saxons known as Wessex want to fight! Very well then, if war is what they want, then war is what they shall have!"* He then ordered his army to invade Wessex. The three kings of Wessex managed to escape from Edwin and soon afterwards, they met with Saint Birinus, who was a bishop.

Forty years after the arrival of Augustine, known as "Apostle of the Engels", the three kings of Wessex were converted to Christianity. That marked the twenty-fifth year of their joint reign of Wessex. The first of them to be converted was Cynegils who swallowed his pride and agreed immediately to receive the holy rite of baptism. Cuichelm resisted for some time before he also was converted. Two years after his brothers had died, Cynegils also died. In the year of 643 A.D., Cynegils was succeeded by his son called Kenwalh.

Kenwalh of West Saxons or Wessex

From the moment he assumed power, he was obsessed by it. He wallowed in regal luxury and began to rule with a great

115

arrogance. He was discussing religion with his generals, and they objected to him having converted to Christianity. They said, *"Kenwalh, if you wish to remain the king, you need to go back to the worship of Woden and Thor! It is high time to return to the correct Gods of our people! If you do not return to the worship of Woden and Thor, we the senior warriors of this nation shall not support you!"* Kenwalh then publicly rejected Christianity and returned to the pagan worship of Woden and Thor. He carried on with his dishonourable and self-indulgent ways often indicating to women that he may marry them if they consented to have sex with him. After he got his way with the woman concerned, he would cast her aside and dishonour her in general.

Kenwalh saw the beautiful Blaedswith, and he instantly became enchanted with her. He went to her and spoke. He said, *"Beautiful Blaedswith, I am Kenwalh the King of the West Saxons, and I very much want to get to know you a lot better! I just love to make a woman happy, and I shall look after your needs if you make love to me!"* Blaedswith said, *"You say that your name is Kenwalh, and it seems to me that I know of your reputation which has preceded you! Let us be frank about this! You have the reputation of using women for your own sexual gratification and then casting the poor women aside like a piece of soiled clothing and never having anything to do with her again. I shall not have sex with the likes of you! However, I know that the sister of King Penda of Mercier may be more inclined to fall under your charms! I am about to go into an Abbey where I shall become a nun and be safe from predatory males like you!"* That bothered the King of Wessex, and he decided to try his luck with Seaxburh, the sister of King Penda of Mercier.

Do Not Dishonour the Sister of Penda!

While I was researching this part of the history of the ancient English people, it was very apparent that that king called Kenwalh was also known as Cenwahl, Kenald, Kemal, Kendal, and Kendall. I have chosen to call him Kenwalh because he is listed under that name in three references and only once under the other names in other books.

Kenwalh happened to be at the castle of King Penda of Mercia when he met and began flirting with Seaxburg, the sister of Penda. He said, *"Seaxburh, the sister of my host, King Penda of Mercia, how very beautiful you are! I am Kenwalh, the King of the West-Saxons! I would very much like to be with you for all time!"* She answered, *"I hope that you are honourable Sir, for if you are not and if you hurt me or compromise me in any way, then not only will you face the wrath of a woman scorned, but you will pay the penalty for your acts to my brother, Penda. He will most surely kill you after he has degraded you and taken everything off you first! So, remember that if you want to be with me and you want to know me sexually, then you must marry me as well as the fact that you must love and honour me! Nothing else will do as far as both my brother and I are concerned!"*

Kenwalh desperately wanted to have sex with Seaxburh, so he spoke to her. He said, *Seaxburh, the sister of Penda of Mercia, I shall amaze you by my honour! So, please come with me on a horse ride into the fields and woods during which time we can discuss our present and future relationships. There will be much to be gained by both of us in doing this! Also, your brother Penda will benefit if we form a union between us!"*

She thought that Kenwalh was hinting that he desired to marry her and to make her his queen. So, she said to him, *"Kenwalh, are you saying that you desire to marry me or are your words just those of someone who wants to fuck me and then cast me aside like a piece of soiled linen?"*

Kenwalh was both a smooth talker and womaniser. He said, *"I am very attracted to you, Seaxburh, that is true! It is also true that I wish to have sex with you because your looks are divine and you are most appealing! I am willing to do whatever it takes to be able to see your beautiful and naked body and the make passionate love to you! We are currently a long way from Penda's castle and right here is a lovely spot where we can each come to know each other much better. No then, if you are attracted to me and if you want me, then please undress and we shall make love immediately!*

After foreplay had been in progress for about fifteen minutes, they made love. After they had made love, they returned to the castle of Penda. They both spoke to Penda. It pleased him when his sister said, *"Penda, my brother, Kenwalh is going to marry me, will you give us your blessing?"* Penda replied, *"I am happy to hear that you two shall marry. I think a marriage between the two of you will benefit both West Saxony[11] and Mercia. I shall speak to our priests of Woden and Thor, and they shall organise the wedding! Kenwalh, I understand that you will be returning to your kingdom today. Make sure that you return here and marry my sister as soon as I notify you to come here and take her!"*

Having returned to his castle in West Saxony, Kenwalh began boasting about how he had sex with Penda's sister and how he would now leave her and have nothing further to do with her. His closest advisor was Aldrich. He said, *"Kenwalh, have you gone completely stark raving mad? Do you not realise that you cannot just go to other kingdoms and fuck the sister of the king there and then toss her aside like a piece of soiled cloth? By Woden and Thor, I suggest that you honour your word to Penda the king of Mercia and marry his sister! You must do that because my boy, if you cast her aside like you have done to many other women, Penda will make*

---

[11] West Saxons was later called Wessex.

a war upon us, and you cannot beat him and his forces! You will lose any war against Penda!"

Kenwalh Dishonours Seaxburh

Kenwalh replied, *"Very well, I shall marry her, but I am not afraid of her brother!* So, it was that Kenwalh married Seaxburh, and the ceremony was celebrated with great prompt ad ceremony in what we now call Wessex. After a year it became very apparent that Seaxburh would not give a son to Kenwalh, and he began to chase other women. That became known to Seaxburh who spoke to Kenwalh about it. She said, *"Kenwalh, you must instantly stop dishonouring me by playing around with other women. I resent what you are doing, and you now have the chance to change your ways immediately!*

If you do not stop your affairs with other women, I will tell my brother Penda about you have done to me, and then, he will remove you from your kingdom for at least three years. During that time all the income and taxes of West Saxons will be taken and used by Mercier to pay for your folly and to provide me with a secure income! I will now leave here and reside with my brother, Penda!"

It was not long before the war between Mercier and West Saxons began. That resulted in the forces of Kenwalh losing the war, and the defeated. Kenwalh, who had shunned the Christian faith and the ideal of marriage now fled to the protection of Anna, the King of East Anglia in 645 A.D., and he stayed there until 648 A.D., serving King Anna in his army. After living at the court of East Anglia, Kenwalh returned to West Saxons, and he was in conversation with both nobles and priests of the Christian faith. That led to him finally returning to the folds of the Holy Church of Rome. He was discussing his return to the church with some friends.

He said, *"Albrecht, at midday of the morrow, I shall be baptised and that will signal my return to Mother Church! To pay correct homage to the church, I have granted it some land! I have also given three thousand hides[12] to my relation called Cuthred, who is the son of Cuichelm!"*

That angered the Britons who were still living within the kingdom of West Saxons because they were furious that land Kenwalh was giving to others was in fact land belonging the Britons. That resulted in the Britons taking up arms against Kenwalh. He had been closely informed about that, and he was in conference with his military advisors. He spoke to the advisors. He said, *"Gentlemen, it is high time for us to resume our military actions against both the Britons and the Welsh. Both people are not just untrustworthy, they are both pains in the arse! We are going into action against them, and the objective is to get rid of both pests immediately and permanently!"* So, began the military operations against both Britons and the Welsh in earnest.

A leader of the Briton warriors called Armel was speaking to a sub-chief called Elisedd. He said, *"Elisedd, we are going the battle the army of Kenwalh who has arrogantly just given away our lands to the Church of Rome! We cannot allow the arrogant English to continue to just appropriate our territory to whoever they want, whenever they want to do so! I need you to go to the area around Witeornesburg* (Bradford on Avon), *See to it that you and your warriors occupy the high ground before the English King Kenwalh does so!*

Elisedd answered, *"Very well, Armel, it shall be as you have ordered!"* Having said that, he left to carry out his orders. Meanwhile, Kenwalh and his army had taken the high ground before Elisedd, and his Briton warriors could get there. With his army

---

[12] A hide was a measure of land. Approximately 120 acres.

camped on the high ground above the river, Kenwalh and his men could plainly most of the Briton and Welsh warriors below them. There were also other Briton warriors who were out of the line of sight of the English. That is because they were in the woods lining the riverbanks. Kenwalh realised that he needed to know the strength of the Briton forces as well as their locations.

At an orders group[13] King Kenwalh spoke. He said, *"Gentlemen, we must know exactly how many enemy soldiers are facing us. They all appear to be encamped down there along the river. I want you to send out small scouting detachments of our warriors to reconnoitre the enemy positions, making sure that they make accurate maps of where the enemy units and sub-units are located and, how many enemies there are!*

See to it that you send out the best warriors we have and that they all know exactly what to do and how to do it! Their main duties are to provide us with accurate counts of the enemy forces and their exact locations! They should also make notes about how our army can approach the enemy positions unseen for as long as possible! When we have all the information, including routes for our soldiers to get close to the enemy while remaining unseen, we shall launch a night-time attack upon the enemy just as the evening twilight turns into darkness!"

His orders were carried out and that resulted in the commanding general of the English again going to King Kenwalh to confer with him. Having been ushered in to see Kenwalh, the general spoke. He said, *"Sir, the enemy has vast numbers! However, they all are camped in the woods lining the riverbanks. All the low-*

---

[13] An orders group is a meeting of commanders and sub-ordinates to discuss ad issue orders about a military situation.

land areas including the woods lining the riverbanks appear to be very dry!

If our army was to completely encircle the Briton/Welsh army, we could set fire to the trees under which the enemy is camped and so use fire to do much of our work of annihilating enemy for us! As the combined Briton/Welsh army tries to flee from that area, our men shall wipe them out using battle-axes, swords, arrows, and spears! By making our approach to the enemy position a silent one, we can be close to them when we attack and set the woods alight!"

Kenwalh though that over for a brief time and then he spoke. He said, *"General, see to it that everyman who is not an archer, is issued with at least six spears. Also make sure that every archer is issued with at least twenty-five steel tipped arrows per man. Also see to it that all archers are issued with either swords or battle-axes for their use once they have shot their arrows! Go and prepare your men for the coming fight by training them in all forms of combat, but make sure that they only use sticks and not the real weapons. We must make sure that we do not get casualties from training! Go to our supply officers and ensure that the men have issues of flint and fire-consumable fuel like tar and pig-fat so that we can ignite the woods under which the enemy is camped. After the woods have been set on fire, we shall wipe out the enemy!"*

Kenwalh now walked around the position of his army and talked to his soldiers. He said, *"With your various units and their leaders, make sure that every one of you rehearses what must be done tonight until all of you know it! Tonight, we shall firstly get close to the enemy positions, and then we shall set fire to the woods under which they are camped! We will surround the enemy before we set fire to the woods. As the enemy flees from the fire, we shall wipe them all out!*

Kenwalh had said that during the early hours of the morning. He added, *"Everyman who is not an archer shall be issued with six spears to throw at the enemy. As well, you shall all have either a long broadsword or a battle-axe with which to complete the work of closing with and killing the enemy! We shall not take any prisoners!"* After he had finished speaking to that grouping of warriors, he moved on to a different group of them further along his perimeter and then he said much the same sort of things to each one of them.

The result of that was that his soldiers all knew what was expected from them and how to do it! An hour before the dusk was to set in, Kenwalh who was repaying King Anna of East Anglia for his hospitality by commanding his army, moved his soldiers into position along the perimeter of the joint Briton and Welsh army. His sub-units were silently going about the business of pouring tar and pig-fat into open vessels and mixing these substances. Next, his archers dipped their steel arrowheads into the mixture. Everything was now ready for the attack.

Kenwalh walked along the line of archers and spoke to the groups of them. He said, *"Archers, our success tonight depends in a great deal on how well you perform your duties! As the twilight of the evening begins to turn into darkness, you must make sure that your arrowheads are well covered in the sticky tar and pig-fat combination. You must set fire the arrowheads and then shoot your arrows into the treetops lining the river in front of you. You are to turn all your arrows into flaming arrows and all of them must be shot at the treetops before you all! When you have used all your arrows in this way, you are all to take up either swords or battle-axes and then you must close with and kill all remaining enemy warriors!*

Siegehelm approached Kenwalh, he then spoke to him. He said, *"Sir, my Lord, and your friend, King Anna of East Anglia instructed me to scout ahead and find out what the enemy forces are doing. He also told me, that when I know the enemy strengths and locations, I am to report my finding directly to you, Sir! I closely observed the Britons and the Welsh, and I cannot help but wonder that they think that they are doing! They are milling about, and they have no idea of military matters, because they have not even taken up defensive positions and they appear not to have posted any sentries! They also seem to have no idea of how to 'Stand To[14]"*

Suddenly, there was a very loud horn blast, which was followed by the English setting their arrows on fire and then shooting the arrows into the treetops in front of them. Due to the tinder dry nature of the forested banks of the river, fires quickly spread and engulphed most of the area where the force of Britons and Welsh warriors were located. Many of the Britons and Welsh warriors tried to flee from the forest fire but they were killed by the English warriors who attacked them as they fled.

With the forest fire in the woods lining the riverbanks, now causing a mass panic among the enemy, the English from East Anglia gave shouts of joy and victory as they closed with and killed their enemies! At the conclusion of the battle, the joint Briton and Welsh force was wiped out, and there were no survivors! Now then remember that Kenwalh had been a Christian who rejected his faith and returned to the pagan worship of Woden and Thor. While he was at the court of king Anna of East Anglia, he found that theology was often discussed.

The other members of the court were all practising Christians, and these things combined to make Kenwalh desire to again become

---

[14] Stand-to is the traditional time to attack an enemy force. the attacks take place during the morning and evening "twilight".

a Christian. Accordingly, Kenwalh was baptised and was again, become a devout Christian king. He spoke to the members of his army. He said, *"Men, you have all performed very well today! You have wiped out the enemy to a man! Brother Justus shall now lead us in prayers of thanksgiving for our great victory over the enemy!"*

Brother Justus now spoke. He said, *"Let us all pray! Holy Father, we thank you for this wonderful victory over the vastly numerically superior force! We rejoice that you have given us your blessing and the victory!"* Next, he went on with an explanation of the ancient form of the 'Lord's Prayer. He spoke to many assembled warriors. He said, *"Many of you have been baptised and are now practising Christians! It is important that you all know and understand the Lord's Prayer, which was originally explained to you by Saint Augustine before me!"*

Having said that, he took a drink of water and began preaching. He said, *"The lord Jesus Christ died in great pain on a Roman cross to save you from your sins! Together, let us now say the prayer that Jesus taught us!"* He has another swallow of water and said,

"Our Father who is in heaven

Hallowed be your name

Your kingdom come

Let your will and not ours be done

Here on earth, as it is in Heaven

Today, give us our daily bread

And forgive us our sins

Just as we forgive those who sin against us

And do not lead us into temptation

But lead us away from all evil!

So be it!"

The good brother now said, *"That my friends was the 'Lord's Prayer', do any of you have any questions as to what it all means?"* No-one spoke and Brother Justus happily assumed that all men present understood the Lord's Prayer.

Kenwalh was soon again in conference with his officers. He said, *"Gentlemen, soon we will be at the mountain called Pen in Somersetshire and we shall immediately take and hold the high ground, for we shall be in direct battle with Wulfhere, the son of Penda, who is allied to the Britons, and we must wipe them out and take the greater part of Mercier away from them! We shall extract revenge for what Mercier has done to my father and me!"*

So, it was that the army of the West Saxons took the high ground of the mountain called Pen in Somersetshire and made their camp there. They were waiting for the advancing army of Mercia. When the Mercians arrived, they found that the West Saxons were well established and that they had formidable defences already prepared. That gave the West Saxons the upper hand because they were out of the sight of the Mercians as well as having cover from the arrows and spears of the Mercian Army. Therefore, the West Saxons remained unharmed, while the Mercians were slaughtered.

Eventually, Kenwalh who was well, and truly fired up, could contain himself no longer and he called out. He yelled, *"Wulfhere, Wulfhere, the son of Penda, come and face me, Kenwalh of the West Saxons, or die like the coward that you really are! I am Kenwalh and I want my battle-axe to show everyone the colour of your blood and brains when I slice you into two pieces by bringing my battle-axe vertically down from the top of your head towards your feet! Do*

126

not be shy, come over here and face me and then die as an honourable warrior instead of the coward that you are!"

Wulfhere was nowhere to be found, and the battle now fizzled out because the Mercians and their Briton allies were running from the mountain which had been the scene of their Army's destruction. Kenwalh asked for Brother Justus to see him, and soon, the brother was with Kenwalh.

Kenwalh said, *"Brother Justus, the West Saxons have achieved great victories in our last two battles! I now want to give something back to God and thank him for the divine assistance he has granted us! I want you and other monks such as yourself to now move among my warriors and to speak to as many of them as possible about God! I want you to convert as many warriors as you can to the Christian faith and to baptise them all in public! I want you to teach the words of God to all West Saxon warriors! My warriors do not understand Latin, and so, I need you to teach my soldiers the words of God in their own Germanic language! We are all going to Winchester! When we arrive there, I shall build the most beautiful of cathedrals and I want you to officiate the opening and blessing of the cathedral. After that, I plan to do homage at the monastery in Glastonbury!"*

So, it was in 670 A.D., during the twenty-ninth year of his reign that Kenwalh was talking to the Archbishop Theodore. Theodore said, *"Kenwalh, the monastery at Glastonbury, which you profess to hold dear is struggling financially and it cannot feed its monks or buy food in for them. In the name of God, I beseech you to help the monastery which you say that you hold dear!"* That had the desired effect, because Kenwalh immediately said, *"On this piece of parchment is my Royal Seal, granting to Berthwald. The Abbot of Glastonbury, and Ferramere, two hides of land which shall be the property of the monastery for all time. As two hides of land is consists of two hundred and forty acres, that should be sufficient to feed the monks and to produce crops for sale. Now take this Royal Deed conferring ownership of the land to the monastery and give it to the Abbot and let him know that his financial troubles are over because the Church has my alliance!"*

After ruling Wessex for thirty-one years, Kenwalh in 674 A.D., fell ill and he realised that he was dying. He was still alert, and he organised for his wife, Queen Seaxburg, his advisors, and his legal representatives to all be present as he dictated his last will and testament. After issuing directives about some family matters, Kenwalh spoke. He said, *"I hereby name my queen, Seaxburg as my Successor! She is a fine warrior in her own right, and she will lead my army and my kingdom with both courage and zeal. You must now all pledge allegiance to Queen Seaxburg who shall rule on my behalf. She has full authority, and she shall rule!"*

A Challenge to Queen Seaxburg

She immediately took up her duties as the leader of Wessex. She ruled with courage, fairness, and moderation. Fourteen days later, she was seated on her throne with her court around her when there was a challenge to her leadership from a warrior called Adolthrip. He strode into the throne room yelling, *"I am Adolthrip, and I do not give a tinker's cuss about what King Kenwalh has or has not decreed! I shall not obey the orders of any woman, and I hereby challenge Queen Seaxburg or her champion for the crown and the government of West Saxons!"*

Upon Adolthrip saying that, there was a loud shout coming from Alfrid who the champion of Seaxburg. He yelled, *"Adolthrip, Adolthrip, I am Alfrid, the champion of Queen Seaxburg! You shall have to fight me! Are you ready to die?"* That dismayed Adolthrip because Alfrid was a very big man who had enormous battle skills.

At that point, Queen Seaxburg herself spoke and amazed everyone with her statement. She said, *"I am Queen Seaxburg, and it is me who you shall face in combat for the crowns of my husband, Kenwalh and myself! You, Adolthrip, are typical of the men who consider themselves to somehow be better than women yet are both lazy and cowardly! You shall find that in fighting me, you have made the greatest mistake of your low-life! For, I am strong and totally without any fear of the likes of you! We shall settle this here and now! Prepare to die, you low-grade arsehole!"* that had the effect of impressing everyone who was present.

It was now that Seaxburh's champion took over and very firmly said, *"I, Alfrid, shall not let my queen, whom I am sworn to protect with my life, take on this cowardly challenger! And so, Adolthrip, it is me whom you shall be facing, and I say that it is time for you to die!"* That having been said, Alfrid rushed forward and when he got close to Adolthrip, he swung his long broadsword, cutting off the head of Adolthrip. A short time later, Kenwalh died and Seaxburh completely took up the governing of West Saxons. She was good at running the country, but she died after reigning for a year in her own right. She was succeeded by Escwin who ruled for two years before he also died, being succeeded by Kentwin, the son of Cynegils.

A warrior prince called Ceadwall became a victim of a conspiracy among princes, who were envious of his military skill and his skills in governing. The warrior prince was so popular with the members of his army, that when he was sent into exile, the entire army accompanied him.

Ethelwalch King of South Saxons

The region that was formerly called South Saxons is now known as Sussex. We start that story with Ethelwalch, who was king of the South Saxons, he was seated on his throne when he suddenly yelled out. He shouted, *"My general and officers get over here to me now! There is much to discuss of the most serious nature!"* That resulted in the general and his higher-ranking officers immediately going to the king. Ethelwalch received them and spoke to them. He said, *"We have the enemy Wessex King Caedwalla near to us and that is a threat that I cannot tolerate! You are to immediately find him and his army. You must all hunt down and find Caedwalla and his forces! When you have found him, destroy him and his army!"*

Caedwalla of Wessex

Caedwalla was speaking to his senior commanders. He said, *"We are making war upon the Ethelwalch and his South Saxons! After we have wiped them out, we shall return to our own country! We will kill the invading rival princes who have driven us from our lands!"* That was followed by military action which resulted in the entire South Saxon army being wiped out. It also resulted Ethelwalch repenting his attack upon the West Saxons.

With his spirit being elated as were those of his warriors, he suddenly returned to his country and either killed his rivals or drove them out of the region now known as Sussex. For two years he enjoyed the governing of his kingdom as he continued to wage war upon the South Saxons. His hatred and hostility towards the South Saxons were immeasurable and resulted in the destruction of Edric, who had succeeded Ethelwalch. Edric had opposed Ceadwalla with a great boldness. Like most other rulers, he had the services of advisors, warriors, and spies, who were everywhere.

In year 686 A.D., Caedwalla was sitting on his throne, when a messenger came to him. The messenger said, *"Sire, there is a man outside who wishes to have a closed conference with you. His name is Gwrtheyrn, and he says that he has important information about the security of this realm and that he will only speak to you about it!"* Caedwalla said, *"Show him in to see me immediately!"*

Gwrtheyrn entered the throne room and bowed before his king. He said, *"Your Majesty, I am Gwrtheyrn, and I gather intelligence on behalf of your warriors! So far you have been successful against the South Saxons. Your problems are no longer confined to the South Saxons. The Kimbern living in Kent have entered an alliance with the South Saxons as well as the Mercians. As well, the population of the Isle of Wright is in revolt and they have also joined the alliance of Mercia, Kent, and South Saxons against you!"*

Caedwalla called for his messenger. When he arrived, Caedwalla said, *"Messenger, go immediately to the senior commanding officer of my warriors and bring them here for an immediate orders group which must be kept secret! Our kingdom is in great danger!"* The messenger said, *"Yes, Your Highness, I should be able to have them here for you in about two hours, depending upon where there are. I leave now!"* He then departed.

Two hours later, he had returned with the senior commanders, and he ushered them into the throne room. After the officers had started their conversations with Caedwalla the messenger withdrew from the area. King Caedwalla spoke to the commanders of his warriors. He said, *"Gentlemen, we have a very serious situation that must be closely controlled for we are in great danger! We have fought the South Saxons to a standstill, but they are again a threat to us because they have formed alliances with the kingdoms of Kent and Mercia. Not only that, but the population of the Isle of Wight is in revolt against us, and they have also joined the alliances against us! As far as I am concerned, the treason shown by the people of the Isle of Wight must be punished by the raping of their women, the plunder of their homes and the killing of their men! See to it that all of that is done! Also, seize some of the most fruitful land and pepper it with large amount of salt, so that it will become useless for generations to come! Show the rebels and all those who oppose me, no mercy!"*

Mull of Wessex

These orders were followed, and there was much suffering in both Kent and the Isle of Wight as the instructions of Caedwalla were carried out. That night, Caedwalla's brother called Mull spoke to the king. He said, *"Caedwalla, please grant me the command of your army so that I can also perform great military deeds as you have already done! That would make the reputation of our country and army even greater that it now is. I am also eager to become known as a slayer of the Kimbern living in Kent just like you already are known!"*

Caedwalla said, *"Very well Mull, I hereby grant you command of my army. You will find that it is made up of young and able soldiers who will not flinch in battle! See to it that you always lead the army from in front of it so that your men will be inspired by the example that you set them. When you have subdued all of Kent, I want you to make war on the population of the Isle of Wight!"* So it was that was that Mull found himself leading an army of young and capable soldiers who made up the greater part of the army of Caedwalla into Kent, which did not have a force capable of stopping him.

As Mull was leading this force through Kent and finding that there was no-one to stop him, he laid waste to the land by peppering it with large volumes of salt. That made the fertile land become barren for generations as little could be grown upon it. On the order of Caedwalla, he inflicted the horrors of war upon the populations of both Kent and the Isle of Wight. He even used a tactic during which the unoffending ministers of the Christian Church were killed. He thought of his enemies as being weak and effeminate to the point where he took no precautions against the anger of his enemies.

During the spring of 687 A.D., Mull was in the company of twelve warriors and a long way from his army. The thirteen men had discovered a house which was in a forest, near its edge. Upon getting near the house, all these men rushed into it. They were all intent on plundering the house and raping any women within it. As the men were plundering the house and raping the women of it, a woman managed to escape. She ran into the dense forest and began walking when she noticed that no-one was pursuing her. In time she met some warriors who formed part of the army of Kent.

She noticed a warrior sub chief called Bietsung who was leading a small army Kent army unit. He said, *"Lovely lady, I am Bietsung, and I can see that you appear to be rather upset, what is the matter and can my friends and I help you in some way?* She answered, *"Thank you for asking, Bietsung, I am Lydia, and I am fleeing from the minions of Caedwalla and Mull of Wessex who have attacked my home. There are at least thirteen of them in number and perhaps more whom I have not seen. They are plundering everything in house, and they are raping all women and girls. They have also killed two men of the house, including my husband!"*

Bietsung said, *"My fellow warriors and I are part of the army of Kent. We shall gather more warriors and proceed to your home which you indicated is about one thousand paces from here. I suggest that you accompany my men and I as we get our reinforcements. So, do you wish to stay with us, or do you want to just get out of this area?"* Lydia replied, *"Bietsung, if you guarantee my safety, I shall be happy to stay with you."* Bietsung said, *"Yes, of course I guarantee your safety. Also, I am obtaining an additional twenty warriors to add to the ten warriors that I have with me. Then, all of us, including yourself, shall go back to your house. When we get there, we shall surround it and slay the aggressors from West Saxons who have caused you so much hardship! It will be best if you guide us to your home."*

Lydia agreed to that and Bietsung obtained his extra twenty warriors. The all of them went to towards Lydia's house. As the group got closer to the house, Bietsung could plainly hear the raucous and drunken laughter of Mull and his companions.

He said, *"Lydia, we are at the point of no return now. The duty of my men and I is to wipe of the forces of Wessex where-ever we find them. I cannot guarantee the safety of the other members of your family who may still be alive within the house!"* Lydia replied, *"Bietsung, just do what you must do! At the very least, I shall have revenge for what the West Saxons have done!"* Bietsung now addressed his warriors. He said, *"Friends, it is time to surround the house. Do it now! No-one from the force of West Saxons must be allowed to escape! As soon as the house is surrounded, set fire to it and burn the drunken West Saxons out!"* And so died the young general Mull together with his twelve other soldiers!

Caedwalla Learns of Mull's Fate

Caedwalla, upon hearing of the death of his brother, again invaded Kent where he slaughtered much of the population and plundered their homes. Next, he landed on the Isle of Wight and again, he slaughtered many of the people there as well as plundering their homes. Then, one night after a victory feast, Caedwalla who was tired and drunk after much eating and drinking of wine and ale, went to his bed. Soon, he was dreaming. As he was dozing off, he became sure that he was seeing a vision of Saint Peter, the Apostle and the first Pope of the Roman Catholic Church.

Saint Peter said, *"Caedwalla, Caedwalla, you have been a great warrior king, but you have killed many of the true righteous believers and servants of God! You and your armies are guilty of bringing war and famine upon the people of God in Kent and the Isle of Wight! I am telling you that these people are the true believers and servants of God and that you must not ever molest them again! These people are now under the direct protection of God, and you must now atone for your actions against them because God has commanded that!*

You must make good the harm you have done, and you must again become a practising Christian! You were baptised as a child and although you have been of the true faith, you have only been an occasional worshipper of God! I now command you to again be baptised in public at Glastonbury or Canterbury! I shall now give you a vison of what will happen to you if you do not become a practising Christian and beg God to forgive you for your sins in the name of the saviour, Jesus Christ!"

Saint Peter now installed the scenario he had prepared of Caedwalla descending into hell and having demons all around him. As Caedwalla was dreaming, he could see his body was being fed to groups of demons who were biting on his arms and legs. They were interrupted by their leader called Satan. So, Satan spoke to Caedwalla. He said, *"Caedwalla, welcome to my world of hell complete lava, fluid rocks and fire! From here, there is no escape, and you shall suffer for all eternity as we eat your body repeatedly! Your soul shall be made to suffer eternally unless you can join God, Jesus Christ, and Saint Peter in heaven!"*

That so greatly disturbed him that King Caedwalla who was so successful in war, abandoned his crown and went to Rome where Pope Sergius received him. The Pope spoke first. He said, *"Greetings King Caedwalla of Engel-land, from the letters that I have received about you, you have renounced your crown, and you are coming back the Saviour, Jesus Christ, and God the Father! I understand that you have been a mighty warrior and that you have*

135

seen the error of your ways. Your religious teachers tell me that you have changed your ways and that you now wish to reconcile with God! Today is Thursday and tomorrow shall be Good Friday. The next day is Easter Saturday, and I shall baptise you during a church service that I shall be leading on the banks of the Tiber River on Saturday.

We shall use the shallow part of the Tiber, just past the point where there are two bends in the river, which have resulted in a good build-up of clean sand, and it makes the river very shallow at that point. Be here in Saint Peter's Basilica at mid-morning of Easter Saturday, and I shall take you to the Tiber where we will baptise you. See to it that you are wearing these white baptismal robes which I am now giving to you!

A day and night passed and on Easter Saturday, King Caedwalla of the Britons was wearing the white robes issued to him by the Pope. He was at Saint Peter's Basilica at mid-morning as he had been instructed. Pope Sergius walked to him and spoke. He said, *"Come with me King Caedwalla and we shall go to the Tiber to baptise you!"* So, they set off by horse drawn carriage and arrived at the bend in the Tiber that the Pope wanted to use for the church service and the baptism of King Caedwalla. The pope waded towards the middle of the shallow part of the river and waited for Caedwalla to reach him. When that happened, he held the king and spoke to him.

He said, *"Caedwalla, do you hereby renounce the devil called Satan and all of his follows and temptations?"* Caedwalla said, *"Yes, I do! I also swear total allegiance and obedience to God the Father, his only Son, the Saviour Jesus Christ, and the Holy Ghost! I swear before God almighty that I shall full-fill my duties as a Christian and that I shall always try to live as God wants us to!"* The Pope said, *"Caedwalla, lean backwards and do not be afraid of falling in the water because both of my hands are under your back. I will now lower you into the water and then I shall bring you back to the standing position. Now take a deep breath!"*

Caedwalla did so and the pope thrust him very briefly underwater. He then pulled Ceadwalla to the standing position and spoke to him. He said, *"King Caedwalla you are now baptised in the name of the Father, The Son, and the Holy Ghost!* Soon after that event, during a feast which was attended by both men, Caedwalla died on the 20th of April 689 A.D., he was buried in Saint Peter's Cathedral.

King Ina of Wessex

In the territory of the West Saxons there was some unrest because their king was dead. In 689 A.D., there were many public meetings called to discuss what many people felt was a growing crisis. The West Saxons wanted a good and warlike king to lead them and provide protection against the Engels of Mercia and the incoming Danes who were becoming a problem. After a long time of being a leaderless nation, the bishops of West Saxons met for a conference which was held in London. The bishops met and conferred with each other. After some time, they decided that they should find a man called Ina to be their king.

These bishops did not know of anyone who was called Ina and so, they sent messengers to all parts of Wessex to find a man called Ina. A man called Ina was nowhere to be found. Then, a little later, the messengers were near Somerton on the way towards London, when they heard a farmer who was calling out to his son. He was yelling, *"Ina, Ina, come here this instant Ina!"*

The messengers were astounded that soon afterwards; a handsome young man was walking towards the farmhouse leading a team of horses. The messengers went to him and spoke to him. They said, *"Sire, it is with great joy that we, the messengers of the*

137

bishops of West Saxons, hereby inform you that God has chosen you to become the new King of West Saxons (Wessex). God has commanded that you shall be king! Now then, do you accept this great honour and awesome responsibility?"

The young farmer called Ida answered the messengers. He said, *"Yes, indeed, I do accept this call from the heavens, I shall become one of the best kings ever to have ruled West Saxons!* So, Ina was made the king of West Saxons, and his queen was called Æthelburga. She was a regal and nice-looking woman who was both fair in her dealings with her people and she was also courageous.

King Ina passed laws which were a considerable help to King Alfred the Great when he formed his laws for the whole of England. He waged war upon the South Saxons (Sussex) and the East Angles (East Anglia), wiping them out in battle. Ina was also a religious man. He founded monasteries at his own expense and ordered that the bodies of the martyrs Indract and his followers be taken from their place of martyrdom. He ordered the remains of the martyrs to be taken to the church at Glastonbury where they were put into a stone pyramid on the left side of the altar and Saint Hilda was put there as well. His other followers were placed under the pavement without any planning or design in mind. Ina also granted more gold and land to the church at Glastonbury.

In 716 A.D., Ina died after having reigned for twenty-seven years. The government of Wessex was succeeded by Ethelard, who was the cousin of Ina. Ethelard quietly ruled the kingdom for fourteen years before he was succeeded by his kinsman called Cuthred. Cuthred took up the duties of being the king of Wessex and he immediately showed everyone that he had similar courage and abilities as King Ina, who had ruled before him. He thought that it would be a good move on his part to pledge in public that the grants made by his predecessors would be honoured by him, so at the church near the monastery at Glastonbury, he spoke to the congregation.

He said, *"In the name of our Lord Jesus Christ, I, Cuthred, King of the West Saxons, hereby declare that all the gifts of former kings such as Kenwalh, Baldred, Ina, Ethelard and Ethelbald, who was a king of the Mercians, shall be honoured by me! The church shall continue to hold country houses, villages, and lands according to confirmation made to the ancient city of Glastonbury and confirmed by autograph and by the sign of the cross, I do hereby decree that all grants made by former kings shall remain firm and inviolate as long as the revolution of the pole shall carry the lands and seas with regular movement around the starry heavens!*

But if anyone confiding in tyrannical pride shall endeavour on any occasion to disturb and nullify this, which is my testamentary grant, may he be separated by the fan of the last judgement from the conjugation of the righteous and joined to the assembly of the wicked forever, paying the penalty of his violent acts. But whoever with benevolent intention strives to approve, confirm, and defend my grant, may he be allowed unfailing immortality before the glory of him that sits on the throne with the happy company of angels and all saints!" Cuthred began re-organisation and retraining of his army and after a great deal of work, he was able to lead successful campaigns against the Britons and then against Ethelbald, king of Mercia.

With that in mind, Cuthred spoke to his army commanders. He said, *"Gentlemen, we have some problems to do with the organisation of our forces and the weapons used by the men. For these reasons, we shall now re-arm the army with new weapons and we shall teach our warriors new tactics! From now on, the smallest sub-unit in my army shall consist of a ten-man section commanded by a junior non-commissioned officer. The next higher sub-unit shall be thirty men commanded by a junior commissioned officer and a senior non-commissioned officer[15].*

I want every man in the section to know how to perform the duties of everyman who is next to him. For example, if an archer becomes disabled or is killed, his place must immediately be filled by the soldier nearest to him, who must immediately assume the duties of the archer. The same things must apply to ordinary infantry soldiers and members of cavalry units! In all cases, if a soldier becomes disabled or gets killed, his closest companions must resume his duties and carry on the attack! Not only that, but every man must know the duties every other man who is one rank above him or one rank below him! Now see to it that it is done, for in twenty-four days from now, we shall attack the Engels, utilising the aid of Ethelbald of Mercia!"

In 743 A.D., the orders of Cuthred were carried out and the resulting campaign against the Engels with help from Ethelbald of Mercia was completely successful. Time passed and in 752 A.D., there was a falling out between Ethelbald of Mercia and Cuthred of Wessex. Due to the efforts of his re-organised and now very efficient army, Cuthred wiped out most of the army of Ethelbald at the "Battle of Burford in 752 A.D... During the following year, Cuthred and his West Saxon army found themselves fighting against the patriots of Wales. As usual, Cuthred's army won.

Sigebert the Gutless

In 754 A.D., Cuthred died, and the leadership of Wessex was taken up by Sigebert. He was a man who used inhuman cruelty among his own subjects, and he was known far and wide as being both a coward and a very cruel tyrant. Many people of Wessex were

---

[15] In the modern armies of most English-speaking countries, the sub-unit is the platoon, and it is commanded by either a lieutenant or second lieutenant. The second in command of a modern platoon is normally the platoon sergeant.

openly discussing their new king. They said, *"We had a good king in our previous one called Cuthred! Too bad for us that he died and has been replaced by 'Sigebert the Gutless and cruel'. Let us put our heads together and work out the way of getting rid of that worthless and pitiless arsehole!"*

Soon, the situation of Wessex was discussed by the West Saxon Council who debated the bad situation among them. Typically, they said, *"Things cannot continue as they currently are, our people are suffering greatly from the cruelty and viciousness of 'Sigebert the Gutless.' This council of nobles hereby gives notice that "Sigebert the Gutless' has lost the support of the 'Council of Nobles' and calls upon his relative called Cynewulf to take up the reigns of governing Wessex!"*

All of that resulted Sigebert being driven from the throne of Wessex in less than a year after he had taken it up. He had been driven out of most of his territory by Cynewulf who was following the directive of the council to remove him from power. In 755 A.D., Sigebert was removed from power and was alone in the forest of Andred, where he lived for some time. Sigebert, did however, manage to sway some of his former followers to his cause and that enabled him to hold on to the province of Hampshire.

Through the aid of these followers, he kept up his former habits and quickly made enemies of all his subjects by the murder of a Cumbrian who was immensely loyal to him. Now that he no longer had friends or associates, he fled and tried living among the wild beasts in the forest for a while. He quickly tired of living in the forest and then he approached a swineherd who was living near the forest's edge. Sigebert said, *"I am Sigebert the King, serve and obey me and in return, I will enrich you greatly!"*

Edgar the swineherd, was an honourable man who had heard of the many wrongs that Sigebert had committed against the people of Wessex. He had also heard of a reward from the 'Council of Nobles' that was payable to anyone who brought down Sigebert. He said, *"I am Edgar and as you can plainly see, I must tend to my herd of pigs. I have heard of you.*

The people of Wessex all call you 'Sigebert the Gutless and cruel'! Very well, I shall support you, but I need you to come over here and for you to help me lift this heavy piece of timber, so that my pigs can pass through that narrow opening!" So it was that Sigebert walked over to where Edgar the swineherd was and he said, *"Alright, I am now here, please let me know what it is that you want to have done, and it shall be so!"* Unknown to Sigebert, Edgar the swineherd had an original Saxon sah attached to his belt and it was hidden from view by his cloak. Edgar said, *"Over here my liege, pick up the end of this piece of timber nearest to you and help me to get it over there if you want my help!"*

As he said that, Edgar was reaching under his cloak, and he withdrew the sah from its scabbard. As Sigebert moved around to pick up one end of the timber and bent over to pick up one end of it, Edgar moved to behind him and then placed his left arm around the neck of Sigebert. In his right hand, Edgar was holding the sah. Edgar now stabbed Sigebert and then proceeded to cut his throat with the sah.

As he was killing 'Sigebert the Gutless' Edgar said, *"You who have filled everyone with disgust at your lusty lifestyle, your cruelty and your cowardice are being killed by a lowly swineherd whom you despise so much! As well as stabbing you, I have opened your veins and you shall now bleed to death, so, your fucking majesty, you can sit there and watch as your blood and life slowly drains away! So please die and take a long time to do so, your arsehole-ship!"*

Cynewulf

Now that Sigebert was gone, Cynewulf became the king of Wessex and undertook the governing of the kingdom in 729 A.D... The reputation and deeds of Cynewulf were of great distinction, and he was everything that his predecessor, King Sigebert was not! He had the respect and loyalty of his commanders and soldiers. For example, he was constantly leading his soldiers into action against the Welsh who were a continuing security problem insomuch as they were trying to invade English territory. In year 753 A.D., the twenty-fourth year of his reign, he lost a battle against Offa, a king of the Mercians, but he continued to lead his warriors from in front of them. His reputation among his soldiers was such that he was able to call upon their loyalty and to get it unto their deaths, at any time that he wanted.

In 755A.D., Cynewulf was actively in conference with his generals and advisors when he said, *"Gentlemen, it is I who has led our armies many times into hard battles against the Welsh, and we have won the day every time! I have now been on the throne for twenty-eight years and news has reached me that the Ætheling[16] of 'Sigebert the Gutless' whose name is Cyneheard, is actively working against me and my kingdom. He must be brought to heel or die!"*

His audience was very supportive of Cynewulf, and he had the love and loyalty of his soldiers. He said, *"Early in the morning, I and twenty-five of my best warriors are traveling to Merton, where I will visit my wife!"* He did not know that there was a traitor within his palace, who sent word of the meeting of Cynewulf and his wife at Merton to Cyeheard, the Ætheling of the deposed King Sigebert. The message sent to Cyneheard read, *"Your majesty, please take note that you are now able to destroy Cynewulf, who deposed your father! Cynewulf is going to a small house at the edge of the forest*

---

[16] Ætheling (21st century spelling is atheling) means the prince/heir apparent of the Royal Family.

near Merton. He is leaving here in the early morning, and he and his escort should arrive at the house near Merton by about midday! If you were to immediately leave for Merton, you could be at the house before him. That way, you could ambush and kill him, thus avenging your father!"

So, in 757 A.D., Cynewulf and his escort left his castle for Merton before the onset of the morning twilight. Both he and his escorting warriors took their time travelling as they were unaware of the plot that was being put into action by Cyneheard the son of 'Sigebert the Gutless' and that it would result in a hard fight. As Cynewulf and his escorting warriors were advancing towards the house near Merton, they were surprised to see a bare breasted young woman running towards them and away from Merton's direction. Cynewulf saw her and had her brought before him. He said, *"Edelbrock, get this girl some cloths to cover her torso!"* Edelbrock was soon back with the requested garment and Cynewulf said, *"Here you are young woman, go ahead and put on this shirt. Now then, I am King Cynewulf on the way to visit my wife near Merton. Please introduced yourself to me!"*

She said, *"King Cynewulf, it is good that I have found you! Your wife and all other females in your house near Merton either have been or are in the process of being raped and killed by Ætheling Cyneheard and his foul men! I managed to get away after Cyneheard's soldiers tore off the top of my dress and then began to fondle my tits! I saw your wife being raped repeatedly as were the other women present in your home! The Ætheling Cyneheard has about twenty men with him inside your house!*

King Cynewulf was dismayed by what had happen to his wife. He said, *"So, the son of 'Sigebert the Gutless' has attacked my home and raped and or killed the women of my home! The time has come for him to die!"* Having said that, King Cynewulf went through the doorway of his house. Just inside the door, he saw the

Ætheling and yelled, *"Cyneheard, Cyneheard, you are the son of 'Sigebert the Gutless'! You have proven yourself to be as cowardly as your father! Come here and face me in mortal combat or die the death of the coward that you are! You are the son of a coward, and given that your mother was a dog, it all makes you a 'Cowardly-son -of-a-bitch'!"*

Having yelled that out, King Cynewulf rushed forwards and swung his long broadsword downwards in an arc from the head of the Ætheling towards his feet. Cyneheard the Ætheling, sprang sideways and therefore became severely wounded instead of dying immediately as he would have if the King's sword hit him in the head. While the fight was in progress, the prince cried out for assistance from his followers many times.

The cries of the Ætheling drew many of his warriors to the fight between the two leaders. Three of these rushed up and got themselves into position behind the king. Then one of them swung his battle-axe in an arc downwards from the head of the king towards his feet, thereby cutting him in two. As he did so, he yelled, *"Now die, Cynewulf, the enemy of my leader, the Ætheling Cyneheard!"* More of King Cynewulf's escort warriors were coming to the aid of their king. The Ætheling now spoke to these men. He said, *"I will give each of you much money and ensure that you are well-off for life as well as sparing your lives and granting all of you pardons!*

However, you must immediately abandon your King Cynewulf who is lying dead over there and pledge your loyalty to me instead! You must quickly make up your mind to serve me, because if you look through the door towards the forest edge, you will see my re-enforcements arriving in great numbers! So, serve me or die!" The warriors of King Cynewulf all refused to leave their king and join Prince Cyneheard. They all fought on until such time as they had all died trying to protect King Cynewulf! The body of King Cynewulf was buried at Winchester and the body of Prince Cyneheard was buried at Repton, which at the time was a noble monastery.

Kings of Northumbria

Ida

Hengest set up his own government in Kent. He also sent his brother called Otha and his son Ebissa to seize northern parts of Engel-land. All three of these men were active as the leaders of their warriors. They always led their men from in front of them, inspiring their warriors by the example of their own actions. Being the elder of the two, Otha said to Ebissa, *"My nephew Ebissa, we are frequently coming into action with the inhabitants of this part of Engel-land, and we have already dispersed all those who attempt to resist us! If we continue to do that and let those who submit to us have uninterrupted quiet, then through their own address and the good will of their followers, we will establish a good degree of power over them."*

That was answered by Ebissa. He said, *"Uncle Otha, Hengest, my father has only commanded that we make subjects of the people in this, the northern part of Engel-land. I fully agree with you that that by wiping out all those who oppose us and being lenient to those who submit to us, we will be able to subdue this part of Engel-land and by also protecting all of the locals from outside dangers such as Picts and Scots, we will generate such a large amount of goodwill with these people that it will become easy to set up a principality as has been ordered by my father, Hengest!"*

Otha was pleased with that outlook of his nephew. He said, *"Alright then, let's begin setting the principality of this part of Engel-land immediately."* And so, the principality was successfully set up and it continued to function as a principality which was subject to the kings of Kent for ninety years. After that, these arrangements ceased because the Germanic race of people are naturally ambitious. Therefore, the was intense competition between the Engels who had settled in large areas of what would become Northumbria, subject to the Kimbern rulers in Kent. Therefore, in 547 A.D., which was the sixtieth year after the death of Hengest, the principality was converted into a kingdom prior to it being incorporated into Northumbria. Before it was incorporated into the region, we now call Northumbria, that region was made up of the independent kingdoms of Bernicia and Deira. In the year 517 A.D., a son was born to the wife of King Eoppa. Filled with joy at this birth of a fine and healthy son, Eoppa called for celebrations to begin.

With great joy he spoke to the members of his court. He said, *"It is with great joy that I, Eoppa, now proclaim that your future king has been born! His name is Ida, and you shall all now come forward, one at a time and pledge your homage to him forever!"* And so, the members of the court of Bernicia came forward singly and pledged their loyalty and allegiance to their future King Ida. The people of Bernicia had originally been the Engels who were one of the first Germanic tribes to settle in Britania. As we have already seen, when these people left their original homeland on the Jutland peninsula, they went as a mass migration which left original homeland completely deserted.

Although some historians have called the members of the Kimbern tribe Jutes, the fact remains that that name can be used to describe all the Germanic tribes that came to Britania because they all came from the Jutland peninsula of Northern Germania. The Kimbern came from the north of it, the Engels came from the middle of it and the Saxons came from the south of it. Therefore, if someone wishes to apply the name of Jutes to the incoming Germanic tribes, then that person should apply that name to the Kimbern (called

Cimbri by Romans), the Engels and the Saxons. Also bear in mind that the three tribes confederated into one powerful tribe which became known as Saxons to most people. The tribes operated under the direction of their own nobles, but always under the banner of the Saxons!

As he was growing up. Ida was strictly supervised with his every move being watched and commented upon. He was an able student and was taught to read and write in both Latin and Greek. That was of benefit to him and his people as those two languages were the only completely written languages in Europe at that time.

Bear in mind that what was thought of as decent and proper behaviour during the time frame of 500 to 1,000 A.D., was vastly different to the morality (or the lack of it) of the twenty-second century. So, when Ida was aged twelve years, he was introduced to his future wife, called Bearnach. He was smitten by her presence and they both enjoyed each other's company. The two of them continued to meet with the full approval of both sets of their parents. The parents then decided that their children should marry immediately. Despite them both being only twelve years of age. So, at the wedding, the amazing sight of a twelve-year-old boy being married to a fourteen-year-old girl took place. Like all Engels (Angles), Ida was a pagan who worshipped the goddess Hertha or Mother Earth.

The very young couple went through the rituals of marriage of their religion and became husband and wife. During the year of 530 A.D., when Ida was thirteen years old, Bearnach was in labour. She spoke to Ida. She said, *"Ida, I Can feel that your son is about to come into the world! What name would you like to call him?* Ida thought the matter through for a while before he answered her. He said, *"I want my first son to be called Adda, who shall become the king of Bernicia after me!"* So it was that Adda became the Ætheling and the future King Adda of Bernicia. Seven years later, Bearnach again gave birth, and she again asked Ida to name the child. He said, *"Let this son become known to as all as Æthelric! He shall become king of Bernicia after myself and his brother, Adda!"*

That quickly became public knowledge and the population of Angles in Bernicia rejoiced that they now had a second heir to the throne of their country. Two years later in 539 A.D., another son was born to Bearnach and Ida. He was named as Ocg. Over time, Ida fathered twelve children and he became known as *'Ida the Great Knee.'* He was often at war and always led attacks upon the Britons and other enemies in person and from in front of his warriors. In 547 A.D., on the Engel-land coast was the Briton stronghold of Din Guyaroi (Bamburgh) located on the northeast coast. That fortress was an impediment to anyone who wanted to pass through the area and that was beginning to give problems to Ida because it interrupted his supply and communication lines.

He called for an orders group with his commanders. He said, *"Gentlemen, before us is the coastal stronghold of Din Guyaroi! It is fast becoming a major problem, and it interferes with our lines of communications and supply! We must take this fortress, and we must do so quickly! I do not want great number of casualties among our warriors, so please produce some ideas of how best to take the fortress without our warriors suffering immense casualties, although I fully realise that some casualties are inevitable!"*

One of his senior officers now spoke. He said, *"Sire, I have been with you through many campaigns against the Britons other enemies including the Welsh, so you know that I speak true! If you would like to wipe out the Britons before you, with a minimum of your own casualties, then I recommend that we use a three-pronged attack involving the use of catapults from directions of the north, south and west simultaneously!*

Your reputation among the Britons is already that of 'Ida the Flame Bearer', so let it be known to the Britons that they are facing the 'Flame Bearer' and that your will burn them out if you must, but that you consider it to be far better to be merciful. That you will have mercy upon them if they submit and become part of Bernicia. I also think that they will reject your advances and that you should consider the use of a sea-borne attack simultaneously with the land-based attacks upon the fortress. The sea-born attack could easily be launched using our Engel longships or Saxon ceols. In this way, we can launch simultaneous attacks from every direction at once, with the result that the enemy fortress will fall!"

Ida answered, *"Very well general, that is a well thought out solution to the problem. I agree that using a combination of a sea-borne assault, with assaults by catapults from the other three directions and infantry assaults backing these up, we shall be successful! We must make sure that the Britons realise that it is futile for them to mess with Engels, Kimbern or Saxons! I have authorised the use of twelve Engel longships to help in our attack upon the fortress!*

Alaric, I want you to organise and synchronise the positioning of the ships and the warriors to board them ready for the sea-borne attack to take place. As well, you and the other commanders are to pull back our army to positions located no more than half a day's march from the enemy fortress. The catapults all have wheels, and they shall be moved into position during the night. We shall launch the attack upon the Briton fortress in the morning, while it is still dark, and before the morning twilight!"

Alaric did as he had been ordered and soon found that there were only six longships available for use. He therefore decided to assign small groups of thirty warriors to each longship and simply add the commanding officer of the sub-unit and his second in command who was a senior non-commissioned officer. That resulted in the sea-borne strike forces being like the platoons of modern-day armies. He was successful in getting the six longships into a small, sheltered bay just eighteen miles from Din Guyaroi. The longships now waited to be boarded by the warriors making up the sea-borne assault teams. Alaric now went to Ida, and he was ushered in to see him. Ida was seated upon a throne and Alaric knelt before and then he spoke to his Ætheling. He said, *"Sire, I have only been able to get hold of six longships, but by having the invading units that I have organised on them, it will work to our advantage!"*

Ida answered, *"Alaric, please explain about the invading units that you say you have organised!"* Alaric answered, *"Sire, I have organised the sea-borne invading units selected to attack Din Guyaroi to be small highly trained units of thirty warriors. Each of these units is commanded by a junior officer and his second in command is a senior warrior of non-commissioned rank. That brings the total strength of the sea-borne invading units to thirty-two men if counting the officer and his second in command! These thirty-two warriors are different from the normal crew members of the longships. That will allow the longships to depart for the bringing of reinforcements after they have landed the warriors attacking the Briton stronghold!"*

That answer satisfied Ida of the Bernicia region of Northumbria, and he now spoke to Alaric. He said, *"Thank you, Alaric, you have done well, I am most happy with your organising the ship-based attacking units to be semi-autonomous warrior units which can operate independently of their ships when they attack hard to crack enemy positions from the sea! The problem as I see it becomes one of timing of our attack! By that, I mean that in order for us to be successful in launching simultaneous attacks from four directions at once, and one of them being a sea-borne attack, we need to rehearse and co-ordinate them in a secure area which is not too far from the locations of our warriors who are acting as blocking forces and keeping the enemy sealed up within their own positions! Now get out there and organise things so that attacks upon enemy positions can be rehearsed using attacks by three different land directions and one sea-borne attack from the east!"* That pleased Alaric, who spoke to Ida. He said, *"Sire, thank you for this opportunity to serve you! Consider that everything you have just asked of me shall be done, or by the Goddess Hertha, my name is not Alaric!"*

So, for the following month, the forces of the Ætheling Ida, were in the region of Tyne, Wear and Tees. Wheeled catapults were built, crewed, and tested. A mock enemy stronghold was set up very close to the coast and then it was used repeatedly to rehearse and co-ordinate the attacks from the three different land directions as well as the sea-borne attack from the east! The preparation and rehearsals were being watched very closely by Ida and his staff. Ida spoke to his senior officers. He said, *"Gentlemen, your attacks are disjointed, and they are not co-ordinated! That is simply not good enough! If we went into action in this current state of unpreparedness, we would suffer many casualties, which I do not want!*

So, go back to your units, organise, and drill them until such time as all units can attack simultaneously and effectively! Double the number of catapults and covered battering rams and completely train all warriors to use them effectively! See to it that all of you practise launching co-ordinated attacks using our three-pronged attacks by land and the sea-borne invasion from the east! Now get out there and make sure that everything I have ordered is done and quickly!

I want to launch the attack on the Briton stronghold in five days from now! The day before the attack, I want to give to the warriors as their own free time during which they can do whatever they want. However, make sure that they do not consume too much

152

wine or beer! I do not want them so drunk that they will not be able to function on the following early morning. We will move into position during the night. The attack shall commence a short time before the darkness of the night turns into twilight! So, from now on rehearse the night-time getting into position and the attacks themselves! That applies to equally to the catapults which are a critical part of this assault!"

So, over the next four days, the warriors of Ida practised getting the catapults into position over all kinds of terrain at night, while at the same time, other warriors practised moving into position and that included those who were to launch the sea-borne attack from the east. At last, during the fourth night of rehearsals, Ida was satisfied that all his units were fully trained and synchronised, ready for battle. He therefore said, *"Men, you have learned to time and synchronise with all other units and sub-units, including the sea-borne warriors! Take tonight off and enjoy drinking of beer or wine, but do not overdo that! For during the night, we will move into position, ready to wipe of the Britons in their stronghold of Din Guyaroi."*

And so, his army took the evening off and relaxed with some drinking and even fighting among the warriors as well as feasting. They then went to sleep in the knowledge that they would be required to move into position while it was still dark. Some of them would be moving the catapults and covered battering rams into position for the attack.

The six longships with their invading warriors upon them were anchored at an inlet out of sight of the defenders at Din Guyaroi. They were to move to their positions off the Briton stronghold soon afterwards, while it was dark and before the attack. It had been agreed among all commanders that the signal for the attack to begin was to be the sight of a flaming arrow coming from the longships which were now anchoured just outside of Din Guyaroi. That was to start the covered battering rams which had wheels and the catapults moving towards the walls of the Briton's fortress. The war machines and the army of Ida was moving towards the Britons from three land directions at the same time as the longships landed their warriors on the shore near Din Guyaroi. As the army of Ida was moving forward, the flaming arrow from the landed shore party was plainly seen by everyone.

The war machines had been brought into place using horses and men. As soon as the machines were in place, the valuable horses were led away to safe areas. The final approach to the walls of Din Guyaroi was only fifty metres away. The soldiers of King Ida's army now took over the propelling of both the wheeled and covered battering rams as well as the catapults and the wheeled siege towers to their final positions. The approach worked perfectly because it was a pitch-black night and while that caused concern among the warriors, it allowed them to reach the walls unobserved.

The flaming arrow that had been shot into the night sky by the landing party of warriors at the shore was see by all and the order of *"Attack the Britons!"* was given. Another flaming arrow was shot into the night sky as an answer to sea-borne invaders that the land attacks were starting. The alarm was raised at the Briton fortress, and soon, its ramparts were manned. Three more flaming arrows were seen; these being shot skywards again to inform the landing parties of Warriors. That resulted in King Ida's army loading its catapults with large rocks which were coated with a mixture of straw and pitch and fire was set to them. These large burning rocks were then thrown at the buildings within the fortress. As well, Ida's archers were ordered to fire flaming arrows onto the roof of any building that within the fortress if they could be seen. The combined effect of the flaming arrows and the burning rocks thrown by the catapults was to start many fires within the fortress.

The covered battering rams had breached the gates of the fortress allowing the future King Ida's warriors to rush forward and close with their enemies. As well, other war machines used were wheeled mobile assault towers. They were taken up to the walls when a hinged ramp was dropped down and that provided a firm footing for Ida's warriors to run across the ramp and to set foot upon the ramparts. Now, they only had to run along the ramparts and close with the Briton defenders. The result of all of this was that although Ida's soldiers suffered numerous casualties, they won the fight and Ida's soldiers took over the stronghold of Din Guyaroi. When the soldiers of both sides discussed the action, the reputation of 'Ida the Flame Bearer' was further enhanced.

It was during the afternoon that a messenger arrived from Bernicia with an urgent message for the Ætheling, Ida. The messenger was brought before Ida. He said, *"Sire, you are required back in Bernicia because your father, King Eoppa has died! There is much upheaval in the castle and plotters who are actively working against you are many in number and they all want your crown, even though you are the rightful heir to the throne!"*

Ætheling Ida calmly said, *"Messenger, I thank you for this information! You have done me a great service by letting me know that my throne is in danger! Now, go to the field kitchen, eat, and refresh yourself in general, because you shall be returning to where you have come from as soon as you are refreshed! You are to tell my wife and the other loyal members of my household that I will sort out the faithful from the traitors when I get back!"* The messenger left, and Ida organised his army to move back to Bernicia. Ida hurried back with his army and took control as the first independent king of Bernicia. He was to reign for fourteen years before he was succeeded by his son called Adda.

Adda

Adda took over the government and conducted it well, even further expanding his borders a considerable distance. During his time, some youths from the Northumbria region were sold as slaves in Rome to gain financial advantage for their families. When the Romans saw these fine-looking young men, many of them asked about them. They asked, *"Of what race are these young men?"* and *"From where do they originate?"* Their questions were answered with, *"They are by birth, from the province of Deira in Northumbria, they are Angles, the descendants of Engels who now live in Engel-land! They are the subjects of King Adda, and they worship the goddess Hertha who is also called Mother Earth!"*

Adda, (sometimes he is known as Alla in the Saxon Chronicle) having succeeded Ida to the throne in 560 A.D., became the main cause of the introduction of Christianity among the Angles, but he remained a pagan and continued to worship the goddess Hertha or Mother Earth, ruling for thirty years. He was succeeded by another of Ida's sons called Æthelric. He died in 593 A.D. and was succeeded by Ethelfrid.

Ethelfrid

Ethelfrid having inherited the kingdom, chose to vigorously defend it, and expand it. He invaded his neighbours and quickly established the reputation of being a noteworthy king among all who encountered him. Many feared him and were in awe of his warrior reputation.

Edan the King of Scots

He was greatly envied by Edan, the king of Scots who now spoke the members of his court around him, including his general staff. He said, *"Tell me general, what is the progress of the attack upon the forces of Ethelfrid at Dalston, near Carlisle? Also give me a complete report of the tactical situation!"* His general said, *"As you may recall sir, your army was successful in cutting off and surrounding the army of Ethelfrid and we began to close in on the Northumbrians. The initial success of your army was rendered totally ineffective by the valour of Tedbald, the brother of Ethelfrid! He constantly exposed himself to danger by boldly going the battlefield in person and attacking our warriors. He is highly thought of by the warriors in Ethelfrid's army as well as your own soldiers! At the city of Car-legion[17], he used strategy to take it! When he began his attacks upon the city, its inhabitants rushed out to defend it in huge numbers, preferring death to having to put up with a siege!*

Tedbald simply ordered his men to run away from the defenders until such time as they had drawn the defenders into carefully prepared ambush sites. There were four of these ambush sites around the city. In each one, there were two hundred archers and up to five hundred warriors armed with spears, battle-axes, and swords. So, deceived by strategy, they were overcome and put to flight!" The Scottish king answered, *"Oh, I see, so we cannot even think of taking the fight right up to the Northumbrians!"*

Ethelfrid was aware of the danger posed towards him by others who were his own relations. Therefore, he banished Edwin, the son of Alla from his kingdom. So it was that Edwin wandered all over various countries before he finally came to Redwald, who was king of the East Angles. (East Anglia)[18]

Edwin (d Oct. 632 A.D...)

After he was taken to see Redwald, King of East Anglia, Edwin was ushered in to see the king who was seated on his throne. Upon seeing King Redwald, Ewin said, *"Great Redwald, I am*

---

[17] The city of Car-legion was a city of the Britons, and it is now known as Chester.
[18] East Anglia was another region originally settled by the Engels.

Edwin the son of Alla of Deira. I was dispossessed of my throne and country when Aetheric, the King of Bernicia seized power in Deira in the year 590 A.D... that was followed by me being banished from my kingdom by Ethelfrid and his bullies! I implore you to help me get my country and throne of Deira in Northumbria back. If you aid me in getting back what is rightfully mine, I will always pledge loyalty to you!"

That resulted in Edwin being given the protection of Redwald, the King of the East Angles. Soon afterwards messengers from Ethelfrid were ushered into the presence of King Redwald (also known as Raedwald) and upon seeing him, they said, *"Noble and mighty King Redwald of the East Angles, we have an important message for you from our King Ethelfrid! His message is that you shall immediately hand over the fugitive Edwin, or a state of war shall exist between you and King Ethelfrid! We have been instructed to await your answer and to immediately take it to King Ethelfrid!"*

With the messengers still present, Redwald asked his wife and queen for her opinion of how best to resolve the matter. She replied with, *"Husband, I advise that you do not break the bonds of friendship and that you remain true to your word like the honourable king that you have always been. I urge you not to be intimidated by the vile Ethelfrid and his minions! I think that the best answer to Ethelfrid is to send him the heads of his messengers and to make a proper war against him!"* The resulting delivery to King Ethelfrid of the heads of his messengers enraged him.

Being thus encouraged by his queen, Redwald and his army moved out to engage Ethelfrid and his forces in combat. After his scouts had located the army of Ethelfrid, Regnhere, the son of Redwald and the commander of his army, called an orders group with his officers. He said, *"Gentlemen, we are facing Ethelfrid, who has proven himself to be a great general and his army has great abilities! We must use every means to even up the advantage he enjoys of having his army twice the size of ours and he also has professional soldiers to back up the efforts of his warriors[19]!*

I want you to keep on using our scouts to observe what the enemy is doing and to send word of that to us using messaging aids such as carrier pigeons. That will allow us to receive messages quickly and allow us to deploy counter-measures to whatever the enemy does! Talk to the warriors in your units and make sure that every man can immediately assume the duties of every other man who is above or below him in both rank and stations! In some cases that shall mean extra training for the men involved, but it must be done! No excuses, just get this done!"

The scouts did their duties well and they constantly sent messages even though many of them were illiterate. Therefore, they used agreed symbols to warn of enemy movement by carrier pigeon and sometimes by using flashes of reflected light from objects with shiny surfaces. Also, the length and number of flashes used when using light to convey messages was agreed upon before its use was authorised and that was learned by all warriors. What these people were doing was employing the use of an ancient forms of codes.

Regnhere and Ethelfrid Fight

Regnhere was informed that the enemy army was encamped by a river and so, he decided to move his father's warriors into position around the enemy camp at night. As the warriors moved into position around the enemy camp, some of them stubbed their toes on tree roots and other obstacles, causing some of his warriors to quietly curse, *"Oh fuck it, that hurt!"*

---

[19] In Britania, warriors generally were farmers who obtained their living from what the land could produce, and as well, they were at the beck and call of their king or overlord for service with the army of whoever the king or overlord was.

By the very early morning and while it was still dark, the encirclement of the enemy camp was completed. Soon after that a very bright moonlight was seen illuminating the countryside, much to the joy of Regnhere. He was speaking to his senior officers. He said, *"Gentlemen, we now attack the enemy, take no prisoners and remember that I have a small bag of gold for anyone who brings me the head of Ethelfrid!"*

His warriors now rushed the encampment and immediately began killing the soldiers and warriors of Ethelfrid's army. Typically, his men were yelling in loud voices, *"Kill off the Northumbrians, do not spare any, just wipe the bastards out!"* That commotion was heard by Ethelfrid, who was taken by surprise, but he quickly recovered and set about trying to restore a very bad situation. It was the sort of situation where a man could kill his attacker but also be killed by him. Ethelfrid threw away his shield and instead, he grasped his favourite weapon, the two-handed, double-edged battle-axe.

Having seen Regnhere the enemy commander, Ethelfrid ran into middle of the encampment where the action was most intense and yelled out! *"Regnhere, Regnhere, I am Ethelfrid, and you will now die!"* with that said, he swung his battle-axe in a downwards arc from the top of the head of Regnhere toward his feet. At the same time Regnhere was thrusting his long broadsword into the side of Ethelfrid. For Ethelfrid, that was the end of his life, but not before Regnhere had also died. And so, Ethelfrid, after reigning for twenty-four years and being second to none in battle, was dead.

He had two sons by Acca, the daughter of Alla and sister of Edwin. The names of the boys were Oswald, who was aged twelve years and Oswy who was aged four years. Upon the death of their father, the boys and their governors fled to Scotland and escaped.

With his enemies now dead or else banished from the kingdom, Edwin was installed as the King of East Anglia when Redwald died. During Edwin's exile among them, the East Anglicans had experienced his ardent disposition and ready courage, therefore, they swore allegiance to him. He now granted one of Redwald's sons the empty title of king. It was an empty title because whoever the king was, he had to accept the fact that he was subservient to Edwin. The hopes and resources of the Angles were centred upon him, and he became the ruler of most of England except for Kent.

He left Kent alone because he was for a very long time strongly attracted to Ethelburga who was the sister of the King of Kent and he wanted to marry her, thus uniting the two kingdoms through family ties. After a long courtship, Ethelburga did in fact marry him, but before doing so, she firmly spoke. She said, *"By my marrying you, King Edwin of East Anglia, there shall be one kingdom from the currently two separate ones, united by ties of kindred and there shall not be any rivalry in our powers and no difference between our manners!*

I have for a long time now, been instructing and teaching you the word of God and his son, the Saviour, Our Lord, Jesus Christ! I need you to understand that I am a Christian ad that as such, I must be married to a man who is also a Christian! That being the case, I have organised for Bishop Paulinus to firstly convert you from your current pagan beliefs and then to marry us using Christian rites and practices!"

For quite some time, Edwin found himself mentally battling his pagan religious beliefs in the Goddess Hertha, and because of that he was wavering and doubtful of this newer religion which preached about a merciful god who would forgive the sins of his people. Then, suddenly, he completely went over to the Christian faith, He then built many churches and invited neighbouring kings to take on the Christian faith, and he never neglected God. It was said, *"The Merciful grace of God smiles upon the devotion of our king, and not only here, but also in the other nations of Britania, that is, the Engels (Angles), Scots and Picts, even the Orkney and Mevanian Islands. The Angels both fear the power of our king and venerate him. Because of the way that this king does things, there is no public robber, no domestic thief, and the temper of conjugal fidelity is far distant!"*

12th of October 632 A.D...

When Edwin was aged forty-eight years on 12th of October 632A.D., and in the seventh year of his reign, both he and his son were attacked by the princes he had formerly subjugated. These were Caedwalla of the West Saxons and Penda of Mercia. Now that Edwin was slain, the sons of Ethelfrid wanted to get control of their country back.

These men were also the nephews of Edwin, Oswald and Oswy. They were receiving help and guidance from their elder brother called Eanfrid. By working together, they were successful in regaining their country. That resulted in Oswy, a cousin of Edwin taking over Deira and Eanfrid, the son of Ethelfrid taking Bernicia. So it was that Northumbria was divided and ruled by these men.

Both men had been raised in Scotland where they were baptised. They had scarcely taken up their royal authorities when they both renounced their Christian faith and returned to pagan worship of the Engels, who worshipped the Goddess Hertha, or Mother Earth. During church services, the bishops and priests openly spoke against both kings. They said, *"Look at how God is punishing the Kings of Deira and Bernicia! They are both suffering the just penalty of their apostasy through the hostile action of the King of Wessex called Caedwalla!"* Caedwalla, the King Wessex was often spoken against by the Engels who were now increasingly known as Angles. He was known to say, *"I was born for exterminating the Angles!"*

A year had passed and there was a sudden marked improvement in the religious outlook of Oswald who now returned to the Christian faith and was baptised by Bishop Paulinus. The number of warriors and soldiers available for hostile operations against the Wessex King Caedwalla were few, and so Oswald addressed his little army.

He said, *"Warriors and soldiers of Deira, we are few, but what we lack in numbers we will make up for with ferocity! It is with the help of God and what is right that we will win against Caedwalla's warriors who outnumber us greatly! I shall not make anyone of you fight if that is against you will! I only want volunteers in this glorious mission of God against the low-grade warriors from Wessex!"* He had barely finished saying that to his soldiers and warriors when he drew his long broadsword out of its scabbard and use the sword to draw a line in the sand. He then loudly spoke to his men.

He said, *"Behold, I have drawn a line in the soil! Those of you who Have the courage and ability to do so, and are loyal to me, please cross this line and together we shall teach the warriors of Wessex not to ever try aggression against the Angles, no matter what part of Britannia or other places in the world that the Angles may come from! I now command you to either be with me by crossing the line or else you can depart and save your skins!"*

He had barely finished saying that when all his warriors crossed the line. A cry rang out from his army. He men were pledging their loyalty. They said, *"We the warriors of Deira hereby pledge our continued allegiance to Oswald, King of Deira! Death to the King of Wessex called Caedwalla! Hail Oswald!"*

That so pleased Oswald, that he again spoke to the members of his army. He said, *"I thank you all deeply gentlemen! I thank you for this auspicious show of loyalty to me and your confidence in me! I truly thank you for your support from the bottom of my heart! I shall see to it that your loyalty is rewarded by each of you having equal shares of the booty that we take from King Caedwalla of Wessex! Now follow me to battle! We are going to teach the silly Wessex warriors a lesson that they never forget!"* So, it was that the two sides met in battle, resulting in the defeat of King Caedwalla and the complete destruction of his army. So complete was the route of the Wessex army that it never again was it able to recover and challenge the Angles. Oswald, the King of the Angles, was very joyful at this great victory. So, Oswald addressed his men.

He said, *"I thank you all for your fine and courageous efforts! The army of the Wessex has all but been wiped out and it will not recover to threaten us again! The booty that we have captured from Caedwalla of Wessex shall be equally shared among you all this evening! We have been granted victory not just by our own efforts, but also by the help of God! As my way of saying Thank you to God for this great victory, I have decreed that from this day onwards, there shall be no idols and that where these are found, they shall be destroyed!"*

From that time, the idols fell into the dust where they remained. These effects and the courage of the king now combined, and he extended his borders without any loss of his people, for he now ruled all of Northumbria. Such was the increase in his power that justice and peace met each other and reigned, allowing the impartation of mutual acts of kindness. It was well known that when there were frequent entertainments, the king would forgo his own desires for food and drink, insisting that the poor be given these things.

He was seated at a table and about to commence his dinner when the Royal Almoner[20] spoke to him. He said, *"Your majesty, it is with regret that I must inform you that there are a great number of people assembled outside in the street who are hungry, and they are asking that you, their king will feed them!"*

That was immediately answered by the king. He said, *"Look here Father, they are my people and I, Oswald, shall not let my people go hungry while there is food within my reach! You now have the responsibility to give all the food within this castle and all the food upon this table of the banquet to the poor whom you have informed me about! You will immediately see to it that all food here is distributed among the poor outside! As well, the silver dishes upon which the food had been placed, shall be given to the poor afterwards and after the dishes have been cut into small pieces and shared among the people! The wealth of Northumbria shall be spread among our people! It will be a commonwealth! Now get out there and implement my orders immediately!"*

All of that was done and the actions of King Oswald were much appreciated by his people. The virtue of Oswald is well known, and it needs no further explanation. The envious eyes of Penda, the King of Mercia fell upon Oswald and his small escort just as Oswald and his bodyguard warriors dismounted to rest themselves and their horses.

Penda Orders the Killing of Oswald

The envy of Penda was such that he spoke to a sub-unit of his warriors that specialised in the killing of selected enemies of King Penda of Mercia. He said, *"I want you to immediately take whatever action is necessary to ambush and wipe out the bodyguard*

---

[20] An official dispenser of alms, who was often a household Chaplin such as the Chaplin for a prince.

of Oswald and to kill King Oswald himself! However, if it becomes possible to isolate him from the help of his warriors, please do so and I shall then have the pleasure of dispatching him to the afterlife myself!" And so, the assassination units of the army of Penda sent out small groups of warriors to reconnoitre the country-side. After some time had passed, the assassination units of Penda's army found Oswald and his unit bodyguards.

The members of Penda's army did not immediately engage the bodyguard unit of Oswald. They scouted the region and completely reconnoitred the region until they knew for sure that Oswald was in the company of only ten of his bodyguards. The lead scout of one of Penda's assassination units reported to the King of Mercia He said, *"Your majesty, my men and I have located King Oswald, and we are sure that he has only ten men with him! Would you like us to wipe out his bodyguard and leave him alive or should we kill him as well?"*

King Penda of Mercia said, *"Yes, please wipe out the bodyguard unit of Oswald, but although you may wound him as much as you like, make sure that he stays alive so that I can chop his head off in front of his people! I shall be on my horse waiting to catch sight of him! If you see Oswald, shoot darts and arrows into him to slow him down and to make him an easy mark for me to wipe out! For now, concentrate on killing of all the members of his bodyguard unit, so that will leave us free to catch Oswald!"*

Those orders were carried out and it resulted in Oswald leaving the site of the ambush now that his companions were all dead. However, he did not get very far because he was carrying a forest of darts and arrows in his chest and back. He was dying, but even so, he was praying for the souls of his faithful companions. After a short time, Oswald found that no matter how much he tried to get away, he could no longer avoid the warriors of Penda, and they caught up with him. He was surrounded by the warriors of

Penda and Penda now issued orders. He said, *"Archers, fit arrows to your bows and keep Oswald covered. If he moves at all while I am walking towards him, shoot your arrows into him and kill him. When I reach him, I shall remove his head from his body!"* Penda walked to Oswald and then swung his long broadsword at his head where it joined his neck.

Speaking to his army, Penda said, *"I do not care who does it, but you shall put the head of Oswald on a spike and the spike with the head on it shall be mounted on a large stake in the middle of that large forest clearing. Again, I do not care who does it, as long as it is done, but you shall now also cut the arms off Oswald and place them at the bottom of the stake which is surmounted by his head! Also cut off his legs and place them with his arms at the bottom of the stake. That way, people will see what happens to those who oppose Penda of Mercia!"*

The head was then obtained by his brother at Lindisfarne, and it is said to be preserved in the arms of the blessed Cuthbert[21]. His arms and hands were also obtained by his brother and placed into a shrine at the city of Babenberg[22]. The head was then obtained by his brother at Lindisfarne, and it is said to be preserved in the arms of the blessed Saint Cuthbert[23]. There are stories about how Oswald is a martyr and how his blood and bones could invoke miracles, we shall look at these now. When Ostritha, the wife of Ethelred, and the daughter of King Oswry, was informed that her uncle Oswald had been killed, she was upset.

She said, *"I am most anxious that the bones of the trunk of my uncle's body shall be immediately taken to my monastery of Bardney, which is in the territory of the Mercians and located close*

---

[21] St. Cuthbert is represented as holding the head of Oswald in his arms.

[22] Now called Bambrough in Northumberland.

[23] William of Malmsbury, 1847

to the city of Lincoln and then interred there!" And so, the remains of Oswald were taken to the monastery. However, the monks at that place at first refused to allow her request because they all hated her uncle who had obtained their country through the force of arms. At midnight of the same day, a miraculous light from Heaven began shining down upon the bones which the monks had refused to bury within their monastery. A monk had been praying in the chapel that night and he was on his way back to his lodgings when he beheld a wonderful sight. He hurried to his prior and spoke to him. He said, *"Joseph, Joseph, come quickly, for there is an amazing sight that you should see between the chapel and here! There is a great heavenly light shining upon the bones of Oswald whom we have refused burial here within our walls!"*

Prior Joseph replied, *"Please lead the way to this apparent miracle. If what you say is true, then this monastery has done a great dis-service to King Oswald and to God!"* By the time the monk and his superior returned to the sight of the light shining upon the bones of King Oswald, the intensity of the light had increased markedly and that resulted in many more monks bringing more of them to view the miracle. When that became common knowledge and most of the monks had seen it for themselves, the monks became converts to reason and allowed the remains of King Oswald to be buried within the monastery.

Soon after that, it appeared that miracles abounded from the relics of King Oswald and every sick person who asked for good health from him immediately received it. At the spot where the head of Oswald was spiked, the grass grew ever greener from his blood. A warrior who was riding a horse had his horse become sick and it lay down in agony at the spot where Oswald's head had been placed on the stake. The horse now quickly recovered after it had rolled over at that place and had eaten the grass growing there. After a long time, the remains of King Oswald were removed to Gloucester. The monastery received income from people who wanted to see the relics of Oswald in the hope of improving their health.

King Oswy of Northumbria

Oswy had two sons, the elder who was illegitimate, was rejected, and so, Oswy was succeeded by the younger legitimate brother called Egfrid. He was legitimately born and was more highly valued because of the good qualities of his pious wife, Etheldrida, rather than his own qualities. He did allow his wife to dedicate herself to God[24] and promoted Cuthbert to a bishopric[25]. He was overbearing towards all who were meek or suppliant and overwhelmed the Irish, a nation of men who were harmless and not guilty of any crime.

Egfrid was present at an orders group during which problems with the Mercians were discussed. A senior officer was in earnest conversation with him. The general said, *"Your majesty, you must stop being inactive against those who rebel against you! Unless you take immediate action and follow-up the triumphs of your father, you stand to lose Northumbria to the Mercians and I received word that Ethelred, the son of Penda is marching towards us! I am sure that you shall suffer a great defeat unless you act decisively now!"*

Egfrid chose to ignore what he had been told and so, he was defeated in battle by Ethelred, the son of Penda. So, it was that the news spread as quickly as wildfire all over Northumbria. People said, *"King Egfrid has been killed in battle by Ethelred, the son of Penda of Mercia!"* Over time, that news reached the ears of his elder brother called Alfrid. He spoke to those around him.

---

[24] His first wife was divorced from him because of her celibacy, and she became a nun. While his second wife was Ermenburga.
[25] The office or diocese of a bishop.

He said, *"As far as I am concerned, I am a victim of circumstance! My younger brother, Egfrid, was given my throne just because my mother and my father were not married when I was born. As a result, I find myself called a bastard and instead of me having the crown, it has gone to my younger full brother! That is not and never can be right!*

We both have the same mother and father, the only difference is that when Egfrid was born, our parents had been married, but they were not when I was born! My brother has proven himself to be unworthy of the crown, yet, he has it! He is useless in battle and just rides roughshod over those who are meek or weak willed! Because of that, I have been banished from Northumbria, and all has been taken from me, I am retiring to Ireland, where I should be able to escape the attentions of my greedy brother!"

So, he left Northumbria and lived in Ireland. He devoted his time to study, and he became highly educated. His mind being enriched by much learning. Early one morning, he was approached by representatives of the same people who banished him from his brother's kingdom. They said, *"Your majesty, we are messengers of the Royal Family. We have heard of your many achievements in education, and we believe that it would be for the best of our country to have a man of your knowledge and understanding ruling Northumbria! The King, your brother Egfrid, has died in battle and we have been charged with the task of informing you of that and asking you to rule the country! Your Majesty, if you will do our people the honour of becoming our king, you are to return to the Royal Lodgings with us and begin your reign immediately! Do you accept this great honour and responsibility?"*

Alfrid answered, *"Yes,"* and so, the small group set off for the Royal Lodgings in Northumbria. For the next nineteen years he ruled his kingdom in tranquillity and joy. He did nothing that others could ever accuse him of justly. However, he lost some territory because the Picts were in the pursuit of profit and so they attacked the Angles who had become lazy because of the lengthened peace. The successor to Alfrid was his son called Osred.

Alfrid was speaking to Osred while the latter was aged eight years. He said, *"Look here son, I realise that you are only eight years old, but I am feeling poorly, and you are the next in line to take up the throne. Promise me that you shall govern justly and well!"* Osred answered, *"Father, I shall be as good a king as you are!"* However, instead of that, over the next eleven years, Osred did everything that he could to disgrace the throne. By the time he had turned fourteen years old, he began to make visits to the nearby monastery where he was constantly flirting with the Nuns.

Among these was Ethelbah who was both very attractive and she had just celebrated her fifteenth birthday. Osred saw her when he visited the monastery, and he liked her the moment he saw her. So, Osred walked over to her. He said, *"I am King Osred, your ruler! I like your looks, and I want to get to know you a lot better! Can you please accompany me and spend a pleasurable time with you king?*

Ethelbah answered, *"Your majesty, I am just a poor novice nun, and I must not be seen alone with any man because God is my husband, and I must remain true and faithful to him!"* Even though she had said that to him, her juices were running because like it or not, she was beginning to discover the needs of a healthy young woman. She continued, *"Your majesty, as long as you honour me and protect me, we can go to a seldom used enclave at the dark end of the hallway if you would like to be alone with me!"* That was answered by Osred, who said, *"Of course I wish to be alone with you! So, let's go to the enclave that you have spoken of and do what two healthy young people should do!* Having said that, the couple walked towards the enclave near the end of the monastery building.

171

They now entered the enclave and as they were entering this dark place, Osred gently lifted the chin of Ethelbah and proceeded to kiss her lips.

As a result of that and the fact that they were both young healthy people, Ethelbah completely undressed, and they made love. Osred kept on seducing other nuns of the monastery, and he was at the monastery seeing nuns daily. A meeting of his relatives was called to discuss the outrageous actions of the king. Kenred spoke to Ceolwulf. He said, *"Ceolwulf, you were adopted by Osred and named as his successor a long time ago! We now have the situation that requires us to stop him from being the king because he is committing adultery against God by fucking the nuns at the monastery. The fact is that the nuns are the brides and therefore the wives of God! I and others on the Royal Council have decided to install you as the King of Northumbria if you will do us the honour of ruling over us!* Ceolwulf did as he was asked and became the king. He ruled in a kind and competent manner, for he was highly schooled and was therefore able to give great attention to most things.

He was succeeded by Ceolfrid and under his leadership, the affairs of the monastery flourished. In his old age and before he died, Ceolwulf spoke to members of his court. After being on the throne for twenty years, Eadbert, made an announcement to his court. He said, *"I have ruled for twenty years now, and like my brother before me, I now abdicate my throne and I hereby appoint as my successor, my son, who you all know as Oswulph. My abdication shall take effect immediately and Oswulph shall rule in my stead. I am assuming the monastic habit as soon as I get to the monastery! It is beneath the dignity of a Christian to only be immersed in earthly things! I must now answer to the higher authority of God! I therefore shall abdicate my throne. To guard against the possibility of the country becoming endangered, I hereby decree that my cousin*

Eadbert shall from this day be the king! He shall immediately have full control of my armies, and he will take up his duties as king immediately! I am going to the calling of God, and I am taking the position of a monk at the Abbey at Lindisfarne. I shall be leaving here and going to the abbey immediately!"

While he was travelling to Rome, he stopped at the city of Langres, and he died there. After a long time had passed, his bones were taken to his monastery in England. And so it happened that Eadbert[26] took up his throne and ruled for twenty years. During his rule, he was a model of singular moderation and virtue. Eadbert had a brother with the very same name who was the Archbishop of York.

And so it was that Oswulph now ruled for about a year before he was killed by his own subjects and he was succeeded by Moll. He, in turn, governed in a good and commendable way from 759 to 765 A.D., when he fell victim to the treachery of Alcred. Ten years after he had usurped the throne, Alcred was forced to retire from the government of his country. The son of Moll, called Ethelred, was called upon to become king. He ruled for five years before he was expelled by his countrymen.

Alfwold

The next king was Alfwold. After he had ruled as the King of Northumbria for eleven years, his action caused many unfavourable comments about him to be openly discussed by his people! Typically, the people said, *"This Alfwold is quickly becoming a real pain in the arse! Taxes are much too high; the country is nowhere near safe enough and it is high time for us to be rid of him!"*

---

[26] Also called Egbert.

A band of conspirators was now setup in the Royal Court. An officer of the army of Alfwold was addressing the soldiers. He said, *"Gentlemen, I bring you grave news! Overwhelmingly, our people are demanding the end of the present governing administration of Northumbria and the doing away with King Alfwold! He has a small but very strong effective unit of assassins who always remove his opponents for him! Therefore, the only way to oust him is to murder him! So, please join with me now and let us work together to have a fair and just king upon the throne of Northumbria!"* The assassination of Alfwold was organised and he was succeeded by his nephew called Osred[27].

Most of the Northumbrian kings had their reigns cut short by their deaths. That resulted in no-one wanting to take up the throne after Ethelred. Although Osbald had been elected as king by the nobles, he was deposed after a short time. During the time from 796 to 827, Northumbria had been without a sovereign for thirty-three years. It was mainly because of those circumstances, that there was no organisation or direction, resulting in Northumbria becoming the object of constant incursions by its neighbouring countries. Next came the Danish Vikings, who laid waste to the Holy places and upon their return to their homes represented to their countrymen the fruitfulness of the island and what they saw as the lazy unworthiness of its people.

The Danes now came over to England in great numbers and took possession of parts of England. They even had a king of their own for many years, However, he was sub-ordinate to the King of West Saxons.

---

[27] Osred, through the conspiracy of his own nobles, was deposed and sent into exile. Two years later he returned with the help of Northumbrian warlords, but upon being deserted by his forces, he was made a prisoner and put to death on the orders of Ethelred. (William of Malmsbury, 1847)

Kings of Mercia

Penda – died 15th of November 654 A.D... During the year of 626 A.D., which was one hundred and thirty-nine years after the death of Hengest, Penda[28] rose to power. He was the son of Pybba and the tenth in descent from Wodin. Being of noble lineage, he was also an expert soldier and commander. His wife was Queen Kyneswith, who bore his children. His sons were Peada, Wulfhere, Ethelred, Mercelin and Merwal. His daughters were Kyneburg and Kyneswith, both of whom were distinguished by their chastity.

It is known that his religious beliefs were those of pagan Engel worship of Hertha or 'Mother Earth' At the age of fifty years, he seized the crown of Mercia. Having taken the crown, he called a meeting of the Royal Court and when its members assembled, he spoke to them. He said, *"Mercia shall become well known and feared! I want more lands and people to rule and to provide both money and luxuries for Mercia! All of you shall help me to achieve that goal or else you shall die! That choice is yours and yours alone!*

That prompted one of his officers to speak. He said, *"Your highness, you know that you can always count on the support of my soldiers and myself! To attain the many things that you now require, we must age war upon all of those who may oppose us, including our own countrymen. For these reasons, we must immediately attack our surrounding neighbours, and we must take their cities and invade the kingdoms surrounding them! By doing all those things, we shall make the name of King Penda of Mercia known far*

---

[28] Penda was not the first king of Mercia, but he was the first one who completed any noteworthy acts. Before him were the original king, Crida. He was succeeded in in 600 A.D., by Pybba, followed by Ceorl in 610 A.D... Penda took the throne in 626 A.D...

and wide! We shall make your name become highly respected and feared by all people!"

It turned out that there was little that Penda would not do or try to do. By his courageous daring he had wiped the out the light and luminaires the English, Edwin and Oswald, and kings of Northumbria, Ecgric and Anna. He was also very effective against Kenwalh, king of the West Saxons whom he frequently harassed and finally drove in exile because Kenwalh had deceived and repudiated the sister of Penda. Some early historians have thought it irksome to record how Penda eagerly took opportunities to wreak havoc among his enemies and how he loved to watch as his enemies were dying. He was spoken to by an officer from his army. The officer said, *"Your majesty, we currently have far too many enemies and it is high time for us to obtain allies! An alliance with King Caedwalla of Wessex could be of immense benefit to you, so I urge you to confer with him and hopefully set up an alliance that will be of great benefit to both of you!"*

Penda was impressed with the logic and outspokenness of his young officer. Penda said, *"Soldier, what is your name, and from where do you come?"* The young officer answered with, *"Your majesty, my name is Adelathel, and I am one of your subjects of Mercia. I joined your army a year ago as a private soldier and I am now a sub-altern, a junior officer."*

King Penda said, *"Well Adelathel, seeing how this proposed alliance with the king of the West Saxons called Caedwalla is your idea and also an idea which I heartily endorse, I think that you should go to the camp or the castle of King Caedwalla of the West Saxons with me and my court so that we can enter into meaningful discussions and have a lasting alliance! By both of our sides doing this, it will greatly benefit us both and make our enemies wonder what has hit them! You are to leave for the journey to Caedwalla immediately. When you return, I want details on when, where and how this critical meeting about our alliance is to take place!"*

Adelathel departed for the castle of Caedwalla, taking ten soldiers with him. In due course they all arrived at the stronghold of King Ceadwalla of Wessex. An alert guard challenged Adelathel and his men. Adelathel told the guard who he was and that he had been sent by King Penda of Mercia to arrange an alliance between himself and Caedwalla. The guard sent a messenger with this news to King Caedwalla and that was answered a short time later by a messenger who spoke to the guard. He said, *"The King has asked for me to escort this party directly to him. He thanks you for your devotion to duty."* With that having been said, the messenger and the eleven envoys from King Penda departed to see Caedwalla.

Finally, being ushered in to see King Caedwalla, Adelathel and his ten comrades were spoken to by Caedwalla. He said, *"So, King Penda of Mercia has sent you, young Adelathel to see me to arrange an alliance between us? I think that such an alliance would benefit both of us greatly!"* Adelathel said, *"My Lord, my king, Penda of Mercia is involved in campaigns against many of the surrounding kingdoms and most of them are enemies of both of you! Both my king and I feel that it will be in the mutual interests of both of you to form an alliance which will enable you both to overcome your enemies and to take back what is yours!*

If my Lord Caedwalla is likewise minded, please give me the word and I shall be most happy to immediately travel back to where I have come from and let King Penda know the time, date and venue for the discussion of the proposed alliance between the kingdom of Mercia and the kingdom of the West Saxons which is ruled by yourself, Your majesty!"

Caedwalla of Wessex thought about that for a while and then he spoke. He said, *"Adelathel, I am most happy with the idea that some-one of the Engel stock is comfortable with the idea of helping our people of this land to take back what has been their own land! Can you please go back and see your King Penda and ask him to meet me here in my castle in twenty-one days from now during the early afternoon?"*

Adelathel answered with, *"Your majesty, my King Penda has anticipated that you would want to get the alliance up and running as quickly as possible! To save time, he is an encampment less than half a day's ride from here, awaiting your response. You could travel to his encampment or have him come here and see you today, if that is you will!"* That was answered by Caedwalla who said, *Adelathel, we shall go and see King Penda of Mercia immediately. You shall lead the way because you know where he is. When we arrive, we shall immediately confer about the alliance with Penda!"* An armed escort of warriors as well as Adelathel's escort was quicky organised and soon, they were at the camp of King Penda. Upon arrival there, Adelathel took Caedwalla to see Penda, who was seated on a chair in his tent.

After being ushered inside, Adelathel spoke to Penda. He said, *"Your majesty, this is Caedwalla, the King of Wessex and you shall be pleased to know that he is of like-mindedness to yourself!* Speaking to Caedwalla, Adelathel said, *"Caedwalla this is Penda, about whom you have heard so much, and you will find that he will support your aims of getting back as much of your territory as possible! I will now leave you two kings to discuss the proposed alliance and what each of your forces shall do for the other. I am now taking my leave of you both, my kings!"* Penda started talking first. He said, *"Caedwalla, welcome to my over-all plan. I am attacking all the neighbouring kingdoms! I first started doing this when Kenwalh of the West Saxons did the wrong and dishonourable things to my sister!*

Caedwalla said, *"Mighty Penda, I have heard of your many deeds! Yes, Penda, I, Caedwalla have also heard how you have dealt with Kenwalh of West Saxons. I believe you were too lenient with him and that you have treated him too well! If Kenwalh had done to any member of my family what he did to your sister, I would have cut off Kenwalh's head in public! Now, getting back to the matter at hand, I hereby pledge my warriors and soldiers to your service if you will likewise pledge your soldiers and warriors to my service!"*

These things were agreed to by both men now that mutual understanding had been reached between them. Next a formal alliance document was drafted in Latin because there was no written English language at that time. The document was read out to both kings in their own languages and then they both applied their royal seals to it, thus making it a binding legal document. Both kings were of great service to each other and Penda eagerly watched all opportunities of the slaughter that came from attacking his own countrymen.

Peada

After thirty years of these attacks upon his countrymen, Penda was finally beaten by Oswy, who had succeeded his brother, Oswald. The son of Penda was Peada. He succeeded his father and governed apportion of his kingdom by permission of Oswy who let him form the government of South Mercia.

The reason for Oswy to do that for the son of a former enemy was that Peada had married the daughter of Oswy and was now his son-in-law. Peada married the daughter of Oswy on the condition that that Peada renounced his pagan ways and fully embraced the Christian faith. He did so and then set about getting other people in his province to convert to the Christian religion. As a result, Peada ruled as a puppet king of Oswy, and he was later poisoned by his wife. Upon the death of Peada, Oswy resumed government as was

179

his right because of him being victorious over Penda. However, after three years, the local people rebelled, and they expelled his generals before finally installing Wulfhere as the king of Mercia. Wulfhere was another son of Penda, and the province recovered its liberty.

Wulfhere

Wulfhere immediately acted with energy so as not to disappoint the hopes of his country and showed himself to be an efficient prince by performing great exertions both mental and physical. He helped to spread Christianity, which had been introduced by his brother. In the early years of his reign, he was greatly opposed by the King of West Saxons, but at later times he fought the West Saxons, and he took the Isle of Wight off them. After he was tempted into pagan rites again, he returned to Christianity and bestowed the Isle of Wight to his godson called Ethelwalch, who was the King of the South Saxons.

His good qualities were stained however, because he sold the bishopric of London to the ambitious man called Wini. His wife was Erminhilda, the daughter of Erconbert[29]. Together with his wife, he produced Kinred and Wereburga, who was a most holy virgin who lies buried at Chester. Her brother married Ermenburga, the daughter of Ermenred, the brother of Erconbert. By her, he had three daughters; Milburga who lies at Weneloch; Mildritha in Kent, who lies in the monastery of St. Augustine; and Milgitha, and one son called Merefin.

Alfrid, a king of the Northumbrians married Kyneburg, the daughter of Penda. After a time, she became absolutely disgusted with wedlock and became a nun in the monastery which had been founded by her brothers, Wulfhere and Ethelred. Wulfhere died

---

[29] Also known as Erkenbert, the King of Kent.

after nineteen years on the throne, and he was succeeded by his brother called Ethelred.

Ethelred

Ethelred was more famed for his pious manner than his skill in battle. He was satisfied by displaying much valour during his single but illustrious expedition into Kent and passed the remainder of his life in quiet except for attacking Egfrid, the King of Northumbria who had invaded his kingdom. He convinced Egfrid to return home by organising the murder of Egfrid's brother called Elfwin. He was confessing his sins to Archbishop Theodore. He said, *"Holy Bishop, I have sinned! I have organised the murder of the rival king called Egfrid but that did not happen! Instead, his brother called Elfwin was murdered!"*

Theodore was silent for a while and then he spoke slowly and with great deliberation. He said, *"Ethelred, I have deeply considered that you have had murder in your heart and that it is due to the will of God that the man whom you wanted to have murdered survived, but his brother died in his place! For you to have the forgiveness of God, you must do penance and, you must make amends. You shall have to atone for your murderous act by paying Egfrid a very large sum of money[30]! Also, when you are entering your thirtieth year of your reign, you must abdicate your throne and become a monk at Bardney.*

He did as he had been instructed and was forgiven his sins. After abdicating his throne, he became a monk at Bardney where he was promoted and became the Abbot. He was a close contemporary

---

[30] This was paying what was called paying weregild, for the legal price of his blood. All from the King to the slave had their estimated values. One half of the weregild went to the family of the murdered person and the other half of it went into the public purse.

181

of Ina, King of the West Saxons. His wife was Ostritha the sister of Egfrid. Their son was called Ceolred.

Ceolred

King Ceolred, the son of Ethelred, was inspired by his uncle, who was conspicuous for his valour against Ina. After ruling for eight years, he died and was buried at Lichfield, leaving Ethelbald, the grandnephew of Penda by his brother Alwyn, his heir. It was to Ethelbald that Boniface[31] the Archbishop of Mentz who was an Engel, sent an epistle which is reproduced below:

"To Ethelbald, my dearest lord and to be preferred to all other kings of the Angles, in the love of Christ, Boniface the archbishop legate to Germania from the Church of Rome, wisketh perpetual health in Christ. We confess before God that we heard of your prosperity, your faith, and good works, we rejoice; and if at any time we hear of any adversity that has befallen you, either in the chance of war or jeopardy of your soul, we are afflicted.

We have heard that devoted to almsgiving, you prohibit theft and rapine, are a lover of peace, a defender of widows and the poor; and for this we give God thanks. Your contempt for lawful matrimony, were it for chastity's sake, would be laudable; but since you wallow in luxury and even in adultery with nuns, it is disgraceful and damnable; it dims your glory before God and transforms you into an idolater, because you have polluted the temple of God.

Wherefore, my beloved soon, repent and remember how dishonourable it is that you, who by the grant of God, are sovereign

---

[31] Boniface, whose original name was Winfred, after much work in converting the various tribal nations of Germania to Christianity, acquired the appellation of "Apostle of the Germans" After a long time he was martyred in Friesland. One of the original churches built by him in Saxony still exists at the little village called Gicrstedt.

over many nations, should yourself be a slave of lust to his disservice. Moreover, we have heard that almost all the nobles of the Mercian kingdom, following your example, desert their lawful wives and live-in guilty intercourse with adulteresses and nuns. Let the custom of a foreign country teach you how far distant this is from rectitude.

For in old Saxony, there is no knowledge of Christ, if a virgin in her father's house or a married woman under the protection of her husband, should be found guilty of adultery, they burn her, strangled by her own hand and then they hang up her seducer over the grave where she is buried; or else, cutting of her garments to the waist, modest matrons whip her and piece her with knives, and fresh tormentors punish her in the same manner as she goes from village to village until they destroy her.

Again, the Winedi[32], the basest of nations have this custom – the wife, upon the death of her husband, casts herself onto the same funeral pile to be consumed with him. If then the gentiles who know not God, have so zealous a regard for chastity, how much more ought you to possess, my beloved son, who are both a Christian and a king?

Spare therefore your own soul, spare the multitude of people perishing by your example, for whose souls you must give account. Give heed to this to, if the nation of the Angles, despising lawful matrimony give free indulgence to adultery, a race of ignoble people who despise God must necessarily proceed from such a mixture, will destroy the country by their abandoned manners, as was the case with the Burgundians, Provencals, and Spaniards, whom the Saracens harassed for many years on account of their past transgressions. Moreover, it has been told to us that you take away

---

[32] The Winedi were living on the western bank of the Vistula near the Baltic.

from churches and monasteries many of their privileges and that you excite by your example, the members of your nobility to do the like. But recollect I entreat you, what terrible vengeance God hath inflicted upon former kings guilty of the crimes that we lay before your charge.

For Ceolred, your predecessor, the debaucher of nuns, the infringer of ecclesiastical privileges, was seized while splendidly regaling with his nobles by a malignant spirit, who snatched away his soul without confession and without communion while in converse with the devil and despising the law of God!

God also punished Osred, King of Deira and Bernicia, who was guilty of the same crimes, to such excesses that he lost his kingdom and perished in early manhood dying an ignominious death. Also, Charlemagne of the Franks, a subverter of many monasteries and appropriator of ecclesiastical to his own use, perished suffering pain and a fearful death."

Time passed and then Boniface again wrote to Ethelbald. This time the letter read as: *"Wherefore, my dearest son, showing you good counsel, we call you to witness and entreat you by the living God, and his son, Jesus Christ, and the Holy Spirit, that that you would recollect how fleeting is the present life, how short and momentary is the delight of the flesh and how ignominious for a person of transitory to leave a bad example to posterity. Begin therefore to regulate your life by better habits and correct the past errors of your youth, that you may have praise before men here and be blessed with eternal glory thereafter. We wish Your Highness health and proficiency in virtue!"*

In reply, Ethelbald wrote, *"Wherefore I Ethelbald, King of the Mercians, out of love to Heaven and having regard for my own soul, have felt the necessity of considering how I may by good works, set my soul free from every tie of sin. For since God, through the*

184

greatness of his clemency, without any previous merit on my part, has bestowed upon me the sceptre of government, therefore I willingly repay him out of that which he has given me.

On this account, I grant as long as I live, that all monasteries and churches of my kingdom shall be exempted from public taxes, works, and impositions, except the building of forts and bridges from which none can be released. And moreover, the servants of God shall have perfect liberty in the produce of their woods and lands and the right of fishing, nor shall they bring presents either to a king or princes except voluntarily, but they shall serve God without molestation[33]!"

Ethelbald was succeeded by Offa, who was a man of great mind and who always did what was necessary to succeed at whatever he did, and he reigned for thirty-nine years. His enemies included Cynewulf, King of the West Saxons, and that resulted in war between them. Even though Cynewulf was a celebrated warrior, Offa was victorious over him. He was good at strategy and involved contrivance and cunning to gain victory over his enemies. An example of this being when he held an orders group with his general staff. Offa said, *Well Gentlemen, what have you in ideas of how to beat Cynewulf?"*

No-one spoke and then Offa spoke! He said, *"You call yourselves generals and you cannot even suggest a way to beat Cynewulf? What sort of generals are you? I will tell you what you are! You are all useless! I want messengers to immediately send word to Cynewulf that he is to attend a great banquet at my palace! Let him know that no-one shall attack him and his escort and that he is welcome here if he comes with a minimum of his own warriors!"*

---

[33] William of Malmsbury, 1847

That message was taken to Cynewulf who then arrived at the palace of Offa in Mercia. Cynewulf and his small bodyguard unit rode into the walled palace grounds and all these men were keeping a sharp lookout for suspected treachery. They could not see anything that looked suspicious or threatening and so, they rode deeper into the palace grounds. What they did not know was that Offa had placed well-hidden archers along all vantagepoints and that his soldiers had now sealed off all means of retreat. Suddenly, King Offa of Mercia yelled out to his archers. He yelled, *"Choose your targets and kill everyone in the bodyguard units of King Cynewulf! Let no-one escape, but do not kill King Cynewulf because I have a special treat in mind for him!"*

That resulted in all members of King Cynewulf's bodyguard units being killed. Immediately after that, King Offa issued orders. He said, *"Put King Cynewulf into chains for now! Tonight, we shall have the entertainment of watching him die when he is beheaded!"*

Kenwulf

Kenwulf was the successor to Offa. He wrote this epistle: *"To the most holy and truly loving Lord Leo, Pontiff of the scared apostolical see, I, Kenwulf of Mercia am the King of Mercia by the grace of God and therefore I along with bishops, princes and every degree of under our authority send the salutation of the purest love of Christ to our wonderful Pope!"* He kept on writing and pledged total allegiance to the Church. In due course he received a reply from the Pope. It read, *"To the excellent prince, my son Kenwulf, King of the Mercians, of the province of the Saxons Pope Leo sends a greeting."*

Before that happened, Offa had made sure that the outrages he was performing against his own countrymen would not be to his disadvantage by giving his daughter called Eadburga in marriage to

Bertric the King of West Saxons. He then obtained the friendship and goodwill of Charlemagne, the King of the Franks.

Kenwulf was reputed to be religious at home, while being victorious abroad. He was equally admired for the extent of his power and the presence of his mind. Using the hatred felt by Offa towards the rulers of Kent, he used that hatred successfully to invade Kent. He led away the King of Kent called Eadbert and surnamed as Pren; but shortly after that, at Winchcombe, where he had built a church to honour God, on the day of its dedication, he released the captive king and gave him liberty. He thus earned his reputation for clemency. Cuthred[34], whom he had made king over the Kentish people, was present to applaud this act of royal munificence.

The church resounded with acclamations, the street shook with crowds of people, for in an assembly of thirteen bishops and ten dukes, no-one was refused a largess, and all departed with full purses. As well, in addition to the gifts he made to the nobility, he gave all those who did not have property a pound of silver, to each presbyter a measure of gold, to every monk a schilling and lastly, he made many presents to the people.

After he had given the monastery ample revenues, he honoured it by his sepulchre, in the twenty-four years of his reign. His son called Kenelm, was murdered by his sister, Quendrida and he gained the title of martyr and rests at the monastery. After him, the kingdom of Mercia sank from its prosperity and became almost lifeless, producing nothing worthy of being mentioned in history.

The kings after him were Ceolwulf, the brother of Kenwulf who reigned for one year before he was expelled by Bernulf. He ruled for three years before he was overcome and put to flight by Egbert, king of the West Saxons and was afterwards killed by the

---

[34] Kenwulf made Cuthred the King of Kent in 798 A.D...

East Angles because he attempted to seize East Anglia and make it subject to the Mercians of the time of Offa.

Ludecan, after a reign of two years, was preparing to avenge his predecessor called Withlaf. He was subjugated by the before-mentioned Egbert and governed for thirteen years paying tribute to Egbert and his son. Berthwulf reigned for thirteen years on the same conditions was driven out by Danish pirates beyond the sea.

Burhead married Ethelswith, the daughter of King Ethelwulf, the son of Egbert, exonerated himself, by his affinity, from the payment of tribute and depredations to the enemy, but after twenty-two years, driven by them from his country, he fled to Rome, and was buried at the School of the Angles, in the church of Saint Mary. His wife at that time continued in England but afterwards followed her husband and she died at Pavia.

Next the kingdom was given by the Danes to one Ceolwulf, an attendant of Burred, who bound himself by oath that he would retain it only at their pleasure. After a few years it under the dominion of Alfred, the grandson of Egbert. And so, the sovereignty of the mighty Mercians withered away through the inactivity of a driveller king in the year 875 A.D...

Kings of the East Angles (520 – 905)

The greatest king of the East Angles was Redwald[35], and the Saxons thought that he was tenth in descent from Wodin. All the southern provinces of the Angles and Saxons on his side of the Humber River were subject to his authority. He is the king who out of regard for Edwin, killed Ethelfrid, the king of the Northumbrians. It was because of the persuasion of Edwin that he was converted to

---

[35] Redwald was not the first king of East Anglia, but the first who became distinguished. In year 571 A.D., Uffa was the king, succeeded by his son called Titil in 578. Titil was succeeded by Redwald, who was his son.

Christianity and baptised in public. Afterwards at the instigation of his wife, he renounced the Christian faith. His son was Eorpwald, and he embraced Christianity and poured his immaculate spirit out to God before he was murdered by the barbarian heathen called Richbert.

He was succeeded by Sigebert, who was his half-brother, on his mother's side. He was a worthy servant of the Lord, having been polished from all barbarism by his education among the Franks. He was driven into banishment by Redwald, and after a long time of associating with the Franks, he had received the rites of Christianity. Upon coming to power, he graciously communicated Christianity to the entire kingdom and established schools and centres of learning in different places. The promoter of his studies and the stimulator of his religion was Felix the Bishop, who was born in Burgundy. After he died, he was buried at Ramsey.

After Sigebert, the throne went to Ecgric, who met his death while being attacked by Penda, king of Mercia. The successor of Ecgric was Anna, the son of Eni and the brother of Redwald, involved in similar destruction by the furious Penda.

Anna was succeeded by his brother Ethelhere, who was justly killed by Oswy, the King of the Northumbrians. Oswy an auxiliary to Penda and supported the very army which destroyed his brother. His brother Ethelwald, in various successions left the kingdom to Adulf and Elwold, who were the sons of Ethelhere. Next came Bernred. After him, Ethelred the First. His son was saint Ethelbert, whom Offa, the King of Mercia killed through treachery.

After him, because of the violence of the Mercians, few kings reigned in East Anglia until the time of Saint Edmund. He was killed in the sixteenth year of his reign by Hingwar the Viking heathen. After that, the East angles ceased to command their own country for fifty years. The province was without a king owing to the continued incursions and raids by mainly Danish Vikings. That resulted in both East Anglia and East Saxony being ruled by Guthrum, a Danish king for twelve years during the of King Alfred.

Guthrum had as his successor, another Dane called Eohric, who, after he had ruled for fourteen years, had his reign ended by the East Angles because of his cruelty towards them. However, these people still did not have liberty because the Danish earls continued to oppress them or else excite them against the kings of the West Saxons. That continued until Edward the elder, the son of Alfred the Great, added both provinces to his West Saxon empire, and expelled the Danes, thereby freeing the East Angles.

Alfred is Born

In 848 A.D., Queen Osburh, wife of King Ethelwulf of West Saxons was again in labour and expecting another child to be born. She had previously given birth to and raised a daughter called Ethelswith and three sons. They were Ethelbald, Ethelbert and Ethelred. At midday, she was experiencing some pain, and her labour had started its contractions. Recognising what was happening, she called out for her midwife to attend to her.

The midwife called Mary hastened to her and Osburh spoke to her. She said, *"I am so glad that you are here to help me through this Mary, your presence has a great calming effect for me."* Mary now looked and felt the birth canal of Osburh and found that it was dilated, so she said, *"Osburh my dear, seeing that you already have produced four surviving children, I think that this next one shall not cause you any problems at all, and remember that I am on hand to help you if that becomes necessary!"*

Soon after that conversation, the contractions of Osburh became more frequent and she gave birth to another son. Mary said, *"Congratulations your majesty, you have a fine son, what shall you be calling him?"* Osburh answered with, *"Alfred, I name my son as*

190

Alfred. I had a vision about him during the night and in my vision about him, people called him 'Alfred-the-Great'. Mary said, *"I wish that I would have visions about my children, have you also had visions about your other children?"*

Osburh said, *"Yes, the visions started with the birth of Alfred's brother called Ethelred. Like my dream about Alfred, my visions of Ethelred showed that he would do much to rid our country of invasions of pagans called Danes. I never did have any visions or dreams about the other two children, so I am thinking that Ethelred and Alfred must somehow be special! So, I now have five children, and their father Ethelwulf has decreed that each of them should reign in turn and so, avoid the problems caused by disputes over succession!"* Ethelwulf was a religious man, and so, he sent Alfred to Rome while he was four years old to meet Pope Leo the fourth. The Pope was so impressed with the outlook and intelligence of Alfred that he wrote to Ethelwulf.

His letter read, *"I am pleased to report that you son Alfred, has arrived safely in Rome ad that we have graciously received him in the Vatican. We have taken him to thresholds of the holy apostles, and we have decorated him as a spiritual son, complete with the dignity and all vestments of the consulate, which is customary with Roman consuls. I have taken the liberty of giving him his Royal Unction and his crown which will be held in trust for him by myself and my successor, depending upon when Alfred is ready to ascend to the throne.* It is said that this was the true beginning of Alfred's interest in learning, something which he was delayed from entering until he was a lot older.

Ethelred Becomes the King of Wessex

In 866 A.D., Ethelred the First obtained the kingdom of the West Saxons and ruled it for five years until 871 A.D... This king was personally engaged in the fight against the invading Danes to the point where he was constantly engaged in hostile actions against the invaders. So bravely and vigorously did he fight for his country, that the invaders were amazed by the resistance of him and his people.

He personally led his army against the Danes nine times in one year. His successes were varied, but usually he was victorious. He would constantly launch attacks upon the Danes, and he was quick to use enemy strengths against them by ambushing their long lines of supply and communications. He constantly attacked smaller isolated Danish units, wiping them out. During several of these actions the Danes lost nine earls, one king and many warriors.

At the place called Eschendun, the Danes had a great army which was divided into two groups with a different Danish king commanding each army group. The second army group was commanded by the second Danish king, and he had the support of nine Danish earls. Having sent out active scouting groups well ahead of his army, King Ethelred-the-First of the West Saxons (Wessex) advanced to a short distance from where his brother, Prince Alfred was stationed with his soldiers. The two English brothers decided to hold a conference to discuss how best to defeat the two vast Danish armies before them.

Accordingly, Ethelred spoke to his younger brother, Alfred. He said, *"Alfred, I want you and your soldiers to wipe out the Dane army in front of you which is commanded by a Danish King and nine earls, while my soldiers and I wipe out the second Danish army commanded by a different Danish King. The two Danish armies are commanded by two Danish kings and nine Danish earls. For some reason that I cannot imagine, the enemy army group to your front is under the command of one king and all nine earls. I want you and your army to move into position to attack the Danes while it is still dark in the early hours of the morning. You are to launch your attack upon the invaders just before the morning twilight. Once both of our forces are in position and it is still dark, we shall both let our warriors relax until the cold of the morning approaches. When that happens there shall be a series of trumpet calls which shall signal that the attack upon the Danes must begin immediately. That will happen in the cold of the morning about an hour before the twilight sets in."*

Alfred was not inclined to wait for action against the enemy, he wanted to make them regret ever coming to England immediately. He said, *"My brother, I fully realise that you must perform your religious devotions before you can do anything else in the day. Not so with me, while you are performing your religious observance and saying your prayers, I will already have moved my forces into position and the Danes shall be surrounded during the night before my attack. That way, my warriors can relax and get badly needed sleep before the attack commences in the early hours of the morning. With the Danes surrounded by my warriors who shall be fresh from having sleep in position while surrounding the enemy, as twilight sets in, my forces will drive the Danes back into the sea!"*

So, it was that the army of Alfred moved into position and surrounded the Danes at night. That allowed Alfred and his men to not just be in position while surrounding the enemy, but also to rest there. Great care was taken not to allow noise or light to come from the force of Alfred in case that betrayed the position of Alfred and his warriors to the Danes. That resulted in Alfred and his being ready for battle and fully rested hours before the morning twilight. But it was a different story for his brother, King Ethelred the First of Wessex. He remained in his tent and was carrying out his religious observances. Soon, a messenger went to see Ethelred the First and spoke to him.

He said, *"Your majesty, the pagan Danish Vikings are rushing forward with a great fury, and some of your units in their path are currently in great danger! My commander has sent me to see you so that you can come with me to the areas under Danish attack and repel the invaders!"*

Ethelred the First replied, *"Try to understand that it is by the grace of God that we live and it is by the grace of God that we shall die! I am busy now honouring my commitment to God by performing his services and I shall not move against the enemy until God has received his services from me! I demand that you and all our men have faith in God, for he shall give us victory, because we are the righteous Christians while the Danes are pagans! You may return to the forward areas and let my warriors know that I shall be on the battlefield soon and the Danes shall pay for their crimes against our people!"*

The piety of this king was of great advantage to his brother and Alfred had already advanced far towards the enemy. The battalions of Saxons were now giving way and were close to fleeing from the battlefield because their enemies were pressing down upon them from higher ground. That meant the English Christians were in an unfavourable situation and close to despair when King Ethelred the First unexpectedly hurried forward. At several points around him, his warriors were carrying the cross of Christ. That and the sight of Ethelred calmly issuing orders to his soldiers while personally attacking the Danes resulted in his rallying of the English. The invading Danes became terrified equally by the courage of Ethelred and his zeal, so they fled from the battlefield. During this battle, a Danish king died. Having seen his body, Ethelred asked one of his warriors which of the two Danish king this could be. The warrior answered, *"Your majesty, I think that we have killed the Dane king called Oseg! You will find that there are also five enemy earls lying dead on the battlefield as well huge numbers of their warriors!"*

During this time, the kings of Mercia and Northumberland eagerly seized the opportunity afford them by the arrival of the Danes. Ethelred was fully occupied in fighting them. That relieved the kings of Mercia and Northumberland a little from their bondage to the West Saxons, which allowed those kings to almost regain their original power by siding with the invaders against the West Saxons.

With the kings of the two provinces siding with the Danes, all other provinces were attacked and laid waste by cruel depredations because each king chose to resist the invading Danes within his own territory rather than to jointly defend the country by using coordinated attacks upon the enemy. Because of the absence of a united force acting against them, the Danes acquired even more strength without impediment. That resulted in the country being ruined by their senseless conduct, and the apprehensions of the local people increased, with each successive victory of the Danes.

During 868 A.D., King Ethelred the First and his brother, Prince Alfred were campaigning, trying to rid England of the Danish Vikings. While they were doing so with success, the kingdom of Mercia was invaded by Vikings who camped near Nottingham and that caused King Burghead of Mercia to send a message written in Latin to King Ethelred the first of Wessex, appealing for help in his fight with the Danes.

So it was that King Burghead of Mercia spoke to one of his senior commanders, a nobleman called Æthelred Mucil. He said, *"Ealdorman Æthelred Mucil of Gaini and Gainsborough, I urgently need you to go to the camp of King Ethelred the First of the West Saxons and his brother Alfred to obtain their help to defeat the Danes who are now near Nottingham! Take as big a bodyguard unit as you need to ensure you own safety and return with Ethelred-the-First, his brother Alfred and their armies!"*

And so, having received the Royal Messenger from the King of Mercia, King-Ethelred-the-First spoke He said, *"Æthelred Mucil, please return to your king and tell him that my help is coming immediately! The first thing for myself and my brother to do is to surround the Danes and so make them ineffective by sealing them up in their own positions around Nottingham and that will best be achieved by surrounding them and cutting them off from their supplies and lines of communication!"*

Ethelred and his brother Alfred took their armies to Nottingham where they surrounded the Danes and began the siege. With the English armies now surrounding the Danes, things became more relaxed for the English and that night both King Ethelred and Prince Alfred were invited to the Royal Villa at Sutton Courtenay. Both men attended, and they were met by King Burghead of Mercia and his nobles. King Burghead of Mercia spoke to King Ethelred of the West Saxons. He said, *"It is an honour to have you here, King Ethelred-the-First of Wessex! I hear that Prince Alfred is also here with his own army. I am so very pleased that you have both decided to help us in our fight against the Danes! Now please come with me into the feasting area of this great manor-house and I will introduce you to my people."*

With that said, he then led the way into where the banquet and festivities were being held. Upon going further into the great manor-house, King Burghead of Mercia again spoke. He said, *"Please allow me to introduce you to my Ealdorman, Æthelred Mucil of Gaini, near Gainsborough."*

While that was happening, Prince Alfred Was looking over some of the guests present until his eyes fell upon a lovely young woman and she immediately aroused his interest in her. That was followed by Æthelred Mucil being introduced to Prince Alfred by King Burghead of Mercia. King Burghead said, *"Alfred, this is Æthelred Mucil, please talk to him, because I think that the two of you will be of benefit to each other!"* That resulted in Æthelred speaking to Alfred. He said, *"Alfred, could you please accompany me? There is someone whom I would like you to meet!"*

That was followed by Æthelred leading the way towards his daughter named Ealhswith, which delighted Alfred, as she was the very same young woman who had so impressed him earlier. When they got close to her, Æthelred spoke to Alfred. He said, *"Prince Alfred, this is my daughter in whom I am well pleased! Her name is Ealhswith and I, for one, would be very happy if you two young people happen to like each other!"* To his daughter he said, *"Ealhswith, this is Prince Alfred of the West Saxons, who along with his brother King Ethelred-the-First of Wessex and their armies are here to help us defeat the Danish invaders. Their armies have surrounded the Danish Vikings at Nottingham, and they are laying siege to them!"*

As the evening progressed, these two young people became enchanted with each other, resulting in Alfred proposing marriage to Ealhswith and her accepting it. The resulting marriage ceremony was held at the same Royal Villa, which was a great manor-house. There was much celebrating, drinking, feasting ad gift giving.

As the night went on, Alfred suddenly said to Ealhswith, *"Ealhswith my love, I am not well today. For most of the day, I have been stricken by diarrhea and fever and both of those things have combined, resulting in me being very fatigued and I have a belly pain as well as cramping. I also have a mouth score which is bothering me, and I do not feel very well now. There is something wrong with my belly or gut. I do not know what it is, but it is a painful nuisance! All the same, I shall put up with it and we shall continue our festivities."* He did not know it, but that was the beginning of an intestinal disorder that would last for the rest of his life. Some medical doctors of the twenty-first century looked at his symptoms and they said that they thought he may have been suffering from Crohn's disease!

In 868 A.D., Ealhswith was expecting her first child of five children and was in labour, while Alfred was what many people would call a typical expectant father. About the great event of the imminent birth of his first-born child, his intestinal disorder began to play up and bother him greatly. Ealhswith who was attended by midwives, gave birth to a daughter who was named as Aethelflaed. She grew up and became married to Æthelred of Mercia who was a formidable warrior who fought the Danes and won against them. After she took up her duties of being the wife of Æthelred, she became a heroine among her people in Mercia and was known as "The Lady of the Mercians" to her people.

In year 869 A.D., a second daughter was born to Ealhswith and Alfred. Upon her reaching maturity, she became the Abbess of Shaftesbury. Their next child was a son who became known as Edward the Elder. He succeeded Alfred when he died in 901 A.D... In the year of 877 A.D., Ealhswith gave birth to another daughter called Æthelthryth and who is also known as Elfrida. She grew up and married count Baldwin of Flanders in 893 A.D. and was an ancestress of Matilda of Flanders who married William-the-Conqueror.

King Edmund of East Anglia

The country of the East Angles, including their cities, towns and villages were taken over by many plunderers. The ravaging of the English countryside appeared to be growing with each passing day and that was causing much concern among most of the English people. Then on the 10th of November of 870 A.D., King Edmund of East Anglia arrived with his army and immediately attacked the Danish "Great Army" which was under the command of Egbert the First.

King Edmund called for an orders group between himself and his senior officers to take place. At the meeting thus established, he addressed his sub-ordinates. He said, *"Gentlemen, our country of East Anglia has been invaded by these heathens called Danish Vikings! They are overrunning the entire countryside, and we must put a stop to these horrendous activities! I would like you, Ethelard to go and reconnoitre the land between here and the location of the Danish army units commanded the Danes called Hingwar and Hubba!*

See to it that you obtain as much information as possible about the strengths or otherwise of the enemy forces. Also, their locations and the terrain in which their units are located, and obstacles such as rivers, streams, swamps, and bogs, and even cliffs which could make closing with and killing the enemy difficult for us! We must also know if the invaders are mounted or if they are on foot! If you find the enemy is mounted, try to find out how many horses they have and if they have trained cavalry or not. This information is critical to our success in this fight against the heathen bastards!"

So, it was that Ethelard, who was a junior officer like the sub-altern of the armies of the twenty-second century, left to perform the reconnoitre of the region that the Danes were thought to be occupying. Before leaving the encampment of King Edmund of East Anglia, he collected his small unit of twenty-eight soldiers. He personally inspected all their weapons and armour, in each case making sure that the items were in service-able condition.

During this inspection, he found that some of the battle-axes and swords of his men were in urgent need of maintenance or replacement, so he organised that immediately. Thus, re-equipped and re-armed, the small reconnoitre force left to perform its duty. He addressed his men. He said, *"Men, King Edmund has chosen us for this great and glorious mission to gather intelligence about the enemy. We are to find out the locations, strengths, or weaknesses of the enemy forces the number of men and horses they have. The terrain where the arsehole Danes who spread terror though-out the land are in two major large units. They are commanded by Hingwar and Hubba!*

Our job is to observe the enemy and collect information that can be used against the enemy by our king and his army! We shall obtain the information and that is our only job! We shall not attack the enemy unless we are attacked first! This is a critical intelligence gathering mission and it is a dangerous one! For that reason, I only want to have soldiers who are totally committed to ridding our land of the enemy! So, if any of you is feeling scared or is not totally committed to the defence of East Anglia, depart now! I only want men with me who are willing to fight to their deaths if need be!" No-one moved or spoke and therefore Ethelard was content in the knowledge that his men were committed to the defence of their country and that their equipment was in sound condition.

After leaving the encampment of King Edmund, and riding towards the north-east for some time, Ethelard raised his right hand, thereby calling a halt to the journey of the reconnoitre force and he spoke to his men. He said, *"Soldiers and warriors of King Edmund, from now on, make sure that none of us is visible to anyone at all! We can best do that by making sure that we are never silhouetted by never appearing on the crests of hills and mountains. Where that is unavoidable, we will temporarily detour from our line of march, and we shall blend our silhouettes among taller objects like forests or other suitable things which can be used to breakup our outlines. All shiny surfaces must be kept covered and therefore, not visible to the enemy! We shall have to always keep our horses quiet! The only times that we will engage enemy units in battle is if we outnumber the enemy by three to one, and then only if we are certain that there are no more enemy units within a half day's ride from our location."*

Having spoken to his soldiers, the unit rode forward silently. The two leading horsemen were acting as first and second scouts respectively and these duties were constantly exchanged with other member of the units to keep the scouts both fresh and vigilant. As the force was moving forward in single file, the first scout suddenly raised his right hand. That was the signal for the entire column to stop. Next, he turned towards the second scout and held out his arm so that it formed a straight line from his shoulder to his hand.

He now turned his hand so that his thumb was pointing at the ground. He then pointed his hand towards the north-east, along the ridgeline that all could plainly see. Used in this way, the hand signals were communicating. They said, *"Enemy ahead, to the north-east!"* The forward scout now touched the top his shoulder and then patted himself on the head. That was the hand signal for, *"Officer, come to me".* That was repeated down the line until it was received by Ethelard who now rode to where the two scouts were located. He then asked the forward scout, *"What is happening?"* The forward scout said, *"Sir, ahead is a small enemy unit of about twelve men. I consider them to be a threat to us because they could easily inform their commanders that we are in the area and that could raise a major problem for us! So, what is it that you want done?"*

Ethelard thought about it for a while and then he spoke to his forward scout. He said, *"Firstly, we need to see exactly how many men the enemy unit has and we must make sure that there are no other enemy units within a half day's ride from here! Otherwise, we could all become instant casualties. Because of that, this entire unit shall dismount, and our hoses shall be taken to a secure area under the care of three of our men. The remaining men of our unit shall join us here, and together we shall quietly move forward on foot and then we will see what sort of enemy unit is ahead of us and what its strength is. Now see to it that the information is passed along our line until it reaches the last soldier in it!"*

That was done, and it resulted in the men dismounting and the horses being taken to a secure area under the care of three men. The remainder of the reconnoitre unit now joined Ethelard. He ordered his men to slowly advance on foot and to keep out of sight of the enemy while they did so. The English then confirmed that there in fact only eight enemy soldiers and not the twelve that had been reported earlier. Next, the reconnaissance unit decided to silently ensure that no other enemy units were close to their location.

That was done, and it encouraged Ethelard to order his men. He said, *"Men, the enemy is at hand, and there are only eight of them! We have here, twenty-five men which means that the enemy is outnumbered by about three to one! I want you all to take up your double-edged battle-axes and then we shall wipe out those Danish arseholes who are an ever-present danger to our people!* That was done, resulting in the small unit of Danes being wiped out!

After that action, Ethelard again spoke to his men. He said, *"Men, you have done well, we will now go cautiously forward and locate the main force of Hingwar and Hubba. Once we have the necessary information about their strength of numbers and horses we will return to the encampment of King Edmund.* Then the small unit went forward and soon, they located the armies of Hingwar and Hubba. Ethelard was dismayed at the sight of the two enormous Danish armies.

He spoke to the men who were close to him. He said, *"Oh shit! Look at the size of the Danish armies! Look over there towards the east, the enemy has an estimated eight hundred horses!"* That now resulted in the reconnaissance unit hurrying silently back to the encampment of King Edmund and Ethelard reporting to him.

Arriving at the English encampment, he said to his king, *"Your majesty, the enemy has two very large armies, and we saw an estimated eight hundred horses! From what I have personally seen, there is no way that we can win against the Danes, there are too many of them! I suggest that we perform a quiet withdrawal from this area allowing us to cut down the enemy numbers and making them over-extend their supply and communication lines! After we have harassed the enemy in that way for some time, their number may well be cut down to the point where we can successfully attack them!*

King Edmund now spoke. He said, *"Ethelard, you and your men have done well to find out the strengths of the enemy and for that, I thank you! The enemy is plundering our country and laying waste to much of it while enslaving our people! The people rightly look toward us for protection and my protection is what they shall receive even unto my own death! We shall attack the invaders because it is far better to die as a hero who is defending his country than it is to die as a coward or as a traitor! Even though we are greatly outnumbered, we must attack the enemy! This is the English way! So, Ethelard, you and your men can leave and in so doing, save your-selves or you can join me in fighting the Danes to the death!"*

Ethelard said, *"Your majesty, my men and I shall not desert you in the face of the enemy! We shall stay with you to the very end, even if we all die, it will slow the advance of the Danes and that will allow others to finally deal with them and to wipe them out! My men and I are with you, your majesty, to the end, no matter what befalls us all!* King Edmund said, *"Thank you!"* Then he gathered his senior officers and spoke to them. He said, *"Before us lie two huge enemy armies, which are both much larger than is this one! The enemy is raping our women, killing our children, and laying waste to our countryside while causing havoc and killing our Christian Priests while they destroy our churches! All of that is being done by the Danish pagans and we, the Warriors-of-God are all that stands between those bastards and utter devastation! In opposing the enemy this way, we may all die, but that is highly preferable to living as slave of the pagans! We attack the two Danish armies now!"*

Shortly after that, King Edmund led his army into action against the Danes. The enemy was surprised at the ferocity and the speed by which the English forces of Edmund attacked them, and their outermost units were beginning to give way when there was suddenly a horn blast that signalled the entry of Hingwar and his entire army into the camp. Hingwar was aware of King Edmund and his English army, and he decided to try to cut things short by looking for the English king on the battle-field. So, he went out calling, "Edmund, Edmund, you silly English man, I am Hingwar-the-Dane, and I challenge you in a fight to the death, Englishman! Both men were in fact speaking in dialects of Old German and they could understand what each other was saying.

Accordingly, King Edmund yelled out. He yelled, *"I King Edmund of the East Angles challenge you, Hingwar-the-Dane to a combat to the death because you are a useless foreign prick, and I do not like you, Dane arsehole!"* Hearing that so enraged Hingwar that he rushed towards Edmund, finally closing with him. He now swung his long sword in an arc, aimed at just below Edmund's chin and was gratified to see the head of Edmund separating from his body. That was also seen by some English soldiers and what was developing into a stalemate between the two sides ended up as the complete route of the English.

With this Danish victory, the pagans overran all of Anglia and Mercia, while fixing their winter quarters at Thetford, and very soon afterwards they where they destroyed all the monasteries upon which they came. The Danes went to Medhamsted where they were burning and breaking everything, as well as killing the Abbot and all the monks whom they happened to find. The havoc caused by the Danes changed the monastery from a rich and fruitful place to some heaps of rubble.

The Northumbrians had long been caught up in civil squabbles among themselves made up their differences as the Danes approached. They arrested and replaced their King Osbert and expelled him. They next managed to collect a powerful force and went out to meet the enemy. However, they were easily repelled by the Danes, and they shut themselves up in the city of York. That city was then set on fire by the Danes. That resulted in flames raging to the utmost and even consuming some walls while the defenders died in the fire.

Osburh has Bad News for Alfred

In the year of 855 A.D., Alfred's mother called Osburh, came to her youngest son and spoke to him. She said, *"Alfred, it is with sadness that I must inform you that your adoptive father, the Pope Leo-the-Fourth, has died. Apparently, it is his fondest wish that you remain true to the teachings of the Holy Mother Church, the Apostles and God. The Pope has said that he sees dark days ahead for you and your people, but by having faith and remaining true to God, you shall in the end be victorious over the foreign pagan invaders of your country!"*

King-Alfred-the-Great

King Ethelred-the-First was badly wounded in battle and died from his battle wounds after Easter on the 15th of April 871

205

A.D... he was succeeded by his younger brother Alfred who then became the King of Wessex. As I have stated before, Alfred received the Royal Unction and his crown from Pope Leo-the-Fourth while Alfred was in Rome as a child. In 872 A.D., Alfred succeeded to the throne, and he held it with difficulty using his great courage for twenty-eight years. During this time, Elchere with men from Kent and Huda with men from Surrey took on and defeated the heathen Danish army on the Isle of Thanet.

In 877 A.D., the Danish army marched into Exeter from Wareham. Meanwhile, the ships of the Danish navy sailed west, until they became lost in a great mist while far out in the sea. That resulted in the destruction of one hundred and twenty ships near Swanwich. King Alfred and his army hurried after the Danes, trying to overtake them and thereby engage them in battle before they could reach the safety of their fortress which was impregnable to the English. Alfred and his army did manage to trap the Danes before they could reach the safety of the fort and after the battle, the Danes at that place gave him as many hostages as he wanted and swore solemn oaths to observe the resulting treaty with great honour. Alfred had much to contend with, including the constant attempted invasions by Danish Vikings.

Among the enemies that were trying to take over Wessex were the Danish Viking King Guthrum and his commanders known as Ivor the Boneless, Björn Ironside, Halfdan Ragnarsson and Sigurd Snake-in-the-Eye.

Alfred Uses Guerrilla Tactics

Early in the year of 878 A.D., the Danes led by their King Guthrum overran much of England and seized Chippenham in Wiltshire. For nine years Alfred was battling enemies, and he was sometimes deceived by false treaties, which caused him to sometimes take revenge upon the deceivers. However, the deceivers were many and they were at last successful in reducing Alfred's loyal following to the three counties of Hampshire, Wiltshire, and Somersetshire. Having his loyal following reduced to this level, Alfred and his men were compelled to retreat to an island called Athelney. This island was in marshy ground which made it barely accessible.

One of his soldiers approached and saluted him before speaking. He said, *"Your majesty, our food and provisions are at an extremely low level, and it is doubtful if our small force can have anything to eat! It is rather doubtful that we can alleviate the situation through fishing   because of the ice now on the river and marshes surrounding this place! Even though it is doubtful that we can obtain enough food through fishing, we should at least try it and not just simply let our soldiers starve to death, if nothing else, the attempt to get food by fishing may lift the morale of our soldiers!"*

That caused Alfred to call for an orders group. When his soldiers were assembled, he spoke to them. He said, *"My loyal and gallant soldiers, we are staring possible starvation and defeat by the enemy Danes in the face! To counter that, every one of you must apply yourselves and catch fish, other than those soldiers who are needed to remain on active duty in case of enemy attacks!"*

A short while later, with his companions being stationed along the river side of the island to complete the required fishing, Alfred went to sleep and started to dream. During his dream, he saw the vision of saint Cuthbert, the Bishop of Lindisfarne who spoke to him. Cuthbert said, *"I am the ghost of Cuthbert and God has sent me to announce good fortune to you. Since England has already largely paid for her crimes, God now through the merits of England's native saints looks upon her with an eye of mercy!*

And you who has been so pitifully banished from your kingdom, shall again be seated with honour on your throne! I shall now give you this extraordinary token. Your fishers shall on this day bring home so great a quantity of fish in large baskets that you shall be able to not just eat your fill for this day and the next, but also there shall be enough left over for your people to preserve the fish through smoking the fish and salting them. By doing that, you shall have enough fish to provide preserved food rations for up to three more months for all your people.

That will be even more extraordinary because the river, is at this time, hard-bound with ice, therefore, no-one could warrant any such expectation; especially as the air is now dripping with cold rain which appears to mock the efforts of the fishers. You shall succeed in your wishes and your fortune shall become much better if you conciliate God as your helper and me, his messenger with suitable devotion[36]."

Having said that, the saint relieved the sleeping king of his anxiety and gave the very same dream to his mother who was sleeping near him. Upon both awakening, they were both heard to say that they had the very same dream. Soon afterwards, the fishermen returned with a catch of fish that was so large that it fed the entire army as well as providing the needed extra fish for preserving as future rations.

Now that everyone in his small army had been fed and rested, Alfred launched guerrilla style attacks upon the invading Danes. While at first, that did not worry the invaders a great deal, the repeated and continuing attacks on the more isolated Danish units was resulting in disrupting the lines of communications and supply of the Danes near and around Chippenham. After being continually informed of Alfred's forces disrupting his supply lines,

---

[36] William of Malmsbury, 1847

the Danish King Guthrum was alarmed at the menace to his lines of communication which were under threat from Alfred and his forces.

Since Alfred often hunted in the marshes where he and his small army were taking shelter, he knew most of the area and where there were bogs and places to avoid such as areas of quick-sand. He was absolutely delighted when one of his junior officers called Adulf approached him and spoke after saluting his king.

He said, *"Your majesty, I have been thinking of how to get out of this mess that the Danes have put us into! I have thought about this for a long time and last night, I had a vision from Saint Cuthbert!"* He went on to say, *"Saint Cuthbert said to me, 'Go hither with King Alfred into the camp of the Danes disguised as minstrels and when you are admitted to the banqueting room, put on such a good performance that you will be kept there, entertaining the Danes for several days!*

During that time, you must listen to what the enemy is saying. There will be no problem in you being able to understand what the Danes are saying because both your English and the Danish languages are in fact old German. By you listening to what the enemy has to say to each other, it will give you the advantage of knowing what the enemy shall be doing for some time into the future. You should use that information you can gather in that way and your knowledge of the marshes around Athelney to your advantage and harass the enemy, making them wish that they had set foot upon the soil of Engeland in general and the territory of the West Saxons in particular! That so pleased the adventurous outlook of Alfred, that he spoke. He said, *"Very well, Adulf, can you play any musical instrument, and do you have any of them here?"*

Adulf answered, *"Yes my liege, I can play the lute as you can and yes, I have managed to escape from Chippenham with two of my lutes which we can use as part of our disguises when we go into the Danish fort.*" So, it was that King Alfred and Adulf, the junior officer of his army, went to the Danish fort at Chippenham disguised as minstrels and put their plan into effect. Over the next few days these two daring Englishmen carefully observed was happening and being said among their Danish enemies prior to returning to the Athelney marshes and holding an orders group among the English.

It was during the banquet of the first night they were providing the musical entertainment that they saw seated close to them, the Danish leaders of Ivar-the-Boneless, Sigurd Snake-in-the-Eye, and King Guthrum. All three of these men were using very loud speech and what they were saying was understood by the two Englishmen.

King Guthrum spoke to his assembled commanders and said, *"Men, we have come far since the days when our nation was confined to the area around Copenhagen Island although they may not realise it, some of the best things for the Danish people were the Engels designing their longships and leaving some of them behind when the entire tribe left Anglen and settled in Engel-land! When they left, the whole of the mid Jutland peninsular was deserted! The Kimbern tribe moved out of the northern part of the Jutland peninsular in large numbers as did the Saxons who lived in the southern part of the peninsular! Our people are moving further into the Jutland peninsular as well as the northern parts of Engel-land!*

Since our people have settled in the Anglen area, we have studied the Engel longships and vastly improved the design of their longship. The main modification has been us replacing the keel plank used on the Engel longships with a "T" shaped keel on our longships. That modification has made our ships much more stable during rough weather!

We have developed the longship to the point where like the Engel ships before them, they can be propelled using sails or oars or both. Also, our longships have a shallow draft, and they can now carry up to one hundred men in each ship. These ships also allow us to take our forces into very shallow water, which allows us to land on most shores and keep our ships secure.

Here in Engel-land we have commandeered the horses of the English, and we are using the English horses against them by mounting our infantry so that they can be a very fast reaction force to anything the English try to do. You, Ivor-the-Boneless shall in the early morning in two days from now, take your warriors as well as those of Sigurd Snake-in-the-Eye, Björn Ironside and Halfdan Ragnarsson and look for the English forces of King Alfred, who is fast becoming a real pain in my arse!"

Ivar-the-Boneless was given that name because he was a mountain of a man who had a lot of strength and, he was very fat. Because of his huge appetite, he was constantly eating, and he appeared to be almost shapeless, other than having a large belly over-hanging his belt and he looked like a walking heap of blubber. He also had a vile temper.

He now directly spoke this king. He said, *"King Guthrum, I am most eager to close with and kill these English! I think that Alfred and his warriors have kept us here in this fortified position for far too long! I will welcome the chance to kill them all as slowly and as painfully as is possible! I want to make them pay for interrupting our lines of supplies and making us do without many of the things that we need!*

They have a very strange religious practice in that they say their god is kind and that he will forgive them for their sins against him, but they hanged him up on a Roman cross and killed him! What sort of a bullshit god is he if he could not take himself off the cross,

211

save himself and then wreak vengeance upon those who did that to him? By Odin and Thor, it is high time to get rid of very strange religions like that because they are dangerous to us!"

Halfdan Ragnarsson was so called because he was a midget. He was only 1400 mm (four feet) tall and of a thin build. He more than made up for his physical lack of size by having an aggressive nature, and he now spoke. He said, *"I have heard of this King Alfred, it is said that he and his followers have only a small army and that they have retreated into the swamps and the Somerset Tidal marshes. If that is really where they have gone, it cannot be too hard to find them because we will only have to follow the tracks and trails through the marshes. By being careful and observant, we can in fact wipe out the English by ambushing them, like they have done on numerous occasions to our resupply columns. I want to be with the warriors who wipe out the English!"* That sentiment was echoed by Sigurd Snake-in-the-Eye.

Alfred Returns to the Marshes

With his soldiers and his people assembled before him, Alfred spoke. He said, *"Ladies Gentlemen and children of Wessex, as you can see, Adulf and I have returned from our journey to the Danish fort at Chippenham. While we were there, we were disguised as minstrels, and we learned what the Danes are going to try to burn us out of the marshes which are tinder dry now! We shall let them do whatever they like in the marshes because it will be a total waste of time and resources for them. We are all leaving this locality and we shall firstly go to Wessex where we will organise defences against the expected attack on Devonshire by the brother of Halfdan Ragnarsson and his one thousand eight hundred and forty warriors!*

They will arrive in twenty-three longships, and they shall land at Devonshire. They are so arrogant that they think that they shall have an easy victory! What they do not know is that we shall be there waiting for them and that we shall do to them what they are planning to do to us! That force of Danes in the longships is going to have a large black flag which they call the 'Raven' preceding their forces. I want you to not just wipe out the Danish forces, I also want their flag called the 'Raven' captured so that we can display it as a token of the fact that when Danes come to our country, not only did we kill them, but we have taken what belongs to them!"

The Danes did not know the marshes and mistakenly believed that they could simply go in there and learn the lay of the area whilst there. So, they were seen approaching the river side of the marshes, and Alfred's plan of engaging the Danes was put into effect. A section[37] of infantry bared their behinds and bent over while patting themselves on their bums and calling out to the Danes.

They yelled, *"Hey you fucking Danes – look here, this is what we, the English think of you, you pack of invading arseholes!"* That had the desired effect of enraging the Danes and they chose to give chase to the English. As the Danes closed the gap between them and the English, the English ran off, but they always stopped and make sure that the Danes could see where they were going. As they got deeper into the swampy marshes, the English suddenly disappeared. The pursuing Danes now found that there were no longer any tracks or trails which they could follow and that most of the ground around them would not support their weight. There was much black slim and, areas of quicksand.

Typically, the next thing to happen was that a trumpet blast was heard by the English and that resulted in Englishmen rising from beneath the water under which they were hiding while

---

[37] A small sub-unit in modern times, comprising ten men, commanded by a junior non-commissioned officer such as a corporal in the case of Australian and British armies. In the case of the USA army, the sub-unit is called a squad, and it is an eight-man unit commanded by sergeant.

breathing through hollow reeds. They then began shooting their arrows and throwing their spears into the areas occupied by the Danes, or else the English attacked the Danes using battle-axes or swords. In all cases where the Danes were engaged, they were slaughtered without mercy because the Danes had no mercy for the English people.

In 878 A.D., by constantly using guerrilla tactics the English attempted to draw the Danish invaders into areas where the English had the advantage of knowing the countryside and trails through the marshes, Alfred and his small army were quickly becoming a real menace to King Guthrum and his Daish Vikings. During an evening feast, King Guthrum was heard to exclaim loudly.

He yelled, *"Is there no-one who can rid me of the bloody nuisance called King Alfred and his small army of English! They are a real menace in that they are launching attacks upon our lines of communication and disrupting them! We have lost much in the way of food and weapons resupply to the English foes, and I want some-one here to go and wipe out the English menace to our security here in Chippenham!"*

He had barely finished talking when he found himself approached by "Ivar-the-Boneless, who began to speak to him. He said, *"Your majesty, give me some good commanders and enough capable men and I will drive the English out of their swamps and marshes where they are currently hiding like skulking cowards, only coming out at night or at other times which favour their attacks upon our supply and communication lines. If you give me the commanders of Björn Ironside, Halfdan Ragnarsson and Sigurd Snake-in-the-Eye and their men, I will wipe out the English upstart called Alfred and his followers!"*

That prompted King Guthrum to speak to "Ivar-the-Boneless." He said, *"Ivar, what is it that makes you think that you* can be successful in closing with and killing the English when many others have tried to do that and failed? They only found that Alfred defeated them! Just what makes you think that you can be successful where so many others have failed and some of them had huge armies?"

Ivar-the-Boneless answered, *"Your majesty, it is now high summer and because of that, much of the marshes where Alfred and his band of Englishmen are taking refuge is tinder dry , the only water that is presently near the marshes is from tidal movements and these are likely to stop for a time, allowing even more drying out of the marshes which are presently covered by long dry reeds which should burn easily! If our forces were to set fire to the reeds in the marshes at the places I have marked on this map of the Somerset Tidal Marshes, we should be able to trap the English between here and the river."* As he was saying that he was pointing at the map he had laid upon the table near him.

He continued with, *"When we set fire to the marsh reeds, it should drive the English towards the river at least. When they get to the river, they will find that instead of being safe, they will be facing Danish Vikings and then they will all die! Now then your majesty, do you give me approval to launch this type of attack upon the English?"*

King Guthrum answered, *" 'Yes Ivor-the-Boneless', if you can wipe out Alfred, you have my permission to try doing that, but also, I would like you to know that the brother of Halfdan Ragnarsson is going to take his one thousand and eight-hundred-and-forty-man army force to Devonshire in Wessex and he will take it from the English. After we have taken that from them, and you and your warriors have burned the English out of their hiding places in the Somerset Marshes, we will again go forth and make the lives of the English people even more miserable than it is now by taking all the food from them as well as killing their priests while we burn down their churches and all other places of religious belief! Now stop talking, eating, and drinking and go out there and get things done! Time is wasting!"*

And so, Alfred and his small army soon arrived at Devonshire where the English immediately began preparing for the arrival of the Danish forces under the command of the brother of Halfdan Ragnarsson. Alfred wanted to make sure that his little easily force could throw the incoming enemies back into the sea, killing as many of them as possible and take their black flag which they liked to call 'The Raven.' Alfred called for Adulf to be sent to him. Soon afterwards, Adulf arrived and asked, *"What is it that you want done Alfred?"*

Alfred replied, *"Adulf, take whomever you need to help you build at least ten four wheeled catapults which can throw large rocks at the enemy. Make sure that the bucket part of each of the ten catapults that holds and throws the rocks and other materials is metal lined with metal so that we can cover the rocks with a mixture of pig fat, straw and tar and set fire to the rocks just before we throw them at the enemy longships. As soon as the catapults begin to throw the burning rocks at the enemy longships, our archers will launch a barrage of flaming arrows at the enemy longships and enemy warriors on the battle-field. While all of that is happening, I will lead a cavalry charge straight into the middle of the enemy army! That way, our combined attacks will completely surprise the enemy and even destroy most of the enemy forces other than the ones who manage to get back to their longships and escape by sailing away!"*

Very early in the morning of three days later, the twenty-three longships which were transporting the one-thousand-eight-hundred-and-forty warriors of Halfdan Ragnarsson, and his brother were silently being rowed towards the shores near Devonshire. Alfred knew that the attack would be staged at this hour of the night and because of that he doubled the number of English sentries on duty. He had also ordered that each sentry was to be relieved from duty after completing two hours on watch. That way, the sentries would remain both fresh and alert.

While it was still dark at about an hour before the morning twilight, an alert sentry was looking toward the coast when he saw the very distinct silhouettes of Viking Longships. They were visible because the cloud cover broke and that allowed a bight moonlight to shine from behind them. The sentry took his horn and sounded three long blasts from it. He also ran around his area of responsibility yelling. He yelled, *"To arms! To arms! The Danish Vikings are coming! To arms!"* As a result, the entire English camp was now on full alert.

Alfred, who like many of his warriors and soldiers was sleeping with his chain mail armour and identifying garments on, immediately got up and went to the forward positions. Upon arrival there, he quickly counted the longships, and he was satisfied that there were twenty-three of them and he correctly assumed that two others may have sunk during extremely rough weather. He now hurried to where Adulf had managed to construct not ten, but sixteen catapults which were positioned along the lines that Alfred had stipulated earlier and that they all had metal lined buckets to hold the rocks covered in pig fat, straw, and tar mixture.

The rocks covered with the mixture were then set alight before being thrown at the enemy on the shore and those still on board the longships by the English catapults. Alfred spoke to Adulf. He said, *"Adulf, did you manage to test-fire the catapults, and do you know their ranges?"* Adulf answered with, *"Of course I do, your majesty! We have tested them, and they can easily reach the longships on the shore, would you like us to rain rocks and fire upon the enemy now or do you want the archers to do their work first?"*

Alfred replied with, *"I have already instructed the archers to assemble and get into position to be ready to rain death and destruction upon the Danes as soon as they hear our trumpets and see our burning rocks fall among the Danes and their longships! Shoot the burning rocks at the Danes now and sound the trumpets immediately!"* Just as he was saying that the first of the burning rocks fell among the longships and some of them were on fire, resulting in their crews abandoning them.

Simultaneously, the trumpets sounded, and the English archers shot their arrows at the longships from which the Daish Vikings were still disembarking. Meanwhile, Alfred had gone to where his cavalry forces were waiting for him. To his soldiers Alfred now spoke. He said, *"Fellow warriors, today we take this war right up to the invading Danes! You are all hereby ordered not to show the Danes any mercy, just like they have not shown any mercy to the English people upon whom these poor excuses for men have already done to our people! Now mount up and draw out your long broadswords, after which we shall charge towards the Viking longships on the shore.*

Do not destroy all the enemy longships as the ones that are still in serviceable condition after this fight will form the beginning of a Royal Navy which will patrol our coasts and wipe out the Danish menace at sea! As of now, we will take the fight to the Danes on both land and sea, so, the more longships and ceols we can get, the better!" That having been said, Alfred who was mounted upon his horse waved his sword at the landing Danes, He yelled, *"Over there, where the longships are, is also our target! We shall wipe out the Danes – charge!"*

Having yelled that, Alfred and his cavalry charged the Danes who were still disembarking from longships despite having burning rocks and arrows falling amongst them. The Dane who was carrying the black flag called 'The Raven' was hit by an English arrow in his left eye and fell to the ground. That black flag was taken up by an English soldier who immediately waved it about, thereby calling a lot of attention to himself by doing so.

That was seen by Alfred who immediately rode up to where the soldier was waving the black flag. Upon reaching him, Alfred said to the soldier, *"Well done soldier, what is your name and rank?"* The soldier replied, *"Your majesty, I am the lowest of the low in rank! My name is John of Brixton!"* Alfred replied, *"John of Brixton, you say that you are the lowest of the low ranks! Well, not anymore! As of now, you shall be a colour sergeant because you have captured the colours of the enemy! I, King Alfred, thank you for this valuable service to England, for you have captured the enemy flag called 'The Raven' by the Danes!"*

The brother of Halfdan Ragnarsson saw that things were going against him. So, he tried to order a retreat to where the longships were under attack by Alfred and his cavalry as well as the English archers and catapults. Although the Danes tried to get away, they found that their way was blocked. The Danes had by now lost two of their longships which were destroyed by the English catapults. Also, the Danes were losing many men because of sustained English arrow attacks upon them.

The losses the Danish Vikings were now so great that the invaders had lost eight hundred and forty men, which was a considerable part of the Danish Viking army. The brother of Halfdan Ragnarsson then ordered a retreat, but not towards the shore where the longships were, but towards King Guthrum at Chippenham. That in turn, made the English rejoice and they fell upon the Danes with great fury and slaughtered most of them. Alfred rejoiced at his victory and now ordered that a strong fortress to be built at Athelney. From that strong point, he and his forces attacked the Danes and constantly disrupted their lines of supply and communications, while always taking care to outnumber the enemy by a ratio of three to one.

Alfred spoke to his followers and re-assured them. He said, *"We have dealt the arrogant Danes a severe body-blow from which they shall have difficulty in recovering! The people of Somersetshire have come out and are now serving in our army, for which I am most thankful. During the weeks after Easter, we are going to Brixton by the eastern side of Selwood and on to Wiltshire and parts of Hampshire that are on this side of the sea!"* Alfred and his army went to those places and Alfred was gratified to see that people came out of their homes and rejoiced that he had beaten the Danes!

Alfred was keenly aware that time was both his greatest friend and his greatest enemy. Therefore, when he and his army arrived at those places they pushed on and proceeded to Heddington. Upon arrival there, Alfred held an orders group with his senior and intermediate officers. He said, *"Gentlemen, get all our men and horses out of sight! We have been marching for days, and it is high time to rest our soldiers and their horses.*

It is now early morning and to again defeat our Danish enemies, we must make war upon them in the very early hours of the morning while it is still dark! I therefore want all men and horses rested and fed! See to it that no alcohol is available to the men and that all of them have serviceable arms and equipment, even if it means that the black-smiths must work all night! At about three hours before the morning twilight, this army shall move towards the enemy fortress, and we shall surround it! When it is time to rise and get ready for the march upon the enemy fort, you shall hear my trumpets sounding and that will be you signal to immediately get up and rouse your men! All men will then have a half hour during which they should eat their rations and drink water. Upon you hearing three trumpet calls close together, you must all move your units and sub-units into position and begin our march upon the enemy!

As usual, I shall be leading you all from front in front of you! Now return to your units or sub-units and see to it that all my orders are carried out to the letter! It is critical that everyone is fully rested. Make sure that sentries our sentries are constantly rotated to keep them fresh and alert! After all, we do not want the Danes to be able to sneak up upon us and give us a hard time!"

That was done and at about four in the morning, Alfred woke up his wife and family and he spoke to his trumpeter. He said, *"Trumpeter, sound two three trumpet calls close together after you have eaten and have had your water. Do that quickly for we must soon move out and start surrounding the enemy position."* The trumpeter did as he had been ordered, and that resulted in three trumpet blasts which resulted in the English army moving towards the enemy fort while it was still very dark with Alfred leading it.

While they were moving forwards in the darkness, the eyes of the English soldier were becoming accustomed to being in the dark and the soldiers could see a little of what was around them, due to moonlight. As the English were becoming accustomed to the darkness, Alfred increased the speed of the march. After two more hours had passed, of what was a night-time forced march, a first scout reported to his superior.

He said, *"Sir, I have seen the enemy fort towards which we are marching. If we keep going at this pace, we should be able to surround it before the morning twilight begins to set in!"*

That information was taken to Alfred who now called for a halt and passed the word down the line that Adulf was to join him immediately. Adulf arrived ad said, *"I am here my king, what is it that you want me to do?"* Alfred said, *Adulf, do your men have the rope and grappling hooks that I ordered all units to have with them?"*

Adulf answered that was indeed the case, where upon Alfred said, *"Good, in fact, very good! Adulf, I want you to now assume command of half of this army and I want you and your men to encircle the Danish fortress from the north and east, while I and the other half of our army encircle the Danish position from the west! When all of our men are in position, we shall use the ropes and grappling hooks to scale the walls of the enemy fort. So far, we Have avoided detection by the Danes, and it is still dark! When you hear a single long trumpet call, begin scaling the walls of the enemy strongpoint. Now return to your half of my army and start putting things into place!* Adulf immediately did as he had been ordered and returned to his men.

A long single trumpet call was heard be the English army as the Danish strongpoint was surrounded. English soldiers were climbing up the walls of the fortress using the aid of ropes which were held in place using the grappling hooks which were put into place by firstly shooting arrows with a lead line attached to them into the top of the fort. After some soldiers had scaled the wall, the soldier concerned then pulled the line up until he got the rope and fastened it to the wall of the fort. Once the English soldiers reached the top of the walls, they engaged all Danes that they saw in battle. Most of the Danes were still asleep while the English were attacking the fort.

As more of the unprepared Danes were slain, the Danish King Guthrum spoke to one of his more courageous messengers. He said, *"Olaf, I want you to go to King Alfred of the English forces and offer him my surrender the condition that he will spare the lives of my remaining warriors and myself. Also tell him that I am willing to have him and his priests baptise me in public and that I am happy* to enter a formal peace treaty type of truce with the English that will be binding upon the Danes!"

That was answered by Olaf who said, *"Yes sir, I will leave immediately!"* Having said that to his king, Olaf left to have his meeting with Alfred. He got as far as the portcullis of the Danish castle, when he decided to obtain a white flag which he could use as a flag of truce to avoid being shoot by English archers. After obtaining the white flag, he proceeded towards the English forces outside of the Danish fort, bearing the white flag.

As the Danish messenger was riding towards the English positions, he was quickly surrounded by English soldiers who brought him before King Alfred. Alfred spoke to Olaf. He said, *"I am Alfred, and I understand that you have an important message for me from King Guthrum of the Danes, so speak now and tell me what it is that you Danes want!"* Olaf said, *"Great King Alfred of the English, my king, Guthrum of the Danish Vikings has authorised me to seek a parley between him and you! He is offering to surrender our great fortress to you on the condition that you shall spare his warriors. He is also offering to convert to Christianity and to be baptised in public which shall lead to more Danes following down this path! Also, he says that a meaningful peace treaty and truce can thus be established between the English and the Danes! I am to return with your answer to these proposals later today, so Alfred, what shall be your answer?"*

King Alfred thought of what he had been told and the possible resulting ramifications that such a peace could bring to the people of England, including his own people in Wessex. So, he replied to Olaf. He said, *"Olaf, very well, you may return to your King Guthrum and tell him that I, Alfred the King of the West Saxons hereby accept what he is offering! My army shall be ordered to cease hostile actions against the Danes as soon as the entire forces of King Guthrum surrender and hand your castle over to me! That is also conditional upon Guthrum at once converting to the Christian faith immediately and becoming baptised in public in twenty-one days from today!*

Make sure that he knows that he must go to Aller, which is near Athelney, and he must be attended by thirty of his worthiest men who shall all be unarmed. When he thus attends as stipulated by me, then I shall become his sponsor, and his baptism will take place at Wedmore. As well, I fully expect all Danes to honour the treaty into which we shall enter! As part of my conditions for peace between the English and the Danes, the Danes shall immediately give up the provinces of East Anglia and Northumbria to me! That shall be followed by the Danes moving to other areas! If you Danes break the treaty, then I shall wipe you out, no matter where you go or who you are!

No sooner had Alfred said that, than a messenger hurried to him and delivered a message. He said, *"Your majesty, your queen has ordered me to find you and inform you that she wants you to be with her because she is frightened!"* That caused the highly strung Alfred who was laying down the terms of the Danish surrender to exclaim, *"Oh fucking hell, now what?! Bloody women, they sure know when to bring bullshit into things! Return to Queen Ealhswith and tell her that even though she is my wife and the queen of Wessex, she must remain where I have ordered, and she must do everything possible to help to defeat the Danish enemy, and she must also fight against the invaders! You are to take that set of armour over there as well as that battle-axe and give them to her. Tell her she must now also fight! When you have done that, stay with her and help her out in any fighting that becomes necessary".*

Before returning to his wife, Alfred concluded the negotiations of the surrender to the English of King Guthrum's forces and enjoying the sight of the Danes complying with his demands. And so, King Guthrum was baptised at Wedmore, and he was sponsored by King Alfred of England. Both men stayed at Wedmore for twelve nights. During that time, Alfred was honoured by Guthrum who also gave him and his attendants many presents. Many Danes refused to become Christians and later met at Hastings and left from there by ships to area of France now called Normandy. That was followed by the Danes leaving Chippenham and going to the area around Cirencester. After that, for some time, peace was enjoyed by many of the English population, regardless of whether they were English or Danes.

Danish Pirates Harass the English

In year 882 A.D., a messenger arrived at Alfred's court, and he very excitedly demanded to be brought before Alfred, saying that he was the bearer of important news. He was soon brought before Alfred and upon seeing Alfred seated upon his throne, the messenger prostrated himself before Alfred saying, *"Mighty King Alfred the Great of England, a great calamity has befallen our people in the areas of Kent and Thanet Island! Both places are being beset by pirates and sea-rovers whom most people believe to be either Danish Vikings or else outlaws of the same people! Our people in the places that I have mentioned and in other places must contend with almost nightly raids and assaults by these pirates!"*

Alfred said, *"Messenger, what is your name and from where did you just come?"* The messenger replied, *"Your majesty, my name is Atheldann Markel, and I have come to you as quickly as I could ride my horse from Kent. The pirates that I speak of appear to have taken up residence upon the Isle of Wight and on Thanet Island and some other parts of Kent. Your people are suffering from the activities of the sea-rovers and pirates, and they beg you to protect them and put end to the pirates!*

225

Alfred was alarmed by this news, and he said, *"Atheldann Markel, I thank you for informing us that there are pirates who may be Danish outlaws or even Danes operating against us with the full knowledge of the Danish kings presently here in England! If it turns out that the Danish kings presently living among us know of these pirates and are either aiding them or are benefitting by the actions of the pirates against us, then it means that the Danes have broken the truce between them and us! If that is the case, then the situation is intolerable, and we must take immediate action! The Danish kings can wait until we know for certain if they have broken the truce or not. What is certain and most important right now is that we take the initiative and wipe out the sea-rovers. We shall use the twenty-one Danish Viking longships that we captured from the Danes at Devonshire some time ago!"*

Alfred now called for his commanders to join him and when they arrived, he spoke to them. He said, *"Gentlemen, as you will recall, when we captured the longships from the Danes, I said that these longships would be the beginning of my new 'Royal Navy'. The time to do that and completely refurbish the longships and select crews for them as well as training them is here now! I want those of you who have experience in the sailing and the military uses of ships to come forward and if you know of other men who have such experience and are both capable and trust-worthy, let me and my staff know who they are and where to find them! Also let them know that the 'Royal Navy' is being formed and that we need warriors with sailing capabilities to staff the Royal Navy!*

This body of sea-bore warriors shall have the job of assaulting the crews of pirate vessels and the ships of all enemy forces. The specialised warriors shall be completely under the control of the 'Royal Navy' and the members of the sea-borne warrior units shall be known as 'Special Warriors[38]' I urgently need at least twenty-one men who are fearless commanders and can navigate as well as handle ships to immediately fill the roles as captains of our first navy ships! These men will also have the responsibility of selecting their crews and training them! The captains of the ships shall also be the commanders of the sea-borne warriors! Where there are to be joint sea-born and land force attacks upon enemy forces, the officers of the 'Royal Navy' shall outrank the officers of the land-based army!"

Alfred now called for his confederate, Adulf. When he arrived, Alfred said, "Adulf, you have had a lot of experience in embarking and disembarking ships. You have experience in leading attacks upon enemy positions on land and you can approach an enemy ship and wipe out its crew! I now have both a major job and a new appointment for you. Firstly, let us discuss your new appointment, as of now, you shall command both the army and the 'Royal Navy'.

I want you to personally select and train all the members of the newly formed sea-borne 'Special Warrior' units. I want these men to always specialise in making sea-borne attacks on both shipping and land-based targets where-ever they may be found! So, the skill of navigation will be of extreme importance in the training of these men. This has been made necessary by the activities of pirates who are giving my people on the Isle of Wight, Thanet Island and Kent a hard time. It is possible that the pirates are in fact working with the Danish kings we have allowed to settle in England and to co-rule our country, subject to the leadership of myself and Wessex! If it is found that the Danish kings are working with the pirates, then we shall make war upon them, and drive them out!

---

[38] Centuries later, these 'Special warriors' operating from ships of the 'Royal Navy' would become known as 'Royal Marines'.

I want you to quickly and completely train men to operate form our ships by both night and day. Make sure that they constantly practice the interception, boarding and capture of enemy ships at sea and within our own areas! If an enemy ship cannot be taken over by our own crews, it must be sunk! There is to be no deviation from that! I need you to these special warriors ready for action ten days from now! In ten days, I will personally lead the 'Royal navy' ships in a search and destroy mission against the sea-rovers who are harassing my people on the Isle of Wight, Thanet Island and Kent! My people shall have safety and security, that I swear by God the Father, his son, Jesus Christ the Saviour, and the Holy Spirit!"

Adulf went ahead and trained the special warriors who were under the command of the officers of the Royal Navy. The idea of soldiers operating from ships being under the command of the navy was at first resisted by army commanders who felt that all soldier duties should be conducted by their members and therefore commanded by army officers. However, they ended up accepting what was ordered and so, the tradition of the Royal Navy being the senior service began. On the eighth day after the training had begun, Adulf reported to Alfred. He said, *"Your majesty, I have the pleasure of reporting to you that the special warriors whom you asked to be trained in assaulting enemy ship and land-based targets from Royal Navy ships are now trained to my expectations and they are performing their duties well! I consider them all to be ready for action!"*

This news overjoyed Alfred who now spoke. He said, *"Excellent! We sail immediately for Thanet Island; I have been informed that the pirates are now living there and that they are a permanent menace to my people! That cannot be allowed to continue!"* With that stated, Alfred and the members of the Royal Navy as well as the new grouping of special warriors boarded the waiting twenty-one longships and then they set sail for Thanet Island.

The naval warrior battle group had been underway for some time and Thanet Island was in sight when the lookout of the lead ship called out, *"Four enemy ships dead ahead!"* Upon hearing that, King Alfred ordered, *"Steer towards the lead ship of the pirates and surround all the Danish longships! Now that we have them in our grasp, we will kill all the Danes other than the ones we select to obtain information from! Give the Danes the same mercy that they gave our people on Thanet Island and other places! Just kill them!"*

The English ships drew ever closer to the Danish pirates. Then, the English crews threw ropes with grappling hooks attached to their ends onto the Danish ships and then pulled on the ropes util the English and Danish ships were tied together. Next, the English Special Warriors boarded the Danish pirate ships and engaged the pirates in hand-to-hand combat. That resulted in the crews of the first two pirate ships being butchered to the last man and then their ships falling into the hands of the English naval force. On the other two Danish pirate ships, the pirates resisted the English for some time, but at last, with their crews' strength being severely cut, and wounded and bleeding, they finally surrendered to Alfred, who now had another four longships to add to his growing navy.

In 883 A.D., Pope Marinus sent King Alfred the "Lignum Domini", which was a golden cross studded with gems and it represented the opening vision of "The Dream of the Rood". The Holy Rood being the scene of the crucifix in which Jesus Christ died. It was used in church services and had many copies of it made for use as items on church alters.

In the same year, Alfred said to his son called Edward-the-Elder and to his Grandson called Athelstan, *"It is time for us to take alms to Rome! I need to have two very capable men to do this for me and I would very much like it if you, Edward my son and your son, Athelstan, could do this for me as that way, I can concentrate on matters here."*

Edward replied to his father. He said, *"Sir, I shall do whatever you decide, you already know that, but consider this, the Danish enemy has an army near London, and I feel that I shall be of more use to you here than by going to Rome with alms! I urge you to consider sending my son and his friend called Sighelm to Rome in my place, thus leaving me available to assist you in the suppression of the Danish invaders if that has to again be done, for I do not trust those Danish heathens!"*

Having heard his son, Alfred agreed with him and so, Sighelm and Athelstan went to Rome carrying the alms from Alfred. After they returned to England, both men went to London and while there, they attended church services and performed their vows before God. Next, they both were engaged in watching the Danish army near London. During these times, Alfred successfully engaged all comers, and he extended his dominion of England to all areas that were not held by the Danes.

Speaking to his son, Edward-the-Elder, he said, *"My son, we must act to ensure that we can unite all Englishmen against the invading Danes who should not be here! Now, there is a truce in place between us and them whereby I guarantee that I shall not interfere with the territory currently held by them and they have guaranteed that they shall likewise nor interfere with us or perform hostile actions against us!*

While all of that appears to be fine, I do not trust the heathens to keep their word and I have the feeling in my bones that sooner or later, they shall break the truce and then they shall again attempt to conquer us! For those reasons, we must be ready to fight them! To ensure that the Angles to the east and north of us are in fact loyal Englishmen, we shall go out in the morning to where the Angles are! We leave at first light of the morrow with our entire army!"

Alfred and his son Edward led their army towards the Angles at first light of the following day. Together they marched onwards and finally reached the territory of the Angles. The Angles when they were informed that King Alfred of Wessex was now among them and that he would from this time onwards take over the government of their country, rejoiced that finally, they had in charge of them the man who would lead them to liberty!

Alfred was approached by his son, Edward who was in the company of another man. He said to Alfred, *"Father, this is Ethelred, he is an Angle nobleman, and he says that he would like to keep the main city of Mercia called London away from the Danes."* Ethelred now spoke to Alfred. He said, *"Great King Alfred of Wessex and all of England, as your son has told you, I am called both Ethered and Ethelred! I am a noble of the Angles. What he does not yet know is that I also am a noble of Mercia and I am from the area around London!*

I hereby pledge my loyalty to you and Wessex and all of England! I also pledge before God that my army is now yours and that I swear total allegiance to you and England! I understand that your forces are watching the Danes around London. I think it will be a lot easier for you to hold back the Danes from again threatening parts of England if you were to announce in public that you have granted to me the city of London in perpetuity!" Alfred said, *"Nobleman Ethelred of Mercia, I hereby gladly accept what you have proposed!"*

Alfred then went and introduced his daughter, called Aethelflaed. He said, *"Ethelred or Ethelred, this is my daughter in whom I am well pleased. Her name is Aethelflaed, and I am sure that the two of you can work together to make the union of Wessex and Mercia becoming the greater part of England. Your approaching marriage will be organised by the church hierarchy and shall be at the location and time of their choosing. Do you agree to this?"*

Ethered answered, *"Yes, I do agree!"* that made Alfred happy, and he said, *"Now then, it has been reported to me that the East Angles and Northumbrians are currently plotting rebellions against me! I need you to go to where these people are and sort out the traitors from the faithful. As some of these people have been traitors before, I want you to put down the rebellions now, and I do not care how you successfully sort the faithful citizens from the traitors! Just do it!"*

Ethered was as good as his word, and he conducted himself equally with both valour and fidelity. He conducted a series of operations against both the East Angles and the Northumbrians who were plotting rebellion against Alfred. That resulted in the plotters being exposed and dealt with by having to give hostages to King Alfred. After England had enjoyed thirteen years of peace and tranquillity, and the productiveness of her soil, the pests of the northern barbarians returned, laying waste to some to the countryside and killing many English people. The Danish invaders split their army into halves which resulted in one half of their army making war upon the English in the East, while the second half of the pagan army went to Rochester and surrounded that city.

Battles at Rochester

Soon, the Danish army near Rochester had built a fortress around themselves and from that, they began to harass the English. An alderman called Evan Roberts was holding an earnest discussion with some fellow aldermen and some of the sentries of the city. He said, *"For some reason, you people do not appear to be* appreciating the reality of our city's situation! Some of you appear to think that there is no real problem and that the Danish invaders are somehow not the violent pagan marauders that they really are! None of you appear to have any idea of what these arseholes are capable of!

They will in due course come into Rochester and then kill as many of our males as possible, other than the ones they want to use as salves, and that will be followed by them raping our women and killing all our children. If you think that you can parley with these monsters, then you are very much mistaken! Now look over there! The Danes have built a fort near this city, and they shall use it to keep us bottled up in here until they launch attacks to wipe all of us out! We have the chance to get volunteers to be messengers to our King Alfred, whom I believe is currently at Wedmore. I am therefore calling for volunteers to accompany me on this mission to get the help of Alfred and his armies to save our city, our women and our children!" Having said that, he took out his longsword from its sheath and used it to mark a line in the soil.

Having done so, he said, "We must have defence against the enemy who has surrounded us and that means that most of you must remain here and defend this place! The leader of the city garrison called Ethelwalch shall be in command of the entire city for as long as I am away on this mission to bring back King Alfred and his army! Ethelwalch will brief you later about what you must all do. I am now calling for twenty volunteers to accompany me on this quest to find our king and return here with him and his army! We must leave when it is dark and it must be tonight, before the Danes can complete their fortress and have their forces totally encircling us!

He had barely finished speaking when twenty-five young men crossed the line which he had drawn in the soil with his sword. That pleased him immensely and so he said, "Gentlemen, go to the *city stables and obtain your horses. After you have seen Commander Ethelwalch and he has provided you with chain-mail armour, shields and swords, report tome back here! Be as quick as you all can so that we can leave to obtain the help of King Alfred and his army!"* His orders were followed by the volunteers, and they were soon all armed, horsed and waiting alderman Roberts at the stables. He was wearing his own chain-mail armour and was armed with the old-style two-handed battle-axe so favoured by the early Saxons prior to now.

Next, he yelled more orders. He yelled, *"Form up in columns of two! I need two horsemen to act as our first and second scouts! Those two positions will be interchanged with other warriors every two hours to relieve stresses upon the scouts! The two scouts are to swap between their positions of forward and second scout on a half hour basis so that they remain alert and capable!"* With that having been said he now ordered, *"By the right and at a trot, forward-ho!"* So it was that the small force left Rochester during the night and were not discovered by the enemy.

They had ridden for about an hour when the forward scout said to the second scout, *"I have just located a small group of Danish Vikings ahead of us! I need you to return to the main group with the alderman and inform him of this! Tell him that I think we can easily take these Danes because there are only about ten of them. They are feasting and drinking now near their campfires, and I would like to wipe them out to repay them for what they have done to my brother and the members of his family!"*

The second scout then left to fetch alderman Roberts while the first scout kept watch upon the area where the Danes were eating and drinking. The second scout finally was back with the main group of warriors, and he had found the alderman. He said, *"Sir, my forward scout has found a small enemy encampment not far from here. There are about ten Viking warriors at the encampment. The forward scout is watching the enemy, and he says that they are both feasting and drinking. There are no sentries in place that could be seen, and the Vikings appear to be drunk!"*

Roberts firstly proceeded to inform all his twenty-five men that he would lead them in a cavalry charge straight into the enemy encampment and that total silence was required from all warriors while they advanced towards the enemy. He then spoke to the second scout. He said, *"Thank you for informing me of this, with you leading the way, we shall now all silently ride our horses to the enemy camp! As we get closer to the enemy, you must find the forward scout who will then guide us to the enemy. When we get there, we shall all close with and kill all of them because prisoners will only slow us down! Therefore, we shall kill all Danes we find at their camp!"*

With the second scout leading, the small English force set off to find the forward scout. Before much longer, they found him and alderman Roberts spoke to him. The forward scout said, *"Sir, I have now I have located two sentries whom I did not see before. These men are the only ones who have not been drinking and who are quite sober. They are the only ones in the Danish camp who can challenge us! However, they will be no problem because I know exactly where they are located and what they are doing! Look over there towards the east, under a tree and you will see one of the sentries! The other one is just behind that low tent. They can best be dealt with by us sneaking up on them and then cutting their throats!"*

It made alderman Robert happy that he was about to engage in offensive action against the Danes. He said, *"Very well, scout, you have the rank of non-commissioned officer, so go and obtain some help from your comrades and cut the throats of the two enemy sentries like you have suggested or simply shoot arrows into them!"*

The forward scout now went ahead and obtained help from others and together, they killed both enemy sentries.

Roberts now went silently to his men and quietly spoke to each of them. He said, *"Quietly come with me and see for yourselves what we must do this night."* Having said that, he led them toward the edge of the trees surrounding a small clearing where the Danes were feasting and very drunk by now. He quietly said to each man, *"We shall all quietly go back to our horses, mount them and then quietly ride back here! When we all return to this point, we shall perform a sudden cavalry charge into the clearing and wipe out the Danes! None of you are to do anything before I order 'Charge!'"*

That was followed by the Englishmen quietly returning to their horses, mounting them, and then riding to the enemy camp. Upon arriving at the enemy camp, the alderman ordered, *"Charge! Kill every fucking Dane you find here!"* that was quickly accomplished and so, the English resumed their journey to Wedmore where King Alfred and his army were known to be.

Finally arriving at Wedmore in the afternoon, the small English force rejoiced that they would soon be with King Alfred. Evan Roberts again sent for the forward scout known as Ethelwald. When he arrived, Roberts said, *"Scout, I need you to once again use your amazing ability to find people and things! This time, I need you to find King Alfred and to organise a meeting between him and myself immediately! Please do that without delay because the very future existence of the people of Rochester depends on how quickly we can relieve that city from the attacks of the enemy Danes!"*

That was followed by the scout saying, *"Yes sir, I shall go immediately to locate and speak to King Alfred. Where will you be when I return? I must know where to find you in case the King wants to see you immediately! In fact, sir, I believe that it would be for the best if you come with me right from the start! That way, you could speak to the king as soon as we find him!* The alderman considered that for some time, and then he spoke. He said, *"Ethelwald, that was sound thinking on your part, so very well, let us go forth and find the king together!"*

Soon afterward, both men were dismounted close to a church where King Alfred was performing his devotions to God and praying to the Saviour, Jesus Christ, while giving thanks to God for his victories over the Danish Vikings. As the two men were entering the church, they could both hear King Alfred pray. He prayed, *"Heavenly Father, who is all powerful, I, Alfred, your servant upon earth in England, hereby beseech you to grant me even more outstanding victories against the Danish invaders who you have let loose among us here in England as a form of punishment for our past sins and those of some of our former kings who have wronged you by having sexual relationships and intercourse with the nuns of monasteries thus committing adultery against you! I realise that is so because the nuns are in fact the brides of God and therefore anyone who has sex with them is committing adultery! I, Alfred shall do all in my power to put things right, and for that, I need your love and guidance! Lord God, tell us what it is that you want me to do!"*

That was followed by a period of total silence, and no-one expect King Alfred, the alderman and the forward scout heard God say the following: *"Alfred, Alfred, this is the Lord, your God and I am telling you that your people at Rochester are in urgent need of your presence. The Danes have completed the building of their fortress near Rochester and even as we speak, they are building walls right around that city. They are planning on laying siege to Rochester to make the people surrender due to their suffering from having no food or water!*

You and your army are to go to Rochester and rescue your people! Right now, in this very church and towards the front door

237

of it, are two men from Rochester whom I have sent to you! They are alderman Evan Roberts, and his forward scout called Ethelwald. Both men are highly capable, and they shall be of great assistance to your task of freeing your people at Rochester!

The men I have sent you know the way through the Danish Vikings who are surrounding the city, and they shall guide you and your army into an advantageous position, which will enable the English to overcome the Danes! Now Alfred my son, rise and walk towards the front door of this church and meet alderman Evan Roberts and his forward scout, and discuss the strategic position of your city called Rochester!"

Alfred began walking towards the front of the church, as he got closer to the alderman and his forward scout, Evan Roberts said, *"Your majesty, we are from your city of Rochester, which urgently needs your help! The Danes have already built their fortress near the city, and they are currently building a wall around it, to more successfully bottle up the residents of Rochester and then they plan to starve the people of that place into submission! We know ways of getting through the positions of the Danes surrounding the city and we shall guide you and your army through the positions of the Vikings and into the city! I am sure that just the sight of you and the English army will be sufficient to give hope back to the people! If you were to also bring food for the population with you, then so much the better!"*

King Alfred said, *"Thank you both, gentlemen! Go to your men and horses and make sure that they are all rested and fed well enough to make a forced march to Rochester. After all our men are rested and re-armed where necessary, we shall load food relief for my people at Rochester and go directly to that city. I am hoping that will be in two hours or less from now!*

Yesterday, I engaged an artist to paint the image of the blessed Virgin Mary on the inside of my shield because God appeared and spoke to me, using the image of Saint Peter! He told me, "Alfred, when you go into Rochester, the people shall receive you as their liberator and they shall support you in whatever you must do to retake the city from the Danish heathens!

I want you to do what Arthur of the Britons centuries ago and have the image of the Virgin Mary painted on the inside of your shield! When you lead your army into battle against the heathens, I want you to kiss the image of the Holy Mary, Mother of God! See to it that all your soldiers can see you do it and tell them that you are doing so! That shall then cause me to instil a great fear into the hearts of the Danish heathen invaders who have surrounded Rochester! As soon as you have kissed the image of the Holy Virgin, I shall create the sight of a thousand angels leading your army and they will be preceded by the cross of Jesus Christ. That sight shall be seen by everyone. that in turn, will give the English army hope while also demoralising the Danes!

As you advance upon the enemy, the angels shall be singing, "Hosanna on the Highest!" See to it that you have much more than the normal number of archers! In fact, I want every other man to at least have a bow and twenty arrows and to use all their arrows against the enemy before attacking the Danes with swords and battle-axes! Do what I have told you, and again, you shall be the victor! As soon as you have wiped out the invaders, you and your army must go into the harbours and take over all enemy shipping that you find there. The ships that you find must be added to your Royal Navy and they must be crewed by your people! Your army shall be victorious!"

These words by King Alfred impressed both men of Rochester to the point where both Evan Roberts and Ethelwalch said, *"Thank you Lord God, for your generous gift of King Alfred who is the deliverer from foreign oppression by Danish heathens and you representative on earth!"* And so, it happened that the English now fed their soldiers and horses and closely examined their weapons, making sure everything was serviceable that where items were found not to be serviceable, they were replaced. The English army was resupplied and while that was happening, Alfred was with the artist who was painting the image of Saint Mary onto the inside of King Alfred's shield. Alfred was most impressed with what he saw. He said to the artist, *"I am most impressed with this fine work that you have performed for me and God on this day! Your reward for this amazing work is the payment of one hundred silver pieces."* With that having been said to the artist, Alfred went to a church and spoke to a priest he found there.

He approached the priest and told him about how Alfred had the vision from God and that Alfred now needed to obtain an official blessing of the image of the Virgin Mary painted on the inside of Alfred's shield. So, he said, *"Holy Father, I am King Alfred, the representative of God in England! God has told me to have this image of the Holy Mother of God painted on the inside of my shield and that it must be blessed by you! I must be seen to be kissing the picture of Mary on the inside of my shield before I and the English army attack the heathens! After that, I shall liberate not just Rochester, but all of England between here and London!"*

That was answered by the priest, who said, *"Your majesty, I am most happy to bless the image of the virgin Mary on the inside of your shield! Now please kneel so that I can begin the blessing and we shall immediately proceed!* Without answering the priest, Alfred knelt and that was immediately followed by the priest touching the top of Alfred's head with his right hand. He raised his left hand towards the sky. The priest now said, *"Holy Father who is in Heaven, I beseech you to bless this image of the mother of God which is painted on the inside of the shield of King Alfred! I also beg you to bless our King Alfred and his army and that you shall give us the victory while ensuring that we have minimal casualties! May your power and love for the English people be concentrated in this king and help him to do your will in England!"*

That was now followed by King Alfred re-joining this army and upon being re-united with his men he ordered, *"Get Alderman Evan Roberts and his men here immediately, they must guide us past the heathens as we enter Rochester!"* The alderman and his followers were quickly located and brought before Alfred. The king now ordered, *"Form into columns of twos, with alderman Roberts and his followers leading us, we go into Rochester city where we shall liberate that place from the heathens! At a trot, Forward-Ho!"*

Alfred and his entire army left for Rochester and were guided past the Danes. When they arrived in Rochester, it resulted in the population of that place coming out of their houses and rejoicing that King Alfred the liberator was among them with food for the hungry. Everyone knew that the siege of the city would soon be lifted and that gave the people renewed heart. After entering the city with his army, Alfred ordered, *"Bring the commander of the sentries to me, and also, the garrison commander called Ethelwalch, as we have much to discuss!"*

After some time had elapsed, both the commander of the sentries and the garrison appeared before Alfred. He said, *"Gentlemen, we have much to do! Firstly, I need to know your current tactical situations and I also need your suggestions of how to improve them using local resources and people as well as my army! To start off with, let me hear your thoughts about the enemy, and their strengths and weaknesses as well as the strengths and weaknesses of our own units! So, could you please start this discussion by letting me know things from your perspective, Ethelwalch!"*

Ethelwalch replied, *"Your highness, we have managed to keep the Danes out of the city so far, but we are under great stress from having little food and our water supply is running low! Many of my soldiers are weak from hunger and it is just as well that you are here to aid us in this fight, otherwise it would become yet another victory for the heathens! I implore you to launch a strike against the Danes very soon, my king because you will find that they have some longships on the shore near here. You may want to add these ships to the Royal Navy!"*

Alfred Wreaks Havoc on the Danes

Alfred simply said, *"Oh, I see, I shall deliberate that matter very soon!* He the spoke to the commander of the sentries of Rochester. He said, *"And what are your observances about the enemy, Lothiar? Do you have any recommendations of how to beat them?"* Lothiar said, *"Yes, your highness, my sentries have been getting tried out by the Danish pests on both a daily and nightly basis! They have not tried to get into Rochester every day and night, but they have been sending small armed units to the walls and other defences every few days or nights to probe our defences!*

It looks to me like they are conducting their probing to get a complete picture of our defence because they are always trying out different lines of attack and then quickly withdrawing only to return with another probing attack in a different area later. I observed the same warrior leader being in the lead of six different probes on different areas around the city walls. I know that it is the same leader, because one of the horns on his helmet is missing!"

That caused Alfred to immediately meditate upon the situation and soon afterwards he said, *"Gentlemen, in the very early morning of the morrow, I shall be silently going amongst my commanders and waking them for battle against the enemy. The commanders who are wakened by me will then awaken all their subordinates and get their men ready for battle! Ensure that no alcohol is available to any of our soldiers tonight! I want all soldiers to be completely sober and fit for the coming fight! We shall all be facing the Danes in the morning, so see to it that everyone has serviceable weapons and that everyone is rested! All damaged or unserviceable weapons are to be immediately replaced by my blacksmiths whom we have with us here in Rochester!"*

While it was still very dark in the very early hours of the following morning, Alfred was up and awakening his commanders. Not only was he dressed, but he was also wearing his chain-mail armour, and he had his large round shield attached to his back. He went from one of his commanders to another, awakening them and urging them to quickly get ready for battle and awaken their subordinates. He next assembled his forces and the garrison of Rochester near the city gates which were close to the enemy. He then ordered that his trumpeters sound many trumpet calls to ensure that the Danes would look toward the English army that was now massing by the city gates.

It was now that he yelled out, *"English warriors of God, the heathen Danish Vikings are over there! They, and they alone are responsible for your house being burned down, your woman being raped, your children being killed and your sons being enslaved! Watch now while I kiss the image of the Virgin Mary on the inside of my shield!"* He now kissed the image of Mary and what happened next struck fear into the hearts of the Danes who were watching.

A bright light appeared in the sky and then the very large cross of Jesus appeared in the company of Angels who were singing "Hosanna on the Highest" trumpets sounded from the sky just as Alfred ordered his trumpeters to begin their trumpet calls. Alfred then ordered, *"Charge"* which was followed by the English all rushing forward and attacking the Danes who fled in terror!

That now enabled Alfred to take the Viking longships that were found on the shore near Rochester and London. He had more fortifications built at both places and then set up is headquarters in London to be nearer to where he needed to be, to continue the fight against the Danes. A few weeks later, a messenger came to Alfred from the fortified positions in Kent with urgent news. Alfred received the messenger and asked him, *"Well Messenger, what appears to be the problem?"* the messenger answered with, *"Your majesty, more Viking pirates have been sighted off the coast near Stourmouth, and some of our observers say that the Vikings have sixteen longships and that we should get your help in dealing with the menace!"*

That immediately resulted in Alfred going into action as he said, *"Well, do not just sit there on your bloody arses, get up and come with me! We are going to teach these pagans a lesson using the Royal Navy, its Special warriors in longships and my army!"* With that said, Alfred led the way to where the ships of his Royal Navy were docked and boarded the command ship. His sub-ordinates from the court were assigned to different ships and then the English fleet set sail. About one hour later, the look-out on Alfred's command ship called out, *"Unknown longships ahead to the south-east! I can see that there are about eight of them in view, but there could be many more of them just past that outcrop of land over there in the south-east!"*

Alfred now called for an orders group to be held between him and his naval commanders. With the meeting now in progress, Alfred spoke. He said, *"Gentlemen, we are hunting the sixteen Danish pirate ships which raided Kent, the Isle of Wright and Thanet Island! I believe the group of Dane ships ahead to be part of the group that we are seeking! Plot the necessary course to intercept them and wipe them out! Once that has been done, we shall locate and the wipe out the remainder of that group of enemies!"*

And so, the first group of eight of the pirate ships was engaged by ships of the Royal Navy which had on board them, the ancient form of Royal Marines, whose job it was to board the pirate ships and then close with and kill the pirate crews. Typically, the English ships would get as close as possible to the pirate ships before ropes with grappling hooks attached to them were thrown across their bows and then pulled tight, allowing the Englishmen join the ships together for long enough for the Special Warriors to completely take over the enemy ship concerned! That continued ship by ship until all the Viking pirate ships had been taken over by the English.

Next, Alfred said, *"Very good, we have eight of the Dane Viking pirate ships in our possession and we still have another eight of them to track down and destroy or else convert into ships of the Royal Navy. I wager that the other eight of them will be found behind that outcrop of land, where I believe them to be hiding! This entire naval group shall now steer towards the outcrop! I want my ships to continuously take note of the distances between our ships and the distance between us and the remaining eight pirate ships. Royal Navy ships are to place themselves in such a manner that it will be impossible for the Vikings to escape! See to it that it is done!*

That was done and it resulted in the English being victorious and enjoying taking much booty from the pirates as well as killing most of them. Because the English had now captured anther eight longships, the strength of the Royal Navy increased by sixteen ships, making King Alfred happy. As the English fleet returned homeward, it encountered another large fleet of Danish Viking pirates and fought them on the same day. This time however, the Danes had the victory, even though the English sailed home anyway both larger than it originally had been and carrying the booty taken from the Danes. It was still the year 885 A.D., and due to the Danes breaking the truce with King Alfred, he completed fortifying the city of London, resulting in the whole English nation turning to him for leadership, other than the part of it which was held captive by the Danes.

Alfred committed the city into the care of Alderman Ethered to hold it for England. King Alfred himself was always leading his forces from in front and therefore, he was present at every action against the Dane invaders. He constantly exposed himself in front of the enemy and was always inspiring and encouraging his men by his own actions, always rallying them, and attacking the enemy himself! The Vikings and other enemies always found that just as they thought that Alfred and his men were beaten, the Englishmen would attack them with undiminished courage and extract revenge for what the enemy had previously done to the English. Alfred's health was terrible. He was always subject to a disorder of the intestines[39] and that condition troubled until he died at the age of fifty.

Alfred, Scholar, Reformer, Lawgiver

It was not just in military service that Alfred was supreme, but also in government. Organising the service due to him from then[40] in year 885 A.D., he scrutinised the administration of justice. What he found alarmed him and he discussed the situation with his queen called Ealhswith and his son called Edward-the-Elder.

So, he said to them, *"My dearest Ealhswith and Edward, I wish to discuss with you both the current laws we have which in my view are too often way-laying the innocent and getting off the guilty!*

---

[39] Various medical doctors have studied Alfred's symptoms and diagnosed that he may have suffered from Crohn's disease.
[40] Followers of noble birth.

We have many judges who are either ignorant of the many things including the law and are corrupt or even both of those things! Many of our people have fallen victim to judges such as these and the people are asking for help in correcting that awful situation! I am now asking each of you for your views on how best to deal with these situations!"

Ealhswith answered with, *"Alfred my dear husband, I think that you should make it law that no-one can be a judge unless he has sound independent financial means, a thorough knowledge of the law and is experienced in legal matters and has the reputation of being as honest as a day is long. He must also be a true supporter of the crown of Wessex and indeed all of England that the Danes do not control!"* She then said, to her son, *"What do you think of this Edward, after you take the crown this sort of thing shall become your problem to deal with, so however your father deals with it now will also affect your rule!"*

Edward now spoke. He said, *"Pappa, I tend to agree with my mother about this. I do agree that the judges should all have independent means wherever possible, but I also think that they must be paid an annual salary for the work that they do. All of them must immediately swear total allegiance to you and if someone refuses then he must be removed from the bench because only royal law enforcement must be tolerated! In fact, if a judge refuses to swear allegiance to you, then he must be charged with treason against you and if he is found guilty of that crime, he should be executed in public so that not only will justice be done, but so that it will be seen to be done!*

I think that with regards to the poor and the weak, that you can further protect them by the passing of laws that will make it illegal for anyone to falsely accuse some else of something that the accuser is guilty of. It would be good to have a standard of behaviour and fair treatment which is binding upon all people, regardless of their rank or station in life!"

Alfred thought about what had been discussed between them and was silent for a time. Then he said, *"Thank you both for your input! I am going to study the principles of lawgiving in the book of Exodus and the codes of Ethelbert of Kent, Ina of Wessex and Offa of Mercia with special attention of the weak and dependent. Once I have done that, I will mediate on this matter and then again discuss it with both of you!"*

Soon after that, Alfred called a meeting of his court and announced, *"I want our language of English to be taught in all schools that I am now opening! I shall be opening ten schools throughout the country to start with. All young freemen who have the means to do so, must learn how to read and write in English and that shall begin immediately! In my own case, I can already read and write our English language as well as Latin. I want our English language to replace Latin as our official written language, and I want as many people as possible to learn English. Our language started off as German, but already there are differences appearing between German and our language! Over time, those differences shall become more marked and pronounced! I hereby inform you all that I am currently translating "The Pastoral Care" by Saint Gregory from Latin into English.*

When that is complete, it shall provide a manual for priests in the instruction of their people!" He went on to enact the following statutes, saying, *"All people must familiarise themselves equally to the religious worship of God and also both military discipline and service to England!"* By saying that, he was effectively saying that people from now on had to be a member of both the church and the military forces.

If someone was accused of a crime, then he was legally bound to produce people from the hundred and anything[41] to become his surety. Those who were unable to find such a surety would dread the severity of the sentence. If the accused made his escape either before or after he had found the surety, all persons of the hundred paid a fine to the king. This regulation resulted in such peace in the country that Alfred ordered golden bracelets to be hung up on a public crossroads where they were seen by all, but no-one dared take the bracelets. Alfred's father, Ethelwulf, established the privileges of the church and they were confirmed by Alfred.

One result of Alfred's interest in church matters was that he received a visit from the Bishop of Sherborn, named as Sighelm. Sighelm spoke to Alfred and said, *"Your majesty, I thank God for your father Ethelwulf who has done so much for the church here in England and I also give thanks to God that you are continuing with your father's great work and that you have confirmed the privileges that he gave to the church! The church needs more money and other resources. I beseech your majesty to continue aiding the church to perform its work. I have been informed that there is much the church can do in India by the giving of God's alms. For my part, I am so overwhelmed by the tales of misfortune in India, that I have sent an ambassador to that place for the purpose of helping to alleviate the suffering there and to help Saint Thomas in spreading the word of God in India!"*

The ambassador of Bishop Sighelm went to India and worked there before returning to England. He brought with him many exotic gems and aromatic spices which abound in India. He also brought with him, part of the cross upon which Jesus Christ

---

[41] In an area known as a hundred, a tything was one tenth part of agricultural or other produce, personal income or profits contributed either voluntarily or as a tax, to support the church and/or government. It could also be any levy of 10% and that could be used for charitable purposes.

died. It was afterwards sent to Pope Manus. Alfred erected monasteries with the first being built at Athelney, near the marshes where he and his forces were hidden from the Danes. The next one was built at Winchester. Alfred spoke to his court.

He said, *"Ladies and gentlemen, we have built some churches and monasteries, the first of these at Athelney is my repayment to God for delivering us all from the evil intentions of the invading Danes! It is only through the grace of God that we managed to not only stay alive, but to inflict severe defeats upon the enemy! That monastery is now in operation, and I hereby order everyone in my court to attend the next religious service there and give thanks for our deliverance!"*

At first, a young man at the court of Alfred objected to having to go to the new monastery at Athelney, and he spoke in anger to Alfred. He said, *"I have no wish to travel to Athelney for anything at all, much less than going there to attend a useless church service! I demand that you release us from this useless order!"* Alfred as usual, took things in his stride and simply said, *"So, you do not think that you should give thanks to God for sparing us from the Danish Vikings and giving us victories over them? Do you truly believe that you could have obtained our successes against the invaders without the help of God? Are you so young and arrogant that you think you can do all the things that God has done for us? For if that is your attitude my boy, then you shall be compelled to leave here immediately as an outcast from my kingdom! Do I make myself clear?"*

The young man now said, *"Yes, your majesty, and I hereby apologise for what I said earlier. I was not aware of how things have happened. Please forgive me Your majesty, for I have been mistaken. I pledge my loyalty to you and Mother church for all time, and I shall never doubt you again sir!"* That caused Alfred to say, *"You are forgiven my boy, now report to the monastery at Athelney and tell the Abbot there that I have sent you to him to do penance for the next seven days in any way that the Abbot sees fit! After you have completed the seven days of penance, you shall return here. In the meantime, the Abbot is being informed of this, and I am sure that he will organise some great work for you to complete. Make sure that you apply yourself well, for I shall hear of what you do!"*

Alfred now once more addressed the members of his court and said, *"The second monastery is now complete at Winchester, and I have named this as 'New Minster'. This place is being run by my appointee of Abbot Grimald who has come to us from Rheims in France via the kind influence of Flaco, who is the archbishop of Rheims. This man shall aid me in my study of literature arts plus he and others shall help me to translate books from other languages into English.*

The monastery at Shaftesbury shall be filled with nuns and my daughter Aethelgifu has been appointed as the Abbess of that place. We are also blessed that from Saint David's has come the scholar called Asser! This man is very highly skilled in literature, and I have appointed him to be the Bishop of Sherborn. His ability is so great that he explained the works of Boethius, who wrote about the 'Consolation of Philosophy', and I have already translated those works into the English language!"

Alfred now wanted more learned scholars, and he therefore sent for Werefrith, the Bishop of Mercia to join him at the Royal Court of Alfred. After travelling for some time, the great scholar arrived and Alfred received him gladly. Alfred said, *"I am glad that you have arrived, Werefrith, for there is much that must be done! I command you to translate into the English language, all the books of Pope Gregory's dialogues. This must be done as another step towards having all our people being able to speak, read and write our English language well! You may be interested to know that I have sent an ambassador to the court of Charles the Bald, and I have asked for Johannes Scotus to be sent to us here at my court! That man is known to not just be a great scholar himself, but also, a very good teacher. I feel that he is exactly what is required to teach the young people of my schools and at my court the correct speaking, reading and writing of English upon which all other kinds of education shall be based from now onwards!"*

Alfred confided in auxiliaries with whom he had started the translation from Latin to English of many texts including those used in churches and in the schools located in his court and in other places. He now gave his entire being to the cultivation of the liberal arts and no other man was quicker in comprehending or more outstanding in translating. That is amazing because it was not until he had reached the age of twelve years that he knew anything of literature. It is thought that Alfred's interest in learning may have come about because of the combination of his kind mother, who would disguise the task of learning what was in a book as amusement, and she would give him a present if he could learn what was required quickly. That was combined with the great influence upon young Alfred at an early age by Pope Leo-the-Great. All those things resulted in Alfred having an unquenchable desire to learn. He translated into English the greater part of the works of Roman authors.

The main works being "Orosius", Gregory's "Pastoral", Bede's "History of the Angles" Boethius "Of the consolation of Philosophy" and his own book entitled as "Handbook". He further encouraged the learning of reading and writing in English by ordering, *"Englishmen shall be rewarded for their knowledge and use of the spoken and written English language! There shall be penalties for the use of languages other than English in my court! Let it be known that no ignorant person can ever aspire to any position of any dignitary unless that person is completely fluent in the use of the English language! All people living in this country must learn and use English!"*

In the prologue to "The Pastoral" Alfred wrote, *"I was incited to translate these books into English because of the many churches containing many books that were burnt and destroyed in general by the heathen Danes!"* One night in 901A.D., after he had completed his evening meal and his religious observances, he was just beginning to translate the Psalms into English from Latin when he died. Alfred-the-Great was succeeded by his son, Edward-the-Elder.

Edward-the-Elder

In 901 A.D., Edward the son of Alfred, became known as Edward-the-Elder and succeeded to the government of England. He was very much inferior to his father in the field of literature, but he was extremely good at using power and military matters. Alfred had united the two kingdoms of Mercia and West Saxons, but he was only holding Mercia because he had assigned it to Æthelred, also known as Ethelred of Mercia, who had become his son-in-law.

On their wedding night, Ethered embraced his wife, and they made love. She became pregnant and after a normal gestation, she had a very painful labour. So, whenever Ethered tried embrace her after that, she refused his advances and spoke to him. She said, *"It is unbecoming for the daughter of a king to give a delight which, after time, produces such painful consequences! Even though I quite enjoy sex, I shall not have it again because of the pain caused by the birth of children which are the results of sexual intercourse[42]!"* As a result of that, Ethelred became celebrate, he also died well before she did!

---

[42] William of Malmsbury, 1847

Edward was left to continue with his father's successes against the Danes. While taking the fight to the Danes in the north, he took the time to visit his sister in Mercia, while he was near her location. Upon seeing her, he explained that he was having a difficult time in getting the Danes under his control and that he thought it to be a good idea to have her help in planning and organising the fights between the Danes, Scots, and Welsh. She became a spirited heroine who assisted her brother greatly.

Edward said, *"My sister, I need guidance of how to get the Danes in the north of our country to accept that the whole country is England and to pledge allegiance both to England and to me as the King of England! What would you suggest that I do to completely rule over all people in our county of England?"*

She answered, *"Brother, have you tried the idea of having strongly walled and defended towns and cities, each with its own armed military forces which are both highly trained and fully equipped and armed? Do you remember how our father, Alfred-the-Great passed laws stating that all men must both serve their country by undergoing military discipline and by giving service to the church? By calling upon all men to serve the country and if need be, to fight to their deaths, you must be able to beat all challenges and in time be victorious over the Danes!"*

Edward then used the laws passed by his father that all men must serve and all cities then had a large part of their male populations both equipped and trained as soldiers forming the local garrisons. His sister, Aethelflaed even took to the field with her own army, and it was known that she could both protect her people at home and intimidate those who were abroad. After many military actions against the Danish Vikings in England, Edward-the-Elder was victorious over the Danes and England was his!

Bibliography

Greenwood, T., 1836. *The first book of the History of the Germans: Barbaric period.* Longman, Rees, Orme & Co, London.

King Alfred-the-Great, 1847. *Anglo-Saxon Chronicle.* Unknown publisher, Middleton De USA.

Lacey, R., Danziger, D., 1999. *The Year 1000.* Little, Brown and Company, London.

William of Malmsbury, 1847. *Chronicle of the kings and queens of England.* Henry G Bohn, London.

www.ingramcontent.com/pod-product-compliance
Lightning Source LLC
Chambersburg PA
CBHW062048080426
42734CB00012B/2592